This Book Comes With Lots of
FREE Online Resources

Nolo's award-winning website has a page dedicated just to this book. Here you can:

DOWNLOAD FORMS – Access forms and worksheets from the book online

KEEP UP TO DATE – When there are important changes to the information in this book, we'll post updates

GET DISCOUNTS ON NOLO PRODUCTS – Get discounts on hundreds of books, forms, and software

READ BLOGS – Get the latest info from Nolo authors' blogs

LISTEN TO PODCASTS – Listen to authors discuss timely issues on topics that interest you

WATCH VIDEOS – Get a quick introduction to a legal topic with our short videos

And that's not all.
Nolo.com contains thousands of articles on everyday legal and business issues, plus a plain-English law dictionary, all written by Nolo experts and available for free. You'll also find more useful **books, software, online apps, downloadable forms,** plus a **lawyer directory.**

With
**Downloadable
FORMS**

 **NOLO**
LAW for ALL

Get forms and more at
www.nolo.com/back-of-book/IELD.html

6th Edition

Nolo's
IEP Guide
Learning Disabilities

Attorney Lawrence M. Siegel

Sixth Edition	JUNE 2014
Editor	BETH LAURENCE
Cover Design	SUSAN PUTNEY
Production	SUSAN PUTNEY
Proofreading	ROBERT WELLS
Index	THÉRÈSE SHERE
Printing	BANG PRINTING

Siegel, Lawrence M., 1946- author.
 Nolo's IEP guide : learning disabilities / by Attorney Lawrence M. Siegel. -- 6th Edition.
    pages cm
 Summary: "Children with learning disabilities have different needs than other kids in special education -- let Nolo's IEP Guide: Learning Disabilities help you make sure those needs are met. Learn how to: understand your child's rights, untangle eligibility rules and develop effective IEP goals"-- Provided by publisher.
 ISBN 978-1-4133-2040-4 (pbk.) -- ISBN 978-1-4133-2041-1 (epub ebook)
1. Individualized education programs--Law and legislation--United States--Popular works. 2. Learning disabled children--Legal status, laws, etc.--United States--Popular works. I. Title. II. Title: IEP guide.
 KF4209.3.S573 2014
 371.90973--dc23

                              2013048072

Please note

We believe accurate, plain-English legal information should help you solve many of your own legal problems. But this text is not a substitute for personalized advice from a knowledgeable lawyer. If you want the help of a trained professional—and we'll always point out situations in which we think that's a good idea—consult an attorney licensed to practice in your state.

Dedication

With love to Nancy, my wonderful sister and a heroine (long-standing) in the classroom—I'm not sure which of these two poses the greater challenge to you.

Acknowledgments

The author wishes to thank Jim Orrell and John La Londe for providing an example of a comprehensive IEP document.

Much appreciation to Marcia Stewart for reading the drafts and adding her unique and strong thoughts to the package.

Thanks to Joe Feldman and the Community Alliance for Special Education of San Francisco for their long-standing commitment to providing passionate and highly skilled, low-cost advocacy to children with learning disabilities.

Thanks to Joan Troppmann, the best RSP in California, for her kind and patient help.

Thanks to Beth Laurence, for her insight, patience, and devotion to children in special education.

About the Author

Lawrence Siegel has been a special education attorney and advocate since 1979, and has represented children with disabilities extensively in IEPs, due process, complaints, legal action, and before legislative and policy bodies. Mr. Seigel has consulted with parent groups throughout the U.S. and has worked directly with special education experts in Japan. As a Fulbright specialist, he worked in Sweden at the University of Stockholm. He teaches special education law at Hastings College of the Law, was on the California Special Education Advisory Commission for eight years, and has written and helped enact special education law in a number of states. He continues to travel the country giving workshops to families with children with disabilities. Mr. Siegel was given an endowed chair at Gallaudet University (2004-2005) in recognition of his work for children with disabilities and is also the author of *Least Restrictive Environment: The Paradox of Inclusion* (LRP Publications, 1994), *The Human Right to Language* (Gallaudet Press, 2008), and *Nolo's IEP Guide: Learning Disabilities*.

Table of Contents

All of the following appendixes are available on this book's Companion Page on Nolo's website (free for readers of this book) at

www.nolo.com/back-of-book/IELD.html

Appendix A: Special Education Law and Regulations

Appendix B: Support Groups, Advocacy Organizations, and Other Resources

Appendix C: The Severe Discrepancy Model

Appendix D: Sample IEP Form

Appendix E: Forms

Your Legal Companion for IEPs

Parents want the best for their children, and they're instinctive advocates. When your child is a student in special education, however, that advocacy can be quite challenging. The IEP process is like a maze, involving a good deal of technical information, intimidating professionals, and confusing choices. For some families, it goes smoothly, with no disagreements. For others, it is a stressful encounter in which you and the school district cannot agree on anything. For most people, the experience is somewhere in between.

Whether you face a disagreement with your district or just want to be more informed about your rights, this book will assist you. It will explain the IEP process in great detail, including each step involved and the rights you and your child have in that process. It will teach you how to be an effective advocate for your child. This book provides you with all of the information you need, including:

- what the Individuals with Disabilities Education Act (or IDEA) guarantees for your child's educational needs
- details about the individualized education program (or IEP) process established by the IDEA
- eligibility rules and the role of evaluations in determining whether your child qualifies for special education
- how to gather the information and develop the material you need to determine your child's specific goals and educational needs
- how to develop a blueprint for your child's education that includes the placement, services, and teaching strategies your child needs, and
- how to deal with disagreements that arise between you and your school district in developing and implementing your child's IEP.

This book will explain that, first and foremost, the IEP process is meant to ensure that an appropriate educational program fits your child's needs, not the other way around. The book will help you proceed on your own through the IEP process, whether it's your first time or your fifth time. The suggestions and forms in the book will help you get—and stay—organized throughout the IEP process.

Detailed online resources provide invaluable information, including:

- key special education laws and regulations
- twenty forms, letters, and checklists to help you through every stage of the IEP process
- addresses and websites of national and state advocacy, parent, and disability organizations, and
- a bibliography of other helpful books.

After working through this book, you will be prepared to advocate for your child to receive the free appropriate public education that is guaranteed to all children who need special education services.

Get Forms, Resources, Updates, and More Online

You'll find forms, resources, and other valuable information on this book's Companion Page on Nolo's website (free for readers of this book) at

www.nolo.com/back-of-book/IELD.html

See Chapter 16 for more information.

Introduction to Special Education

What Is Special Education?

The details and reach of the Individuals with Disability Education Act are remarkable—no other law in this nation provides such clear and unique legal protection for children. Congress first enacted the IDEA in 1975 because public schools were frequently ignoring children with disabilities or shunting them off to inferior or distant programs. IDEA set forth a number of legal mandates for children receiving special education. The most important ones are:

- Your child is entitled to a "free appropriate public education" in the "least restrictive environment."
- Your child is entitled to a comprehensive evaluation of his or her needs, and the district cannot evaluate your child without your approval unless it takes you to a due process hearing and prevails.
- Your child is entitled to have a written individualized education program (IEP) that is developed by an entire team, including you and school representatives, on at least an annual basis.
- Your child's IEP must include measurable annual goals.
- Your child is entitled to "related services" that will help your child benefit from his or her special education.
- Your child is entitled to placement in a private school at public expense if the school district cannot provide an appropriate placement.
- Your child is entitled to be educated as close to home as possible and in the school your child would attend if not disabled.
- You can ask for a mediation and hearing before an impartial third party if you do not agree with the district about any component of the IEP, including even whether your child is eligible for special education.
- Your child's IEP cannot be unilaterally changed by your school district. First, you must agree to that change.

What Is an IEP?

The acronym IEP can refer to several different things:

- the initial meeting that determines whether your child is eligible for special education (the IEP eligibility meeting)
- the annual meeting at which you and school representatives develop your child's educational program for the following school year (called the IEP program meeting), or
- the actual detailed, written description of your child's educational program.

The written IEP should include:

- the specific program or class for your child (called "placement")
- the specific services (called "related services") your child will receive, and
- other educational components, such as curricula and teaching methods.

There is one major caveat, however, in the rights that IDEA grants to your child. IDEA does not require that the school district provide the best possible program. The program that is individualized for your child only has to provide an appropriate educational experience. An appropriate educational experience is one that is reasonable, given your child's particular needs. For instance, you may feel that the private school across town would be the best for your child in terms of accelerating his or her growth. But if the district's program can provide a reasonable chance at growth, the law does not require the district to pay for private school placement. Or, you may feel that although three hours of speech therapy a week will work, six hours would be great. IDEA does not require "great."

The key to preparing to advocate for your child is to focus on showing that the program and services you seek are appropriate. This book will explain the crucial steps in doing so, including:

- how to state your child's needs as specifically and narrowly as possible, and how to make sure those needs are reflected in program components. For example, it is one thing to say "my child needs help with his expressive language"; it is quite another to say "he needs three hours a week of one-on-one speech help to work on his articulation and verbal pragmatics." The first statement is much too broad; the second is specific and clearly states what assistance your child needs.
- how to provide specific proof of your child's needs, by using an evaluation, a report, or testimony from an educator or professional who can specify what your child needs, why, and for how long.
- how to provide the evidence that backs up your position. It is always best if someone inside your school district—whether the classroom teacher, service provider, assessor or administrator—agrees with you about what your child needs. But because you may not always have that support, you may need an expert outside of the district to describe your child's needs and recommend placement and services that will address those needs.
- how to use the proof you gather in the IEP process and, if the IEP team fails to agree with you, how to present it in a due process mediation or hearing.
- what to do when the district fails to follow the legal requirements set forth by IDEA.

IDEA Statutes and Regulations

The laws that govern special education under IDEA are primarily found in two places:

- statutes enacted by Congress and codified in the United States Code beginning at 20 U.S.C. § 1400, and
- regulations issued by the U.S. Department of Education and published in the Code of Federal Regulations beginning at 34 C.F.R. § 300.1.

The regulations clarify and explain the statutes. The statutes and regulations you need are on this book's Companion Page; see Chapter 16 for the link.

Being Your Child's Advocate

This book also highlights the practical aspects of being an advocate for your special education child. While these may seem obvious, it is always helpful to be reminded. The tips below can make the difference in whether or not you obtain an appropriate education for your child.

Organization, Organization, Organization

The path to success begins with meticulous organization, starting with knowing when there should be an IEP meeting and keeping track of your child's progress. File copies of all letters you write to the school district, as well as notes you make of what people say and when. For example, suppose your child's teacher tells you on Wednesday afternoon that your child needs speech therapy. You ask why and he or she explains. When you get home, you sit down and record the details (the date, time, place, and content of your conversation). This information may be vital at the next IEP meeting, when the issue of speech therapy comes up.

Always Ask Why

If you don't know, ask. And if an answer is provided and you don't feel it explained things fully, ask again. You are not an expert in IDEA law, but you will know enough of it to recognize the key components. If something does not make sense to you, or if an administrator says, "Well, we just don't do it that way," ask why. If he or she refers to a law (a statute or regulation) or a policy, ask to see a copy of it. If that does not work, write a letter asking for the information. You might phrase it like this: "You said last week [date] that the district could not provide my child with a one-on-one aide; that it was district policy [or because of budget cuts, or because you didn't think my child needed an aide]. I would appreciate it if you would provide me with the basis for that position. Is it part of the district's written policy, is it your opinion, or is it part of the law (if so, please send me a copy of that law)? Thank you."

Style

It is likely that sometime during your child's years in special education, you will go to an IEP meeting or have a conversation during which someone from the school district says something that offends you or makes you angry. Please keep in mind that you are more likely to persuade the district of your position if you act reasonably rather than in anger. Of course, though you have to be true to you own style and there is nothing wrong with being emotional, blowing a gasket does not usually work and only signals that the discussion has come to a close. If possible, in these situations it is best to be clear, precise, and determined. Give your reaction but be as measured and calm as you can, as in "I know you would not want to deny students what they need, but I believe that the reports we have submitted are clear and there is no doubt that my daughter needs a one-on-one aide, two hours a day. Her teacher said as much. I think your position is not based on evidence and I do not appreciate your tone of voice or the manner in which you are treating us. I hope we can resolve this positively through the IEP, but if not I can assure you we will proceed as we must."

Your Child's Teacher

Your child's teacher is your best potential ally. My personal view is that teachers are as important as any working group in our nation. They teach, counsel, police, nurse, and often work all day, most nights, and many weekends to help children develop. And they do it for lousy pay, while shouldering a ton of paperwork (especially if they teach special education students), along with pressures from their own administration.

Your child's teacher knows your child better than anyone else in the school system. If you can work directly and positively with the teacher, you will have a strong ally at the IEP meeting. That does not mean that the teacher will always agree with you; in the areas that he or she does, however, the teacher's input is vitally important. Respect your teacher's intelligence, motives, and time. Be reasonable in your demands.

Setting Realistic Goals

One of the hardest things a lawyer sometimes has to say to a family is that their IEP goals are not supported by evidence. As a parent, I understand how difficult this is to hear. But for the sake of your child, you sometimes need to face it: By looking at the evidence as objectively as possible, and recognizing when there is insufficient support for some or all of your goals, you will more effectively represent your child and eliminate wasted time and resources.

Remember as well that neither party to the IEP—not the parents nor the school district—has to agree to anything, no matter how powerful the support is or how effectively one side makes its point. Parents are often frustrated when the school administrator simply says "No, we don't agree about that." But you want to yell, "My child needs it, the support is there for it, how can you possibly say that!?" Each party to the IEP has the absolute right to make a decision and stick with it. Parents who remain dissatisfied with the school's position do, however, have a next step: They can challenge the school's factual conclusions (such as whether your child is eligible) through mediation (see Chapter 12); and they can challenge the school's interpretation of the law by filing a complaint (see Chapter 13).

As you'll see, significant changes brought about by the 2004 revamp of the Individuals with Disabilities Education Act are called out, which may help you in case you find yourself dealing with someone who, despite the passage of the years, is unaware of the updates.

Getting Help From Others

Other parents, local groups, and regional or national organizations can be of great help as you wend your way through special education. The amount of information these folks have is amazing. Other parents and parent groups can be your best resource. Parents who have been through the process before can help you avoid making mistakes or undertaking unnecessary tasks. Most important, they can be a source of real encouragement. Chapter 15 provides further thoughts on making use of your local special education community.

Note: Reference is made throughout this book to parents, but the term is used to include foster parents and legal guardians.

TIP

Get involved. Like many laws, after its initial passage IDEA was revisited and reapproved by Congress, in what's known as "reauthorization." Reauthorization does not happen every year, but when it does, it's a good time for advocates and others to improve IDEA. If you are interested in that process, contact an advocacy group; you'll find a list in Appendix B on this book's Companion Page on www.nolo.com. See Chapter 16 for the link.

What This Book Doesn't Cover

This book focuses on the rights and procedures for children between the ages of three and 22. Other important issues fall beyond the scope of this book. These include:

- procedures for children younger than three
- transition services that help children prepare for a job or college, including independent living skills, and
- discipline issues, including suspension and expulsion.

Use the resources in Appendix B to get more information and support on these issues. (See Chapter 16 for the link.) If you need help, especially for the complex issue of discipline, you should contact a special education attorney. (See Chapter 14.)

Your Child's Rights Under the IDEA

The Individuals with Disabilities Education Act (IDEA), a federal law, establishes a formal process for evaluating children with disabilities and providing specialized programs and services to help them succeed in school. Parents play a central role in determining their child's educational program. Under IDEA, the program and services your child needs will be determined through the individualized education program, or IEP, process. The term IEP refers to both a meeting that is held and a plan that is written about your child's program. Your ability to understand and master the IEP process will shape your child's educational experience. Indeed, the IEP is the centerpiece of IDEA.

Although parts of IDEA refer specifically to learning disabilities, most of the law establishes general rules that apply to all children with disabilities. This chapter provides an overview of your child's legal rights in the special education process. Later chapters discuss each step in the IEP process in more detail—this chapter introduces the key concepts you'll need to understand how the whole system works.

As you read this chapter, keep in mind the following:

- Don't let the word "law" throw you. The actual language of IDEA and, more importantly, its underlying purpose, can easily be mastered. The legal concepts in IDEA are logical and sensible.
- Developing a broad understanding of the law will help you when you review later chapters on eligibility, evaluations, IEPs, and other key matters.
- While we provide plain English descriptions of special education law in the body of the book, you can find key provisions of the actual law, as passed by Congress, in Appendix A on this book's Companion Page on nolo.com (see Chapter 16 for the link). IDEA is found in the United States Code starting at 20 U.S.C. § 1400.
- The IDEA regulations found at 34 C.F.R. § 300.1 generally parallel the statutes but in some cases provide more detail. We refer to the IDEA regulations when that additional information is relevant. You can find key regulations in Appendix A. (See Chapter 16 for the link.)
- IDEA was revised ("reauthorized") by Congress in 2004. Although the changes are no longer breaking news, you might

find yourself dealing with people who are not aware of the updates. For this reason, significant changes brought about by the 2004 revamp are called out.

IDEA and State Special Education Laws

IDEA is a federal law, binding on all states. The federal government provides financial assistance to the states for special education; to receive this money, states must adopt laws that implement IDEA.

State laws generally parallel IDEA and often use identical language. State laws cannot provide a child with fewer protections than IDEA does— but they can provide additional rights (and some do). IDEA is always your starting point, but you should check to see what your state law says about special education—it may give your child more rights and options.

States Use Different Definitions of Learning Disability

State laws vary considerably in the way learning disabilities are defined; some states use the federal definition of learning disabilities, other states use different language. Your child's eligibility for special education may well depend on how your state defines learning disabilities, so make sure you know your state's rules. Eligibility is covered in detail in Chapter 7.

Each state's educational agency is responsible for making sure that local school districts comply with the federal law. Though yearly federal support for special education has been in the billions, this amounts to only 8% to 13% of the costs of IDEA, even though Congress initially promised the states that it would provide approximately 40% of the cost of IDEA. The significant shortfall in federal funding puts great pressure on states and local school districts, particularly given competing interests for education dollars.

The special education funding process varies from state to state, and is often complex. No matter how your state funds special education, remember this rule: Even though money (and how it gets from Washington to your state to your district to your child) should not determine the contents of your child's IEP, financial constraints affect every school district. This is especially so today, when budget cuts have had a devastating impact on educational funding. As greater legal mandates and responsibilities are placed on schools and teachers, there appears to be no corresponding increase in the necessary dollars.

What IDEA Requires

The purpose of IDEA is to ensure that children with disabilities receive an appropriate education. To achieve this goal, IDEA imposes a number of legal requirements on school districts.

When Congress enacted IDEA, it chose not to tell school districts what they must specifically do for each specific child; for example, it did not establish what a child with a learning disability or a deaf child or a physically disabled child required. Congress left the specific decision making up to the family and the school district. Congress certainly set up parameters and created requirements (for instance, when an IEP meeting must be held, what topics are to be covered in an IEP, how one defines eligibility categories), but the specifics of a child's program is not established in the law.

By placing the emphasis on the process rather than specifics, Congress intended that school districts have strict processes they must follow, including rules for:

- establishing eligibility for special education
- evaluating a child
- holding an IEP meeting
- what must be covered in an IEP meeting and put on the IEP document
- what related services might be necessary for a child
- when an IEP must be in place and what must be done if an IEP is to be changed
- what to do when the family and the school district disagree about anything related to the child's education, including eligibility and assessments.

The importance of school districts' following rules and procedures cannot be overemphasized; being aware of those rules and what to do when they are not followed may be crucial to your child's case. (Please see Chapter 8 for a full discussion of possible school procedural violations and how they may affect your child's education and case.) We'll discuss some of these rules below.

Eligibility and Evaluations

Every school district has the legal duty to identify, locate, and evaluate children who may be in need of special education. This duty extends to wards of the court and children who have no fixed address (such as migrant or homeless children). (20 U.S.C. § 1412(a)(3).) It also includes children who may be advancing from one grade to the next but nonetheless need special education. Once a child is identified as possibly needing help, the school district must evaluate the child's eligibility for special education. The school must provide special education programs and services only if a child is found eligible.

Rules for Eligibility and Evaluation

In 2004, IDEA provided these key changes to eligibility and evaluation:

- Your child's school district must conduct the initial evaluation to determine whether your child is eligible for special education within 60 days of receiving your consent.
- IDEA encourages states to eliminate the requirement for a "severe discrepancy" between achievement and intellectual ability.
- Parents can no longer unilaterally request more than one evaluation in a school year. A second (or third or fourth) evaluation in one school year now requires the agreement of the parent and the school district.

We discuss the details of these and many other rules about evaluation and eligibility in Chapters 6 and 7.

IDEA has 12 distinct disability categories, each with its own set of detailed requirements. You can find the rules for the learning disability category at 34 C.F.R. §§ 300.307–311 of the current IDEA regulations. These rules are covered in detail in Chapter 7.

IDEA defines "children with disabilities" as individuals between the ages of three and 22 who have one or more of the following conditions (20 U.S.C. § 1401(3) and (30); see also IDEA regulations at 34 C.F.R. § 300.8):

- autism
- visual impairment (including blindness)
- hearing impairment (including deafness)
- serious emotional disturbance
- mental retardation
- multiple disabilities
- orthopedic impairment
- other health impairment (including Attention Deficit Disorder (ADD) and Attention Deficit Hyperactivity Disorder (ADHD))
- specific learning disability
- speech or language impairment, and
- traumatic brain injury.

RELATED TOPIC

You'll notice that Attention Deficit Disorder (ADD) and Attention Deficit Hyperactivity Disorder (ADHD), often thought of as learning disabilities, are listed under the category of "other health impairment" rather than as "specific learning disability." Chapter 3 discusses these distinctions.

To qualify for special education under IDEA, your child must have one of the listed disabilities, *and* the disability must "adversely affect" his or her educational performance. (See Chapter 7 for more information on eligibility.)

TIP

The IEP must address all of your child's disabilities, including learning disabilities. Keep in mind that children with learning disabilities often have other qualifying conditions or characteristics. If you suspect that your child has learning disabilities but he or she ultimately qualifies for special education in another category, learning disability needs can still be addressed in the IEP.

Your child has a right to an initial evaluation to determine whether he or she has a disability as defined by IDEA, as well as a reevaluation at least every three years. If you are not satisfied with the initial evaluation or you feel that your child's disability or special education needs have changed, you have the right to request an additional evaluation, and even an independent evaluation conducted by someone other than a district employee. (20 U.S.C. §§ 1414 and 1415(b)(1).) If you ask for more than one evaluation per year, however, the school district must give its consent. (20 U.S.C. § 1414(a)(2).) The school district can also dispute whether it will pay for an independent evaluation. (34 C.F.R. §300.502.)

Evaluations Versus Assessments

IDEA makes a distinction between "evaluations," which are the tests and other methods used to determine your child's eligibility for special education and to design your child's educational program, and "assessments," which refer to the tests your state uses to measure the performance of all children in school. Prior to the rising popularity of statewide assessments, however, these two terms were often used interchangeably (even in previous editions of this book), so don't be surprised if your school district continues to do so. Chapter 6 provides detailed information on special education evaluations.

 RELATED TOPIC

Eligibility for learning disabled children is discussed in detail in Chapter 7. Evaluations are described in Chapters 6 and 8.

Educational Entitlement

A child who qualifies for special education under IDEA is entitled to a free appropriate public education (FAPE), individually tailored to meet his or her unique needs. (20 U.S.C. § 1401(9) and (29).)

IDEA requires the educational program to fit your child, not the other way around. For example, it is not appropriate for a school district to place your child with a learning disability in a class for emotionally disturbed students. The classroom setting, teaching strategies, and services provided for the emotionally disturbed children would not be appropriate for your child. Without evidence that such a placement meets your child's unique needs, this would not be an individually tailored IEP.

Of course, real school programs don't always match legal mandates, so you may have to be vocal and insistent to get what your child needs. Remember, too, that the IEP team must decide together what is appropriate and what constitutes a program that meets the unique needs of the child. One member of the team—be it the parent or the school administrator—can't make that decision alone.

What is a "free appropriate public education?" Perhaps the most difficult question to answer since the enactment of the IDEA in 1975 is what constitutes an "appropriate" education and what are the duties of a school district to provide it?

The question actually has two parts:

- Since "appropriate" is directly related to educational benefit, how is that benefit measured so as to determine whether the IEP offered your child is appropriate?
- What constitutes an education—is it only academic/scholastic work or does it include things like social and emotional growth?

Courts have attempted to provide some direction as to what is meant by an "appropriate" education and therefore what are the duties of your school district to provide an education that has value to your child. In 1982, the U.S. Supreme Court, in a case called *Hendrick Hudson v. Rowley,* said that an appropriate education is one that "opens the door of public education" to a child with a disability, but does not guarantee any "particular outcome" and has no requirement to "maximize" a child's potential.

This set a low bar for what a parent could expect a district to provide and what outcomes were reasonable. A child with a disability should receive "some" educational benefit but there were no standards for what "some" meant.

The *Rowley* standard has been significantly altered since 1982 by courts all over the nation. Courts have ruled that an "appropriate" education is one in which "more than a trivial amount of educational benefit" is required, that "educational benefit must be meaningful," that your child "progress academically," that learning be "significant and meaningful," and the benefit must be "gauged in relation to a child's potential [not full potential]." A child with a disability should also make "measurable and adequate gains in the classroom."

Please note that the concepts of "appropriate" and educational benefit are still more vague than not (for example, what is "significant" learning?), and subject to your child's individual needs. The language courts have come up with is important to be aware of, but will not automatically mean when you tell your school district that your child needs X or Y to receive "significant" benefit, the district will agree. But it also means that appropriate no longer means the minimum effort, or a weak effort, at providing "something" for your child. That said, there is still no requirement to "maximize" your child's potential or that he receive the "best" or "most" appropriate education. That is why we will remind you repeatedly that when describing a program or service you want for your child, never use the words "best," "maximum," or similar adjectives. You want an "appropriate" education as reflected in the detail of your child's blueprint.

The second issue in considering what is FAPE is what constitutes an education? Most state law, federal policy, and court decisions acknowledge that an "education" is more than grades, more than academic work and progress. You can and should insist that the IEP team consider your child's emotional, linguistic, social, behavioral, and other nontraditional academic/scholastic needs. As one court said, the IDEA wants to "foster self-sufficiency" in students. If your school district says that an "appropriate" education is one that only focuses on standard academics, ask them where it says that in the law, where FAPE is defined that way. And remind them that the IEP process talks about goals and objectives, not specific academic classes, and further states that the IEP team must consider the "strengths of the child and the concerns of the parents for enhancing the education of their child…." (34 C.F.R. § 300.324; see also 34 C.F.R. § 300.323.)

How Your State Law Defines an Appropriate Education

It is important to try to have some understanding of your state's special education laws. While some state special education laws duplicate federal special education laws verbatim, many states add a good deal to the requirements of school district. (Remember, state law must parallel federal special education law, but can provide greater protection and more rights for your child.) For example, in relation to what is meant by an "appropriate education," North Carolina has state policy that requires every child has a fair and full opportunity to reach her "full potential."

In terms of what is meant by an education, Maine goes far beyond the federal government in its definition. Maine defines "educational performance" to include academic areas (reading, math, and so on), but also nonacademic areas (daily life activities, mobility, etc.) and extracurricular activities as well as six guiding principles for what students should become:

- clear and effective communicators
- self-directed and lifelong learners
- creative and practical problem solvers
- responsible and involved citizens
- collaborative and quality workers, and
- integrative and informed thinkers.

(Maine Department of Education Regulation 132.)

Do you have to accept special education or related services? The 2004 amendments to IDEA make clear that you have the right to reject special education and related services. As Congress said, you have the "ultimate choice" in these matters; the school district cannot force anything on your child if you don't want it.

"Appropriate" Doesn't Necessarily Mean "Best"

The law does not require your school district to provide the very best or the optimum education for your child—only an appropriate education. "Appropriate" is an elusive but tremendously important concept. It comes up a lot in IDEA and throughout the IEP process. It is the standard for evaluating every aspect of your child's education—the goals, services, and placement. For one child, an appropriate education may mean a regular class with minor support services, while a hospital placement might be appropriate for another.

Educational Placement

Decisions about your child's educational placement—the program or class where your child will be taught—and related services (covered below) will take center stage in the IEP process.

Least Restrictive Environment

IDEA does not tell you or the school what specific program or class your child should be in; that is a decision for the IEP team. IDEA does require school districts to place disabled children in the "least restrictive environment" (LRE) that meets their individual needs. A child's LRE will depend on that child's abilities and disabilities. Although Congress expressed a strong preference for "mainstreaming" (placing a child in a regular classroom), it used the term LRE to ensure that individual needs would determine each individual placement—and that children who really need a more restrictive placement (such as a special school) would have one.

It is important you understand the difference between the concept of LRE and a specific placement for a specific child. The IDEA requires that each school district have a variety of placement options for your child, called the "continuum of placement options" (see "Range of Placements," below). One of those options is indeed a regular classroom (often referred to as "mainstreaming" or "inclusion") and it is the placement Congress preferred when it enacted the IDEA. There are however, other options including separate classes, schools, and even residential placement. The decision on which placement is right for your child should take into account all of his or her needs. For one child, the LRE may and should be a regular classroom; for another it may and should be a separate class or school.

There is a good deal of debate about the LRE requirement in the national special education community. There are those who believe that all children regardless of their needs and challenges should be mainstreamed. This represents a long-standing commitment of our nation to remove any form of "segregation" from our educational system. There are those who are equally passionate and believe that there are children for whom a regular classroom would actually be more restrictive; for example, a deaf child who uses sign language or a child with significant emotional challenges who needs to be in a very small class on a very small and sheltered campus. As an attorney, my first and only responsibility is to my clients' specific needs and not some generic goal. You, of course, have only one goal, the best placement for your child.

How is the least restrictive environment selected? The preference for a regular classroom placement is found in the language of the IDEA, Section 300.114. This section says that the school district must ensure that, to the "maximum extent appropriate, children with disabilities… are educated with children who are nondisabled" and that removal of children with disabilities from the regular classroom should occur only if "the nature of the disability is such that education in regular classes with the use of supplementary aids and services cannot be achieved satisfactorily."

This language suggests that a child should always begin in a regular class and only after it is demonstrated that he or she cannot receive an appropriate education there, should he or she be "removed" to a more restrictive placement. In reality, of course, this does not always happen and in some cases a regular classroom placement could actually be harmful for a child. Again consider a deaf child who communicates through sign language who would be fully isolated in a regular class or a child who is afraid of a large class. It would be cruel to place this child in a regular class first. (The IDEA does add that when an IEP team selects the LRE for a child, the team must consider any potential harmful effect on the child or on the quality of services that he or she needs. 34 C.F.R. § 300.116.)

To sum up, the LRE rules demonstrate:

- a strong preference for mainstreaming, including the requirement to provide aides and services before a child can be removed from a regular class
- a recognition that a different placement may be necessary, depending on the child's individual needs and challenges, and
- LRE is not a specific place but a determination that one of the continuum of placement options is the "least restrictive" for an individual child

Court decisions on LRE. Federal courts throughout the country have long struggled with the tension between the specialized needs of children under the IDEA and the requirement to place those children in the "least restrictive environment." *Daniel R.R. v. State Board of Education,* 874 F.2d 1036 (5th Cir. 1989) is a significant case that balanced the right to be in a regular classroom versus the need for highly detailed services that might preclude mainstreaming. The court held that a school district must consider the following before removing a child from a regular placement:

- If the student can benefit from mainstreaming, the fact that the child may not gain as much as other students cannot be the basis for denying a regular classroom placement.
- The benefits of mainstreaming are not merely educational, but may be social, linguistic, and more. When analyzing the

benefit of mainstreaming, these noneducational factors must be considered.

- The student's impact on other students must be considered.
- The child should be mainstreamed to the "maximum extent appropriate," even if the student must be placed in a nonregular education program (such as mainstreaming for part of the school day).

Placement Versus Program

The terms "placement" and "program" are often used interchangeably, but there are some differences in meaning. As used in IDEA, placement refers to the various classrooms or schools where a child may be. Program has a broader connotation: It includes not only where the program is located, but also the components of that program, including extra services, curricula, teaching methods, class makeup, and so on. Placement and program components should both be addressed in your child's IEP.

IDEA states that a child should be in the regular classroom unless the child cannot be educated satisfactorily there even with the "use of supplementary aids and services." (20 U.S.C. § 1412(a)(5).) LRE further requires that a child should be educated as close to home as possible and in the class he or she would attend if nondisabled. (IDEA regulations at 34 C.F.R. §§ 300.114–120.) If a child will not participate with nondisabled children in the regular classroom and in other school activities, the IEP team must explain why. (20 U.S.C. § 1414(d)(1)(A).)

Because a learning disability is generally considered less severe than some other special education categories, the LRE for many children with learning disabilities will and should be a regular classroom. There is a much greater burden on school districts to prove that a child with learning disabilities should be placed in a more restrictive environment (such as a special class or a special school).

Charter Schools

Charter schools are public schools generally like traditional public schools, but depending on state law, they may have more freedom from state regulations. Charter schools must follow all federal law, however. Therefore, charter schools must meet all the requirements of the IDEA, including "child find," assessments, IEPs, and due process.

A charter school, again depending on state law, may either be an "independent" educational agency, which means the school is its own school district and has direct responsibility for special education, or may be dependent on and formally part of a school district. In this second case, it is the district that is ultimately responsible for all IDEA requirements. In this situation, think of the charter school as merely one other placement option within the district.

Charter schools are intended to give parents more choice as to where to send their children. There is, of course, significant debate about charter schools; there are those who point to significant gains for children in charter schools, while other academicians suggest little or no change in scores whether a child goes to a charter school or a traditional public school. Other concerns about charter schools include anecdotal information that they are less inclined to provide full special education services, may not have qualified staff, and do not know the complex special education procedures. A recent report out of Oakland, California, indicated that charter schools there did not provide the level of special education and related services that public schools normally do. This is not to say charter schools are not worth an investigation, but it is crucial that you fully investigate any charter school:

- Are the teachers credentialed?
- What experience has the school had with special education?
- Is there a special education administrator?
- Is there other staff with the kind of knowledge and training your child deserves?
- Is there any financial incentive for the charter school to limit its programs and services for children with disabilities?

Depending on the state, a charter school may be able to follow different rules regarding teacher certification. This can affect a child's special education possibilities. Since at a regular school, special education teachers and specialists almost always have state requirements in terms of education and demonstration of specific proficiencies in an area of special education, placement in a program where there are lesser requirements can be concerning and often quite serious in terms of the delivery of an appropriate education for your child.

If you have a child in a charter school, you and your child have all the same rights under the IDEA that apply to those in a regular school, regardless of whether the charter school is an independent school or within a specific school district. That also means that the charter school has all the responsibilities under the IDEA discussed throughout this book. But the fact that the IEP/IDEA requirements for charter schools are the same does not mean that the schools may not misunderstand or ignore those requirements. For example, one federal court made it clear that a charter school can be found to violate the requirements of the IDEA, in this case, a change of placement without an IEP. The court in *R.B. v. Mastery Charter Sch.*, 762 F.Supp.2d 745 (E.D. Pa., 2010) stated that the charter school's "attempt to evade its obligations under the IDEA by passing the buck—in this case, a special-needs student's education—to the District is troubling....[the school] is bound by all the obligations of IDEA."

Private School Placement Before a Public School Program

Although the IDEA provides that there are circumstances when a public school must place or pay for a child's placement in a private school, it hasn't always been clear whether a child must *first* receive public school services (or be placed in a public school) before the school district must pay for or place the child in a private educational setting. The U.S. Supreme Court addressed this question in *Forest Grove School District v. T.A.,* 129 S.Ct. 987 (2009). In that case, the parents enrolled their child in a private school before the district had offered any of its own services. The district didn't want to pay for the education. But because the school district had known that the child was having difficulties but failed to offer any services, the court concluded that it couldn't avoid paying for private placement.

Is Mainstreaming a Legal Right?

Court decisions interpreting the least restrictive environment rule have been as varied as the children in special education. Some court opinions have concluded that mainstreaming is required by IDEA; other judges have ruled that it is "a goal subordinate to the requirement that disabled children receive educational benefit." *Hartmann by Hartmann v. Loudoun County Bd. of Educ.,* 118 F.3d 996, 1002 (4th Cir. 1997).

The goals of mainstreaming and providing an appropriate education may conflict if a child needs very specialized curricula, intense services, specialized staff, or a protected environment. In this type of situation, the child's unique educational needs may go unmet if the child is mainstreamed.

What's clear from these court decisions is that mainstreaming is preferred, but there is no absolute right to mainstreaming. The more complex the child's needs are, the more likely the scale will tip toward a nonmainstreamed placement.

Range of Placements

If a regular classroom placement is not appropriate for your child, the school district must provide a range of alternative placements—called a continuum of placement options—including the following:

- regular classes
- regular classes for part of the school day
- special classes in regular schools—for example, a special class for children with learning disabilities
- special public or private schools for children with disabilities
- charter schools
- residential programs

- home instruction, and
- hospital and other institutional placement.

If a child's unique needs dictate an alternative to a regular classroom, the continuum requirement ensures that the school district will make different placement options available. No matter where children are placed, however, IDEA requires every child to have access to the general curriculum taught in the regular classroom. The IEP must specifically address how this requirement will be met. (20 U.S.C. § 1414(d)(1)(A).)

Support or Related Services

Related services, as listed below, are the educational, psychological, therapeutic, cognitive, and other services that will help your child meet his or her educational goals. These services can be of paramount importance to children with learning disabilities, who are often placed in a regular classroom.

IDEA requires schools to provide related services for two reasons:
- to help your child benefit from special education, and
- to ensure that your child has the chance to "achieve satisfactorily" in a regular classroom.

Under IDEA, related services include:
- speech-language pathology and audiology services
- psychological services (for example, for anxiety or low self-esteem caused by a learning disability)
- physical and occupational therapy (for example, help with fine motor skills, like handwriting and drawing)
- recreation, including therapeutic recreation
- social work services
- counseling services, including rehabilitation counseling
- orientation and mobility services
- medical services for diagnostic and evaluation purposes
- interpreting services
- school nurse services
- one-on-one instructional aide
- transportation, and

- technological devices, such as special computers or voice-recognition software. (20 U.S.C. § 1401(26).)

Rules for Related Services

When Congress amended IDEA in 2004, it made a few changes to the list of related services. Here are the key changes:

- **Interpreting services.** Congress added "interpreting services," although it did not specify whether sign language interpreters must be certified, an important issue for deaf and hard of hearing children.
- **School nurse services.** Congress also added "school nurse services designed to enable a child with a disability to receive a free appropriate public education." (See "Is a Medical Service a Related Service?" below, for more information.)
- **Surgically implanted device.** Congress also specified that a surgically implanted medical device, or the replacement of such a device, is not a related service. (20 U.S.C. § 1401(26).) This language refers to cochlear implants.
- **Peer-reviewed research.** The latest version of the law also requires that the related services listed in the IEP be "based on peer-reviewed research to the extent practicable." (20 U.S.C. § 1414(d)(1)(A).) See Chapters 10 and 11 for more information on this requirement.

Some common related services used by children with a learning disability include one-on-one work with an aide, counseling when the learning disability leads to emotional difficulties, speech and language services to assist a child with language processing or speech problems, and occupational or physical therapy for children with small or large motor difficulties.

This is not an exhaustive list. Because everything under IDEA is driven by a child's individual needs, the IEP team has the authority to provide any service your child needs, even if it's not listed in the law.

Is a Medical Service a Related Service?

What constitutes a related service has been debated since IDEA was enacted in 1975. One particularly difficult issue has been whether a medical service constitutes a related service, if it is needed for a child to benefit from special education. In 1999, the U.S. Supreme Court ruled that a medical service is a related service if it is limited to "diagnostic and evaluation purposes."

The Court also ruled, however, that other medical services might constitute related services under IDEA if they can be performed by a nonphysician. In the case heard by the Court, the child needed and was granted the services of a nurse to provide, among other things, daily catheterization, suctioning of a tracheotomy, and blood pressure monitoring. (*Cedar Rapids Community School District v. Garret F., ex rel. Charlene F.*, 119 S.Ct. 992 (1999).)

Congress codified the *Cedar Rapids* ruling when it amended IDEA in 2004. The law now provides that school nurse services qualify as a related service. (20 U.S.C. § 1401(26).) (Oddly, a few courts have flipped the *Cedar Rapids* logic on its head. In *Max M. v. Thompson*, 592 F.Supp. 1437 (N.D. Ill. 1984), a child was receiving psychiatric care from a psychiatrist (a psychiatrist is a physician). The court ruled that this was a related service because the therapy could also be provided by a nonphysician.)

Parents must show that a particular related service is necessary to their child's education, but there's no dispute that services that can be performed by nurses can be required under IDEA. Keep in mind that normal medical services, such as check-ups, other normal diagnostic procedures, and procedures like an appendectomy, are well beyond the reach of IDEA requirements.

Assistive Technology

IDEA requires that a child be provided with assistive technology services. These services include:

- evaluating how the child functions in his or her customary environment
- leasing or purchasing assistive technology devices

- fitting, maintaining, and replacing assistive technology devices
- using and coordinating other therapies, interventions, or services in conjunction with such technology, and
- training and technical assistance for the child, the child's family, and the educational staff. (20 U.S.C. § 1401(1) and (2).)

Technological devices are defined as any item, piece of equipment, or system acquired, modified, or customized to maintain, increase, or improve the functional capabilities of a child with a disability. An assistive technology device or service might be an augmentative communication system, a computer, computer software, a touch screen, a calculator, a tape recorder, a spell-checker, or books on tape. (34 C.F.R. § 300.5, § 300.6, and § 300.105.)

This part of the law may be especially helpful to children with learning disabilities—computer programs alone can provide opportunities for tremendous improvement in the educational experiences of these kids.

Section 504 of the Rehabilitation Act of 1973 and the Americans with Disabilities Act

Separate from any rights under IDEA, your child may also qualify for special services under the Rehabilitation Act of 1973 (29 U.S.C. § 794), more commonly known as Section 504, and the Americans with Disabilities Act, 42 U.S.C. § 12101, often referred to as ADA. Both Section 504 and ADA are intended to prevent discrimination against children with disabilities, although the laws impose different procedural requirements. Section 504 is essentially an access law that prohibits a school district from denying your child access to an educational program or educational facilities. Section 504 is covered briefly in Chapter 7; Appendix A on this book's Companion Page on nolo.com includes key sections of the law. (See Chapter 16 for the link.)

Transition Services

IDEA requires the IEP team to develop a transition plan to be included in the first IEP in effect when your child turns 16 or at an earlier age if the IEP team determines that to be appropriate. (20 U.S.C. § 1414(d), 34 C.F.R. § 300.320(b).) (Before the 2004 amendments, transition planning had to begin when a child turned 14.)

In the transition plan, you and the IEP team must spell out how your child will proceed after high school, whether to college, to work, to a training program, or to develop the skills necessary to live independently as an adult. (20 U.S.C. § 1414(d)(1)(A).) The plan must include "appropriate measurable postsecondary goals," based on appropriate transition assessments focused on training, employment, education, and independent living skills. The IEP must also list the specific transition services that will be required to help your child reach these transition goals.

Due Process

In law, "due process" generally refers to the right to a fair procedure for determining individual rights and responsibilities. Under IDEA, and as used and discussed in detail in this book, due process refers to your child's right to be evaluated, receive an appropriate education, be educated in the LRE, have an IEP, and be given notice of any changes in the IEP.

Due process also refers to your right to take any dispute you have with your child's school district—for example, a disagreement about an evaluation, eligibility, or any part of the IEP—including the specific placement and related services—to a neutral third party to resolve your dispute. These rights are unique to IDEA; only children in special education have them.

There are two options for resolving disputes through due process: mediation and a due process hearing. In mediation, you and the school district meet with a neutral third party who tries to help you come to an agreement. The mediator has the power of persuasion, but no authority to impose a decision on either side.

If you cannot reach an agreement in mediation (or prefer to skip mediation altogether), you can request a hearing. There, you and the school district present written and oral testimony about the disputed issues before a neutral administrative judge. The judge will decide who is right and issue an order imposing a decision on all parties. Both you and the school district have the right to appeal the decision to a federal or state court, all the way to the U.S. Supreme Court. But before you conjure up images of walking up the marble stairs to the highest court in the land, you should know that most disputes with school districts are resolved before a hearing (and certainly before you find yourself in a courtroom).

If you believe that your school has violated a legal rule—for example, by failing to hold an IEP meeting—you should file a complaint (discussed in Chapter 13). The complaint process is quite different from due process (covered in more detail in Chapter 12). A due process matter involves a factual dispute between you and the school district. A complaint alleges that the district failed to follow the legal requirements of IDEA.

Rules for Due Process

When Congress amended IDEA in 2004, it made several important changes:

- **Filing deadline.** Parents must file for due process within two years after they knew or should have known of the underlying dispute. If your state has its own deadline, the state rule will apply.
- **Timing of response.** Once a due process request has been filed, the other party has ten days to respond.
- **Resolution meeting.** Within 15 days after receiving a due process request, the school district must convene a meeting to try to resolve the dispute. The school district cannot have an attorney at this meeting unless the parents bring one.
- **Attorney's fee.** If parents bring a due process action for any improper purpose, "such as to harass, to cause unnecessary delay, or to needlessly increase the cost of litigation," they may have to pay the school district's attorney's fees. (20 U.S.C. § 1415.)

Suspension and Expulsion

Some children with learning disabilities have trouble behaving themselves in school. Like all other kids, children with learning disabilities sometimes act out, try to get attention in the wrong ways, or are more interested in their friends than their schoolwork. But, sometimes, children with learning disabilities have behavioral problems that are directly related to their disabilities. A child with ADD who can't pay attention in class, a child whose reading difficulties lead to immense frustration, or a child whose processing problems make it hard to follow a teacher's instructions can create disciplinary problems. A child who has secondary emotional difficulties because of a learning disability may be disruptive or even get into fights. How can schools balance their responsibility to maintain order with their duty to provide an appropriate education for children with disabilities?

Most states have laws and procedures about disciplinary action—including suspension and expulsion—quite separate from special education laws and procedures. These disciplinary rules apply to all students within a school district. For special education students, however, these rules must be applied in conjunction with the laws and procedures of IDEA, including specific protections that apply when a child with a learning disability is subject to suspension or expulsion. Like all children in school, your child must follow the rules; otherwise, he or she may be suspended or expelled. Before the school district can take this type of action, however, IDEA requires a very careful analysis of whether the disability played a role in your child's behavior and, if so, whether suspension or expulsion is really justified.

In 1997, Congress added many new rules to IDEA regarding the suspension and expulsion of special education students. Although these rules provide specific rights and procedures for children in special education who are subject to discipline, Congress clearly intended to allow school districts to remove students who misbehave or are dangerous.

CAUTION
Get help if your child is in trouble. The IDEA rules and procedures applicable to suspensions and expulsions are complicated—and the stakes for your child in these situations are very high. This section provides an overview, but you'll probably want to contact a parent support group or special education lawyer if your child faces serious disciplinary action. This is one situation in which you shouldn't try to go it alone.

IDEA and Disciplinary Action

IDEA provides that a student with an IEP cannot have his or her program, placement, or services changed unless the school district and the child's parents agree to the change. Absent such an agreement, the child is entitled to remain, or "stay put," in the current program until either a new IEP is signed or a hearing officer decides that the child's program can be changed. (20 U.S.C. § 1415(j).) The school district cannot remove your child or unilaterally change your child's program—if it tries to do so, you can assert your child's right to stay put in the current placement until a new IEP is in place or a hearing officer approves the change. This very broad rule is intended to prevent a school from moving a child without parental approval.

A proposed suspension or expulsion clearly constitutes a change in placement, and this is where state laws on suspension and expulsion run directly into IDEA requirements. Can a school district suspend or expel (remove the child from school) without violating the "stay put" rule? The answer is, as you probably expected, yes and no. The law clearly states that a child with disabilities can be suspended or expelled, but the suspension or expulsion cannot take place unless certain IDEA procedures are followed. (20 U.S.C. § 1415(j) and (k); these rules are further explained in the IDEA regulations at 34 C.F.R. §§ 300.530–537.)

Congress created different rules depending on the length of the suspension or expulsion. This part of IDEA is fairly complex but, generally, children who are facing more than ten days out of school have more procedural protections under the law.

Suspensions or Expulsions for up to Ten Days

Any special education child removed from school for *up to ten consecutive days* is not entitled to the IDEA procedures and protections. Because such a removal does not constitute a "change in placement," the child cannot claim the "stay put" right. Many suspensions are for fewer than ten consecutive days, so most special education students who are suspended do not have the right to contest that removal based either on IDEA's "stay put" rule or on IDEA's specific disciplinary procedures. In short, a child with disabilities can be suspended from school for up to ten days just like any other student.

Suspensions and Expulsions Exceeding Ten Days

If a school district intends to expel or suspend or a special education student for more than ten consecutive days, that *might* constitute a "change in placement." In these situations, additional IDEA procedures kick in before the child can be removed. These procedures might also apply to a child who is removed from school for more than ten nonconsecutive days

Within ten school days of a decision to change a student's placement, an IEP team must hold a "manifestation determination" review. If the IEP team determines that the misbehavior was caused by the child's disability or by the district's failure to implement the IEP, certain steps are required. The district must either develop a behavioral intervention plan for the child, or modify the child's existing plan. The district is required to return the student to the original placement unless the parent and the district agree to a change of placement as part of modifying the student's behavioral intervention plan.

(You can find these requirements at 34 C.F.R. § 300.530(e).)

Dangerous Behavior

IDEA makes an exception to the ten-day rule for disciplinary problems involving weapons or drugs. A special education student who brings a weapon to school or possesses, uses, sells, or solicits the sale of drugs at school or during a school function can be removed for up to 45 days without parental agreement. This means the student cannot assert his or her "stay put" right to remain in the student's current placement pending the conclusion of the required IDEA disciplinary procedures. The student is entitled, however, to an "interim alternative" placement as determined by the IEP team.

Related Requirements

As a general rule, IDEA requires the IEP team to develop a "behavioral intervention" plan for those students whose behavior impedes learning or that of others. (34 C.F.R. § 300.324(a)(2)(i).) It would not be surprising if a special education student facing suspension or expulsion had such a plan in his or her IEP. As mentioned above, if a student is removed for more than ten days, and the IEP team determines that the student's behavior was a manifestation of his or her disability, IDEA requires the IEP team to do a "functional behavioral assessment" and implement a "behavioral intervention plan" if one is not already in place.

For a child with a learning disability whose condition impairs his or her ability to relate to others or behave appropriately, the plan should address those needs and provide strategies for helping improve peer relationships and/or school behavior. For example, a child who takes out the frustration of a learning disability by lashing out at other students might be taught alternative methods to express frustration, such as talking to a counselor, taking a "time out," or expressing anger more constructively ("I don't like it when you interrupt me when I'm speaking in class").

RESOURCE

Want more information on discipline? For lots of great ideas on dealing with disciplinary and behavior problems, as well as detailed information on drafting behavioral intervention plans, check out the website of the Center for Effective Collaboration and Practice (a group dedicated to helping students, teachers, and parents address emotional and behavioral concerns), at http://cecp.air.org.

Additional IDEA Rights

IDEA also gives children the following rights.

Summer School

IDEA requires the school district to provide children with summer school (called an "extended school year" or ESY) if necessary to meet their needs. (34 C.F.R. § 300.106.)

The general rule applied to whether a school district must provide ESY is whether your child will "likely regress" without it. That rule has expanded somewhat: the U.S Department of Education, Office of Special Education Programs, has written that if the child will too slowly "recoup" what was lost without ESY, then ESY must be provided.

Private School

IDEA gives your child the right to be placed in a nonprofit or private (including parochial) school if your school district cannot provide an appropriate program. (20 U.S.C. § 1412(a)(10).) IDEA does not give your child an automatic right to attend a private school, however, and it is generally difficult to get a private placement—particularly for those with learning disabilities, whose needs may not be severe enough to warrant a private school. Under IDEA, school districts are required to show that they cannot serve a child before they are allowed to place and pay for a child in a private school.

Although there are impediments to securing a private placement, it is certainly possible. Your child's needs and the nature of the available public programs will largely determine whether a private school is appropriate and feasible. If you feel that your child needs a private placement, you should certainly pursue it through the IEP process. (See Chapter 12 for more information.)

There must be either an IEP agreement or a due process or court ruling that the private school is appropriate before the school district is required to pay for a private school placement. If you place your child in a private school on your own, your school district is not required to pay. See "IDEA Notice Requirements and Private School Placements," below.

Although the school district does not have to pay tuition costs for children whose parents place them in private school, it must offer special education and related services to these children. The school district need not provide these services at the private school (although it can choose to do so), nor does it have to provide any services different from or in addition to those that would be available if the child were in public school.

Under IDEA, school districts must consult with private schools about whether and how special education and related services will be provided to children whose parents placed them in private school. The private school can file a complaint with the state educational agency if it feels the district is not complying with this "consultation" requirement in a timely and meaningful manner. (20 U.S.C. § 1412(a)(10).) The school district does not have to provide services at the private school, so this consultation or "right to talk" requirement doesn't create or expand rights for children whose parents place them in private school.

IDEA Notice Requirements and Private School Placements

If you plan to remove your child to a private program, you must notify the school district of your intent either:

- at the most recent IEP meeting you attended prior to removing your child from public school, or
- by written notice at least ten business days before the actual removal. (20 U.S.C. § 1412(a)(10)(C).)

If you don't provide this notice, your request for the school district to reimburse you for the cost of your child's placement in a private school may be denied, or you may receive only partial repayment.

Special Education in Prison

Imprisoned children between the ages of 18 and 21 who were identified and had an IEP prior to incarceration are also entitled to a free appropriate public education. (20 U.S.C. § 1414(d)(7).) Children who are convicted as adults and incarcerated in adult prisons, however, do not have certain protections, such as those relating to general assessments and transition planning.

Individualized Education Program

The IEP may seem complicated—after all, the term refers to a meeting, a document, and a description of your child's entire educational program. While the IEP meeting is discussed in detail in Chapters 10 and 11, here are a few introductory concepts to help you get started:

- By law, you are an equal partner in the IEP process. As a general rule, no part of the IEP can be implemented without your approval or that of the school district.

- Your child's entry into special education will follow an initial eligibility IEP. Thereafter, IEP meetings will be held yearly, focusing on your child's current educational program and what next year's IEP will look like. While the procedures for these two kinds of IEPs (referred to as eligibility and program IEPs) are the same, there are some important differences—see Chapters 7, 10, and 11.

- You and the school district must agree to and sign a written IEP document before your child begins special education, and at least once each school year after that.

- Whenever you or your child's school district wants to change your child's current IEP, the district must schedule a new IEP meeting and develop a new written IEP. You and the school district can agree to hold the meeting via videoconference or conference call, or agree to make changes in the written IEP without an IEP meeting. (See "Rules for IEP Meetings," below.)

- You are entitled to an IEP meeting whenever you feel one is needed—for example, if you have concerns about your child's progress, there are classroom problems, or a related service or placement is not working.

- Once signed by you and the school district, the IEP is binding; the school district must provide everything included in that IEP.

This section provides details about the written IEP. Although forms will vary, every IEP, in every school district in every state, must include the same IEP information.

Rules for IEP Meetings

The 2004 amendments changed some of the rules for IEP meetings. Here are some of the provisions added (Chapters 10 and 11 cover IEP meetings in detail):

- Changes to the IEP can now be made without a meeting, if both the parent and the school district agree and the changes are made in writing. If you decide to forgo an IEP meeting, you should make sure you understand the changes and that the written agreement reflects them accurately. (34 C.F.R. § 300.324(a)(4).)
- IEP meetings can now be held by videoconference or conference call rather than in person. (34 C.F.R. § 300.328.)
- Members of the IEP team can be excused from attending in certain circumstances, if you agree to their absence. (34 C.F.R. § 300.321(e).)
- If a child transfers from one school district to another (in or out of state), the new school district must initially provide a program "comparable" to the one described in the existing IEP. (34 C.F.R. § 300.323.)
- A new pilot program in about 15 locations is experimenting with less frequent IEP meetings. (20 U.S.C. § 1414(d)(5).) Each pilot can set up a system to develop IEPs that cover a period of up to three years, rather than the current model, which requires annual IEPs. Participation will not be required—you and your child still have the right to annual IEPs if you wish—but this program bears watching as a possible wave of the future.

Current Educational Status

The IEP must include a description of your child's current status in school, including cognitive skills, linguistic ability, emotional behavior, social skills and behavior, and physical ability. (20 U.S.C. § 1414(d)(1)(A)(i).) Current functioning may be reflected in testing data, grades, reports, or anecdotal information, such as teacher observations. IDEA calls this the "present levels of academic achievement and functional performance." This part of the IEP must describe how your child's disability affects his or her involvement and progress in the general curriculum. Formal testing or evaluations of your child will provide a good deal of the information necessary to describe your child's current educational status.

 RELATED TOPIC

Chapters 6 and 8 cover evaluations and other information-gathering tools you can use to develop useful evidence of your child's needs.

Measurable Annual Goals

Goals are the nuts and bolts of your child's daily program. They generally include academic, linguistic, and other cognitive activities. The IEP must not only detail your child's goals, but also describe how progress toward those goals will be measured.

EXAMPLE:

Goal: John will increase his reading comprehension. John will read a three-paragraph story and answer eight out of ten questions about the story correctly.

While goals are usually academic and cognitive in nature, there is no restriction on what goals may cover or say. They should reflect whatever the IEP team determines is important to your child's education. Goals can relate to specific subject areas—reading, spelling, math, or history—

as well as physical education, how your child socializes with peers, emotional needs, and even how your child will move about the school.

IDEA refers to "measurable annual goals, including academic and functional goals" designed to meet your child's educational and other needs and enable him or her to be "involved in and make progress in the general education curriculum." The law requires your child's IEP to describe how yearly progress toward meeting these goals will be measured. (20 U.S.C. § 1414(d)(1)(A).) This is a change from the former version of IDEA, which required the IEP team to come up with "benchmarks"—short-term objectives that would help a child achieve these larger goals. The new language seems broad enough to encompass short-term, specific objectives (although they won't be called by that name) as well as long-term goals. As to the term "measurable," an annual goal can be measured numerically, by teacher report, or any other method that is appropriate.

Whether or not your child is receiving a "free appropriate public education" (FAPE) may depend on whether the program offered by the school district can help him or her achieve the goals in the IEP. If you and the school district disagree about whether a specific placement or service is necessary, a key issue will be whether your child's goals can be met without it.

RELATED TOPIC
Chapter 9 shows you how to write goals that support your child's placement and service needs.

Instructional Setting or Placement

The IEP must include information about the appropriate instructional setting or placement for your child. Here are a few examples of IEP placements:

- A child with significant learning disabilities might be placed in a regular classroom with support services, such as assistance from a one-on-one aide.

- A child with significant language and cognitive delays might be placed in a special class.
- A child who is terrified of large spaces and crowds could be placed in a small, protected nonregular school.
- A child with serious emotional difficulties might be placed in a residential program.

A child with learning disabilities can be placed in any of these classes or programs, depending on the severity of need, although children with learning disabilities are less likely to be placed in the more restrictive placements, such as separate schools or residential programs. Many children with learning disabilities are placed in regular classrooms; however, those placements may require some fine-tuning to meet your child's needs. For example, your child may need a seat near the front of the class, a note-taker, more time to take tests or complete homework, specialized curricula, or the opportunity to use a computer for writing assignments.

Related Services

As discussed above, related services are the developmental, corrective, or supportive services necessary to facilitate your child's placement in a regular class or to allow your child to benefit from special education. These must be specifically included in the IEP.

Once the IEP team determines the appropriate related support services, the team should give details about each service, including:

- when it begins
- the amount (such as all day, once a day, twice a week, once a week, or once a month)
- the duration (such as 15, 30, 45, or 60 minutes per session)
- the ratio of pupils to related service providers, and
- the qualifications of the service provider.

Other Required IEP Components

The IEP must also specifically address:

- how your child's disability affects his or her involvement and progress in the general curriculum used in the regular classroom
- how your child's need to be involved in the general curriculum will be met
- how special education and related services will help your child attain annual goals; be involved in the general curriculum, and extracurricular and nonacademic activities; and participate with other children with and without disabilities
- whether any program modifications or supports for school personnel are necessary for your child to benefit from special education
- how you will be regularly informed of your child's progress
- how your child will participate in any district or statewide assessment of student achievement used for the general student body, and whether any modifications or accommodations will be necessary
- how your child's transition services will be provided (once your child is 16 years old), and
- how your child's need for assistive technology will be met.

For blind and visually impaired students, the IEP team must provide for instruction in Braille and the use of Braille, unless the IEP determines that Braille is not appropriate. (20 U.S.C. § 1414 (d)(3)(B)(iii).)

In addition, IDEA requires the IEP team to "consider" the following:

- strategies, including positive behavioral interventions, to address the needs of children with behavior difficulties (20 U.S.C. § 1414(d)(3)(B)(i))
- the language needs of children with limited English proficiency (20 U.S.C. § 1414(d)(3)(B)(ii)), and
- the communication needs of deaf and hard of hearing children, including opportunities for direct communication with peers and staff and instruction in the child's language and communication mode (20 U.S.C. § 1414 (d)(3)(B)(iv)).

For more details, contact your school district, your state department of education, or a disability group (Appendix B). See Appendix D for a sample IEP. The appendixes are available on this book's Companion Page on nolo.com. See Chapter 16 for the link.

Optional Components

The IEP may include other components, such as specific teaching methods, particular class subjects, or anything else the IEP team agrees should be included. (20 U.S.C. § 1414(d)(1)(A).)

EXAMPLES:

- a specific methodology or teaching strategy designed to help your learning disabled child, such as a multisensory approach (see Chapter 5)
- pull-out services with a resource specialist to work on specific areas of need, like reading, math, or handwriting, and
- visual aids for a visually impaired child.

More Information on State Special Education Laws

State special education laws (statutes) are normally found in the education code of each state. State departments of education often have their own regulations implementing the law.

You can find the addresses, phone numbers, and websites of state departments of education through the U.S. Department of Education website at www.ed.gov. When you contact your state's department, ask for a copy of your state laws and any publications explaining your legal rights (many are available online). Ask about the state special education advisory commission—IDEA requires each state to have one, composed of educators and parents.

Because laws and policies change, it is important to keep up to date, especially if you are involved in a dispute with your school. For more information on legal research, see Chapter 14.

Working With Your School District

Most, if not all, of your dealings will be with your local public school district, which has the legal responsibility for your child's IEP.

Sometimes, however, special education programs are the responsibility of a larger educational unit, such as a county office of education. This is often the case when a school district is small or there are not enough children to establish a special education class. Always start with the school district where you reside. It has the ultimate responsibility for your child, even if there is a larger, area-wide agency involved. As used in this book, the term "local school district" refers to the responsible educational unit.

Teacher Certification Requirements

When Congress amended IDEA in 2004, it added language to conform the requirements of IDEA with the requirements of No Child Left Behind (NCLB), the education law passed in 2001. (For more on NCLB, see "No Child Left Behind," below.) IDEA now provides that any public elementary or secondary school special education teacher in your state must have:

- obtained "full" state certification as a special education teacher
- passed the state special education licensing examination, or
- completed valid state "alternative" certification requirements, and hold a license to teach in your state.

(20 U.S.C. § 1401(10).)

This rule does not apply to special education teachers in private or charter schools.

Key Players in the IEP Process

The key participants in the IEP process are:

- you
- your child (if appropriate)
- your child's teacher—potentially your best ally or worst enemy in the IEP process. Because many children with learning disabilities will be in regular classrooms, this will often be the regular teacher. Or it may be a resource specialist, for those children with learning disabilities who are pulled out of their regular

class to work with a specialist on particular areas of need. (Older children, particularly those in junior or senior high school, may have a separate teacher for each academic class.)

- a school administrator with responsibility for special education—a site principal or special education administrator
- specialists, such as a school psychologist, speech or occupational therapist, communications specialist, resource specialist, or adaptive physical education instructor, and
- anyone else you or the school wants to attend, such as your child's physician, your lawyer, the school's evaluator, or an outside independent evaluator you selected.

 RELATED TOPIC

Chapter 10 covers the IEP participants in detail, including their roles, who has authority, and who should attend the IEP meetings. It also explains how to prepare for the IEP meeting.

The Realities of Schools and Special Education

School districts and their special education administrators are as varied as parents. Their programs, services, and budgets will differ, as will their personalities. All of these factors influence what programs school districts have to offer and how they deal with children and parents. Depending on the population breakdown in the district, there may be many special education programs or only a few. Philosophical or pedagogical differences may have an impact on programs and services. Some administrators believe very firmly that most, if not all, children with disabilities should be mainstreamed in regular education. Some administrators believe with equal vigor that special programs are important and that children with disabilities, more often than not, belong in special classes.

More Information on Special Education and Local Schools

Your school district is required by IDEA to provide you with a copy of federal and state statutes and regulations and any relevant policies. Be sure to request this information, along with the school's IEP form. Most school districts have some kind of parent guide, as do most states. Contact your school district for a copy.

Finding out what programs are available in your district, and what personalities and philosophies dominate, is important. Ask around. Talk to your child's teacher and other parents; go to a PTA meeting. Many school districts have a community advisory committee for special education; the parents involved in that group will likely know the specific programs, players, and philosophies in your school district. (See Chapter 15 for more information on parent organizations.)

It is not uncommon for parents to view school administrators and other staff as impediments rather than as partners in the special education process. Sometimes school personnel view parents as unreasonable and difficult.

While there are times when these viewpoints are justified, remember that a majority of educators are passionate, hardworking, and caring individuals. They teach in a complicated environment in which there is too much paperwork and there are too many requirements and not enough support or pay. It's not fair to demonize them—and it won't help you secure the best possible education for your child.

RELATED TOPIC

Chapter 8 provides detailed advice on how to explore available school programs. Chapter 15 discusses parent groups.

The Importance of "Process"

IDEA has very specific rules for assessments, eligibility determination, or notifying parents of their rights—basically, for the entire IEP process. Congress believed that establishing a clear procedure was as important, if not more important, than dictating specific IEP solutions for various situations. For example, instead of trying to anticipate and answer every possible special education scenario—"School district, follow this plan for a 14-year-old learning disabled child, use this one for a seven-year-old LD student, and implement this one for a five-year-old vision-impaired student…"—the lawmakers decided that a clear diagnostic process would result in tailored plans that would better serve children with disabilities.

But sometimes school districts fail to follow these rules. For example, school districts may fail to seek permission to assess a child, neglect to hold an IEP meeting every year as required, not provide a fair and open chance to discuss anything regarding your child at the IEP meeting, and fail to inform parents of placement options in the district. The district might not have the appropriate professionals at the IEP meeting; sometimes, even before the IEP meeting, it prematurely decides what it will provide.

When a school district violates any of the procedures of the IDEA, the violation itself may mean that the district has to do what you want for your child, regardless of whether you have sufficient evidence to prove your child needs the specific education program or services you're requesting. For example, suppose your child needs a particular related service, and at the IEP meeting, the district representative says something like, "We don't offer those services," or "We've already decided your child does not need those services," or "No, we don't need to see the outside evaluation you had done about those services." These "the door is shut" statements violate the IEP's requirement that the meeting allow you a full and open chance to discuss your child's needs, without any predetermination by the district.

Or, perhaps you write the district to tell it that your child is having problems, and you would like it to evaluate her to determine whether she is eligible for special education. If the district refuses to assess your child (or does the assessment without your permission), those violations may be significant enough that your child will be found eligible, regardless of what the evidence showed.

When Process Matters

A school district's refusal or failure to follow the rules can result in victories for the child. Here are some examples. Keep in mind that each case is heavily dependent on the precise facts presented to the judge—and no two cases are precisely alike.

In *Deal v. Hamilton*, 392 F.3d 840 (6th Cir. 2004), the school district had determined before the IEP meeting that the *Lovaas* method (a strategy for assisting autistic children) was "too expensive," and also had issued an internal memo that this case was a "sensitive" one. A federal appellate court concluded that the district had predetermined it would not consider the *Lovaas* method, thereby depriving the parents of the opportunity to have a meaningful involvement in the development of their child's IEP.

In *W. G. v. Target Range*, 960 F.2d 1479 (9th Cir. 1992), the school district failed to reconvene to reconsider a student's eligibility for more than two years, and at the belated meeting, provided an already prepared IEP document. The appellate court concluded that these procedural violations were so significant that there was no need to go into whether the private school placement was appropriate.

Courts have handled many more cases involving procedural violations, including the failure to have a regular education teacher at the IEP meeting (as required by 34 C.F.R. § 300.321(a)(2)). For example, in *M.L. v. Federal Way School District*, 394 F.3d. 634 (9th Cir. 2004), the absence of a regular education teacher at the IEP meeting, and the failure of the IEP administrator in charge of making IEP decisions to have ever seen the child, were so serious as to render the process ineffective.

Keep in mind that in just as many cases, the facts did not support a finding of a procedural violation. And sometimes, even when a court finds that a violation has taken place, it concludes that the violation was not significant enough to trigger the "procedural rule."

In short, a school district's procedural failures can be important—be sure to keep track of what your district does, how it responds to you, and otherwise follows the requirements of IDEA. Violations are further discussed in Chapter 13.

When you have a dispute with your school district about some aspect of your child's IEP/education, it may be that you don't have a strong case. For example, you may want your child to have more of a particular related service, more time in a regular class, or even placement in a nonpublic school and yet the evidence supporting that may not be strong. You may not be out of luck. A significant failure by your school or district to follow the "process" can render any dispute over educational services secondary. I want to stress the word "significant" because to result in your getting what you want for your child, the violation of process must directly impact your child's right to have an appropriate education or directly impact your ability to be part of the IEP process.

People often say that attorneys are always looking for technical failures to win a case, suggesting that the real "truth" of the dispute is never reached. We've all heard about the criminal who gets off on a technicality. But there are important reasons for focusing on procedural or "technical" requirements. This is particularly true in special education because the failure to provide the full "procedure" can have a very direct impact on your child's education.

Here are two examples of procedural violations, one not significant, the other significant.

> **EXAMPLE 1:** The school district provides a thorough IEP but a box is not correctly checked on a form. This is not likely going to be a significant procedural violation.

> **EXAMPLE 2:** You want your child placed in a regular classroom with an aide for the start of the new school year. The district does not hold an IEP meeting until midyear even though you have requested one over and over. Your child is unable to access the

regular classroom for a significant amount of time. The procedural violation is significant and has had a direct educational consequence of importance.

Compensatory Education

When a school district fails to provide a child with a "free appropriate public education," including the placement, program, and/or services needed, the child may be entitled to "compensatory" education; that is, additional assistance to make up for the original failure. Compensatory education is not applicable when there is a disagreement between you and the district about some component of your child's IEP, but when the district fails to provide the IEP or violates IDEA procedures.

Compensatory education can take many forms and should relate directly to the child's individual needs. Compensatory ed. represents "replacement of educational services the child should have received in the first place" to place the child in the same position he or she would have been in if it weren't for the school's failure. (*Reid v. District of Columbia*, 365 U.S. App. D.C. 234, 401 F.3d 516, 518 [578] (D.C. Cir. 2005).)

Compensatory education may be payment of private school tuition, one-on-one tutoring, a classroom aide, or assistive technology support (one court ordered a school district to provide 608 hours of compensatory education through tech support).

Compensatory education can be provided after the student turns 21, but compensatory damages—money—is not usually available to make up for the school's failure to provide special education. Note that a failure to follow the procedures—a procedural violation—can have the same effect on a child as failing to provide services, and therefore may justify compensatory education. For example, a school fails to hold a timely IEP meeting and the student loses out on two months' of support. This procedural violation caused an educational failure, justifying compensatory education.

No Child Left Behind

In 2001, Congress passed education legislation called "No Child Left Behind" (NCLB). When amending IDEA in 2004, Congress added language to align it with the requirements of NCLB, primarily by imposing standards for special education teacher qualifications and emphasizing the teaching of "core academic subjects": English, reading or language arts, math, science, foreign languages, civics and government, economics, arts, history, and geography.

NCLB's stated purpose is to increase "accountability" for schools by requiring rigorous state educational standards in reading and math and by mandating state testing to determine whether children are meeting those standards. Test results must be broken out by race, ethnicity, income, English proficiency, and disability. School districts that don't show yearly progress, as reflected in standards and testing, will be subject to corrective action and possibly even forced restructuring. Children who attend schools that are not making yearly progress will have the opportunity to transfer to other schools, including charter schools, and to obtain supplemental services.

The effects of NCLB remain uncertain because of its complex requirements and the federal government's failure to adequately fund the law. Some states are trying to "opt out" of NCLB's provisions, primarily because the law imposes major new requirements without the funds necessary to implement them. Some advocates worry that the lack of funding provided for NCLB could result in fewer dollars available for all educational programs, including special education.

For example, one of NCLB's stated goals is to ensure that all children can read by the end of the third grade. To achieve this goal, the law increases funding for scientifically based reading instruction programs and provides grants for school districts to assess students in the K–3 grades to determine which ones are at risk for reading failure. Because developing reading skills is so important—and often so difficult—for children with learning disabilities, how (and whether) your school district implements this part of NCLB could really affect your child's program. Contact your district and your state department of education to find out how this and other parts of the law will be administered locally.

President Barack Obama has stated that reforming NCLB is high on his education agenda, so there may be more changes to come in the near future.

What Is a Learning Disability?

The term "learning disability" means different things to different people. In the most basic sense, a learning disability is a problem taking in, processing, understanding, or expressing thoughts and information, as reflected in difficulties with reading, calculating, spelling, writing, understanding or expressing language, coordination, self-control, and/or social skills development.

Beyond this basic definition, people use different terms to describe learning disabilities, depending on their area of expertise. The way a parent might explain a child's learning difficulties is often quite different from the labels a neurologist, psychologist, or educational specialist might use. And, as always, lawyers have their own set of technical definitions.

Mastering this terminology can be a challenge; you might wish you'd gotten a double major in law and neurology, with a minor in Latin. But don't worry—while you need to learn the basic terms specialists use for various kinds of learning problems, you don't need to become an expert in complicated jargon. While this chapter will help you understand the terminology various experts might use to "diagnose" your child, always keep your eye on the ultimate goal: to use these various definitions to make sure your child receives the individual help necessary to succeed in school.

The section below covers the legal definitions of learning disability used in IDEA. These terms are vitally important because your child must meet these requirements to qualify for special education. The next section explains some of the technical terms used to describe and diagnose learning disabilities and the basic learning deficiencies and problems these terms cover. The final section of this chapter describes the first hints, signs, and indications that your child might be struggling with a learning problem.

Legal Definitions

Your child will be eligible for special education only if his or her condition falls within the IDEA's definition of a learning disability. IDEA actually uses the term "specific learning disability." IDEA does not classify Attention Deficit Disorder (ADD) and Attention Deficit

Hyperactivity Disorder (ADHD) as specific learning disabilities. IDEA addresses these conditions separately; see "ADD/ADHD," below.

Specific Learning Disability

IDEA defines a specific learning disability as a "disorder in one or more of the basic psychological processes involved in understanding or in using language, spoken or written, that may manifest itself in the imperfect ability to listen, think, speak, read, write, spell, or to do mathematical calculations, including conditions such as perceptual disabilities, brain injury, minimal brain dysfunction, dyslexia, and developmental aphasia." (34 C.F.R. § 300.8(c)(10).)

In order for a child to be eligible for special education based on a learning disability, the IEP team must agree that the child "does not achieve adequately for the child's age or to meet State-approved grade-level standards in one or more of the following areas, when provided with learning experiences and instruction appropriate for the child's age or State-approved grade-level standards:

- oral expression
- listening comprehension
- written expression
- basic reading skill
- reading fluency skills
- reading comprehension
- mathematics calculation, or
- mathematics problem solving.

(34 C.F.R. § 300.309(a)(1).)

In other words, there must be a significant gap between what your child should be able to achieve in school, based on age and general intelligence, and what your child is actually able to accomplish in school, based on grades, test scores, classroom work, homework assignments, and so on.

Also, a specific learning disability cannot be "primarily" the result of:

- a visual, hearing, or motor disability
- mental retardation

- emotional disturbance
- cultural factors
- environmental or economic disadvantage, or
- limited English proficiency.

(34 C.F.R. § 300.309(a)(3).)

In Chapter 7 we discuss in detail how a child qualifies under "specific learning disability." For now, just note that you are basically looking to see whether your child is achieving "adequately" for his or her age or grade level.

> **CAUTION**
>
> **Reading or math difficulties caused by lack of instruction are not covered.** When Congress amended IDEA in 2004, it made a distinction between reading problems caused by a learning difficulty and those caused by poor or no instruction. The law now states that a student with problems in reading or math will not qualify for special education if those problems are caused by a "lack of appropriate instruction in reading or math." If your child is experiencing reading or math problems, you will want to pay careful attention to your school district's interpretation of this language. (See Chapter 7 for more on eligibility.)

ADD/ADHD

Although many advocacy organizations designate Attention Deficit Disorder (ADD) and Attention Deficit Hyperactivity Disorder (ADHD) as kinds of learning disabilities, IDEA does not. Instead, IDEA classifies ADD and ADHD as part of a category it calls "other health impairment."

The "other health impairment" category lists ADD and ADHD as examples of chronic or acute health problems that result in "limited strength, vitality, or alertness, including a heightened alertness to environmental stimuli, that results in limited alertness with respect to the educational environment." As with a specific learning disability, the health impairment must adversely affect the child's educational performance. (34 C.F.R. § 300.8(c)(9).)

Of course, a child with ADD or ADHD might also have symptoms or difficulties that fall within the description of a specific learning disability. In these circumstances, the child might qualify for special education under either category. The important issue is not the name or label ascribed to your child, but how the condition affects his or her ability to learn. Once your child is found eligible for special education— under any of the listed categories—the IEP must address all of your child's educational needs, whether they are created by ADD, ADHD, or a specific learning disability.

What Is the Difference Between ADD and ADHD?

Attention Deficit Disorder (ADD) and Attention Deficit Hyperactivity Disorder (ADHD) both involve the ability or inability to concentrate and retain focus. This can impact every aspect of life, including daily activities and a child's education. As school requirements grow more complex and pressures increase, the inability to focus on schoolwork can be devastating.

ADD is considered a subtype of the larger designation of ADHD. Both ADD and particularly ADHD students have trouble following directions. They have difficulty processing information and finishing assignments. ADHD students are distractable. They may seem to do their work with less care than other students, but they are struggling with a great deal of internal "movement."

Scientific and Professional Definitions

Beyond these legal definitions, scientists, educators, and other experts have their own ways of explaining and defining learning disabilities. You may run across these terms and ideas as you start trying to understand your child's problems (and what can be done to address them).

Organizational Definitions

Organizations and groups that specialize in learning disability education and advocacy use a variety of definitions to describe learning disabilities. The Learning Disabilities Association of America (LDA), for example, defines a learning disability as a "severe difficulty in some aspect of learning, speaking, reading, writing, or spelling." The National Center for Learning Disabilities defines learning disabilities as neurological disorders that affect "the brain's ability to receive, process, store, and respond to information" and create a "gap" between ability and performance.

The Child Development Institute (CDI) acknowledges that there is "no clear and widely accepted definition" and notes at least 12 different definitions in professional literature. The CDI looks to factors that indicate a learning disability, stressing "difficulties with academic achievement and progress" and "an uneven pattern of development" (language, physical, academic, and/or perceptual).

Find Out Much More on the Web

You can find lots of helpful information about specific learning disabilities on the Internet. In addition to the many websites and organizations referred to throughout this book and in Appendix B on this book's Companion Page on nolo.com, you will find websites for many of the definitions and terms used in this chapter. If you go to your search engine and type in ADD or ADHD, aphasia, dyslexia, or any of the many other terms used here, you will find a number of useful sites. Just a few are:

- www.add.org, for the Attention Deficit Disorder Association
- www.aphasia.org, for the National Aphasia Association, and
- www.interdys.org, for the International Dyslexia Association.

You can also go to www.ldaamerica.org (the Learning Disabilities Association of America), which provides a good deal of information about many learning disabilities.

The University of Arizona Strategic Alternative Learning Techniques (SALT) Center states that a learning disability "affects the manner in which individuals take in information, retain it, and express the knowledge and understanding they possess" as reflected in "deficits in reading comprehension, spelling, mechanics of writing, math computation, and/or problem solving."

Specific Learning Disabilities

In addition to the broad definitions of a learning disability found in IDEA and recognized by experts, there are specific learning disabilities whose names may be familiar to you. Some of the more well-known are:

- **Dyslexia:** problems with reading, spelling, and writing (including transposing letters and pronunciation difficulties).
- **Aphasia:** difficulties in processing information; more specifically, a limited ability to use or comprehend words, often as the result of a brain injury or a stroke. Someone with mild aphasia might have difficulty remembering the names of people or objects; more severe aphasia might impair a person's ability to speak or understand language at all.
- **Dyscalculia:** difficulties in calculating numbers or grasping mathematical concepts, such as algebra or geometric equations.
- **Dysgraphia:** difficulties with handwriting (including illegible writing, inappropriately sized or spaced letters, or spelling problems).
- **Dyspraxia:** difficulties with motor tasks, such as large movements (walking) or small movements (picking up a pencil or drawing).
- **Auditory processing disorder:** difficulties in understanding (processing) sounds; a child physically hears the word but can't understand its meaning or usage. A child with this problem might have trouble understanding spoken directions or following a conversation, or be easily distracted by noise.
- **Visual processing problems:** difficulties in understanding visual input; a child has no sight impairment but has difficulties in understanding and using visual information. A child with this problem might

have trouble judging physical distance (including appropriate social distances—for example, the child might physically crowd others), differentiating between similar letters or objects, or understanding spatial relationships.

- **Short- and long-term memory problems:** difficulties in creating or retrieving memories (for example, trouble remembering facts, phone numbers, or assignments, difficulty following instructions).

ADD and ADHD

ADD and ADHD are common behavior disorders characterized by a number of symptoms that often appear in early childhood and can continue into adulthood. The terms ADD and ADHD are often used interchangeably, and the characteristics of each are often quite similar (if not identical). Some consider ADHD a subcategory of ADD.

ADD/ADHD is a syndrome or disorder often characterized by:

- inattention or inability to stay focused over a period of time
- impulsivity—a tendency to act without thinking, and
- hyperactivity—an inability to sit still and focus.

A child with ADD/ADHD may be easily distracted or squirmy, quickly shift from one activity to another, talk excessively and interrupt, have difficulty following instructions, be unable to wait his or her turn, engage in dangerous behavior, or lose things.

Diagnosing ADHD/ADD

Diagnosing any "condition" is complex, but particularly so when we are dealing with somewhat subjective characteristics (what is "distractability" and how do we distinguish a diagnostic conclusion from an observation that someone seems to be daydreaming on a particular day?). In addition, any condition that is based "in the brain" adds additional complexities. Are there other conditions at play? Are there neurological or psychological issues separate from ADHD/ADD?

There are many tools to diagnose ADHD/ADD, including a physical examination, interviews, questionnaires, and direct observation—there is no one test to determine ADHD/ADD. The duration, type, and impact of symptoms add much to the picture. As a general rule, your child should be displaying characteristics of ADHD/ADD for at least five to six months before being diagnosed.

It is imperative that you try to keep a log of your child's behavior and schoolwork. What are the teachers saying? (Ask, if you have concerns and teachers are not reporting any issues.) Is your child able to finish homework and/or finish the work fully? What are the specific signs of lack of focus that your teacher is seeing and how often does it happen? What about your child's written schoolwork? Is she finishing all the work, and what is the quality of the work?

The National Center for Learning Disabilities (www.ncld.org) provides a wide variety of information on ADHD/ADD and all issues involved with learning disabilities.

Treatment for ADD/ADHD

There is no "cure" for ADD/ADHD. Among the more common treatments for ADD/ADHD are medication—Ritalin is frequently used—as well as behavior modification or management training, socialization training, counseling, self-verbalization, and self-reinforcement.

Some children with ADD/ADHD can achieve significant improvement by taking medication. For other children, medication doesn't help—or leads to new problems. Medicating a child is, of course, a very serious matter. You don't want to go that route until you are absolutely sure it is appropriate, as explained by your child's medical doctor. *Your child cannot be forced to take medication without your express permission.*

What Causes Learning Disabilities?

A learning disability can be the result of genetics, a brain injury, neurological problems, biochemical reaction, and perhaps even psychological issues. Current theories on ADD/ADHD, for example, indicate that it may be caused by chemical imbalance in the brain, genetics, brain trauma or damage, allergies, or neurological factors.

The truth is that no one really knows what causes learning disabilities generally, although your physician might be able to pinpoint some of the reasons why your child has a learning disability and the effects of that disability. For more information on what causes learning disabilities, check the online and other resources in Appendix B on this book's Companion Page (see Chapter 16 for the link).

It's important not to get so focused on what "caused" your child's learning disability that you lose sight of the goal at hand: to get help for your child. Your child will be best served by moving forward, not by looking backward. We all come into this world with a set of characteristics, inclinations, conditions, and, yes, difficulties. Granted, some are more serious than others. A learning disability is not a neutral characteristic like hair color or height, but it is an understandable and common condition that does not mark your child for failure or you for blame. By following the procedures and strategies in this book, you can help your child deal with his or her learning disability in a successful way.

Children With Learning Disabilities May Have Other Special Education Needs

Like any other child, a child with learning disabilities can have other special education conditions or needs. A child with learning disabilities can be gifted, have emotional or behavioral problems, or have a hearing loss, limited vision, or physical disabilities.

A learning disability directly affects how a child does in school, including relationships with peers. If the disability goes unnoticed or untreated, there can be emotional and behavioral consequences. A child may withdraw, have sleeping problems, show signs of anxiety or fear, or develop behavioral problems. You should watch your child for signs of secondary emotional and behavioral reactions—and share what you see with your school. If your child is found eligible for special education, the IEP must address all of his or her needs and conditions, not just the learning disability.

Does Your Child Have a Learning Disability?

Many parents have a strong sense, very early on, that their child has problems with learning, while others are surprised to hear from their child's doctor, teacher, or psychologist that the child may have a learning disability. Of course, learning disabilities might manifest in countless ways, depending on the type and severity of the disability, your child's personality, how your child is educated, and other factors.

When Will a Learning Disability Become Apparent?

Generally, the more severe the learning disability, the more likely it will be apparent at an early age. The difficulty for parents is to isolate what's going wrong and why.

As any parent knows, children develop at different paces. This means parents have to walk a fine line between missing a sign of a learning disability and overreacting to a delay that is simply part of your child's normal developmental timeline. Because schoolwork becomes more complicated each year, some learning difficulties may not be evident in the earlier grades. For example, problems understanding abstract concepts may only become apparent when a child begins studying historical movements, scientific theories, or mathematical equations.

The earlier you find out about a learning disability, the better chance your child will have to develop strategies to minimize the disability's effect on his or her educational and social growth. While there is no hard and fast rule, it becomes exponentially more difficult for a child to catch up if a learning disability is identified only in the fourth or fifth grade rather than the first. The longer you wait, the more complicated and demanding school becomes—and the greater the impact of the learning disability on your child. If your child doesn't receive help, emotional, behavioral, and even physical problems may develop over time.

Learning Disabilities for Older and Younger Children

The earlier a learning disability is identified and assessed, the better. But, sometimes, a learning disability may go unnoticed until a child is older. The signs you'll see in a younger and an older child may be different. For example, a younger child will demonstrate problems in more basic processes, such as prereading, speech, listening, simple calculations, and early socialization (sharing, group play, or taking turns, for example). For an older child, the signs may be more complex and even more upsetting. There may have been a slow erosion of confidence, or a year-by-year drop in grades and schoolwork.

Peer pressure and self-awareness is much more intense for a 14-year-old than for a six-year-old; the older child will probably be dealing with both the learning disability and the anger, fear, and embarrassment it generates. Older children with a learning disability may be much more self-conscious, more reluctant to face up to the difficulties they experience, and less willing to share those difficulties with you.

The needs of younger and older children with learning disabilities are also quite different. Younger children will be in one school environment all day, while older children will be going from class to class and perhaps receiving pull-out help for their learning disabilities. And for the older child with a learning disability, particularly in junior and senior high school, it will be important to consider graduation plans, required exit and state exams, and college and/or work plans.

Signs of a Learning Disability

You want to be aware of basic developmental stages and benchmarks so you can identify difficulties as early as possible.

Developmental Milestones and Benchmarks

Early signs of a learning disability include difficulty with spoken instructions, initial reading problems, handwriting difficulties, and spatial confusion. What's important is whether your child is significantly delayed in reaching important milestones, compared to other children of the same age. Here are a few benchmarks most pediatricians agree upon:

- A one-year-old should be able to reach for objects, roll over, stand with some support, follow objects, laugh, respond to "no," and use a crayon.
- By the age of two, a child should respond to other children, walk, use some words, recognize familiar persons, point, and understand some simple shapes.
- A three-year-old should be able to move easily and go up stairs, be understood when speaking, use scissors, and draw pictures.
- By age four, a child should be able to catch a ball, copy shapes, count, identify some colors, dress without help, and play appropriately with peers.

Remember, children who are not learning disabled may meet certain milestones but not others, or may meet some more fully than others. No one milestone—met or missed—should either make you despondent or encourage you to fill out a Mensa application for your child. Try to keep a balance between being aware of important milestones (emphasis on the plural) and assuming the worst because your three-year-old's drawing of a dog looks more like a cow.

Signs of a Learning Disability for Children in School

If your child is already in school, there are some additional signs to watch out for, including:

- educational manifestations—difficulties in reading, writing, spelling, mathematics
- difficulties in processing, understanding, and expressing information through language
- neurological or memory problems, including trouble with auditory memory (remembering what is spoken), encoding information, and attending to stimuli, or limited ability to integrate, store, and retrieve information
- delays or difficulties in language or fine motor skills, or in understanding simple instructions

- social or emotional problems, such as trouble sleeping, eating, or getting along with others
- difficulties paying attention or staying focused, including inappropriate or hyperactive behavior, or
- physical delays or difficulties, such as hearing loss, sight problems, or mobility or handwriting problems.

Misdiagnosis of ADD/ADHD

Sometimes, school representatives misconstrue signs of ADD/ADHD behaviors—including impulsivity, inattention, hyperactivity—as merely "bad behavior." Other times, children (especially boys) who are simply energetic and physical are presumed to have ADD/ADHD, without any further evaluation. Either situation can be detrimental to your child. Armed with information about ADD/ADHD and your child's specific needs, you should be prepared to discuss with your school district why some of the more frequently misdiagnosed or missed ADD/ADHD behaviors are signs of a disability, not of laziness or poor behavior. Or, if you think that the school district has mistakenly tagged your child with the ADD/ADHD "label," you should insist on an evaluation as soon as possible (see Chapter 6).

Keeping Track of Your Child and Securing Professional Assistance

It can be very difficult for parents to figure out whether their child has a learning disability—and, if so, the type and severity of that disability. Your child is having difficulty in school or paying attention at home— what should you make of that? Is it a disability or is it just your child's unique way of doing things? Are your child's reading problems caused by a learning disability or an inappropriate early reading program? What is the difference between a disability and the individual characteristics that may make your child a little less skilled in reading, but a remarkable artist?

How Serious Is Your Child's Learning Disability?

After finding out that their child has a learning disability, most parents want to know how "bad" it is. Of course, the answer depends on what type of learning disability your child has. Certainly, some learning disabilities are more serious than others. If a child has other disabling conditions, the learning disability can have a more complicated impact and be more difficult to address.

Even though your child's learning disability might make school difficult, it may not be as traumatic, ultimately, as many other disabilities. A learning disability is not the same as an emotional disturbance and probably not as life-affecting as the loss of one's mobility, hearing, or vision, for example.

With early intervention and help, your child can overcome the disability and become a successful human being. Your child can go to college, play sports, be student body president, flourish academically, and have friends despite a learning disability. It may be harder than it is for some other students, but children with learning disabilities can go as far as their talents and energies take them, if they receive the help they need.

You should track your concerns about your child's progress, then consult a professional (in or out of school) to get some feedback. Here are some tips that will help you organize your thoughts:

- Keep a record of important benchmarks and milestones— including those listed above and others provided by your pediatrician—and note any areas where your child seems to be lagging significantly.
- Keep track of comments by others about your child's progress, including information provided to you by neighbors, teachers, doctors, or family members.
- Keep copies of all written information about your child, such as reports, report cards, and the statements of teachers and other professionals.

- Find out (from books, articles, and Web resources on learning disabilities) what your child's general skill level should be, and compare that to how he or she is actually doing.
- Ask your doctor, your child's teacher, and others whom you trust whether they think your child might have a learning disability.

As you begin this process, let me offer some advice: Stay vigilant, watch for signs, try to be objective, think things over before you panic, and be sure to talk to others, particularly professionals, *before* you jump to any conclusions.

Learning Disabilities and the IEP Process

As noted in Chapter 2, the rights and procedures provided by IDEA apply to children with all kinds of disabilities. They provide a general structure within which each child's unique needs can be evaluated and addressed. Certain parts of the IEP process are especially important to children with learning disabilities, however. Each of these topics is covered in detail in later chapters of this book. For now, keep in mind that you'll want to pay special attention to:

- **Evaluations.** Evaluations are the tests performed on your child to determine whether he or she has a learning disability—and, if so, what strategies will help address the problem. They provide the evidence of a learning disability necessary to qualify your child for special education. Unlike physical disabilities, which are often obvious, learning disabilities can be tough to detect on casual observation—which is why evaluations are so important. Evaluations are covered in Chapter 6.
- **Eligibility.** To prove that your child is eligible for special education based on a specific learning disability, you must show that your child has a disorder that results in an imperfect ability to listen, think, speak, read, write, spell, or do mathematical calculations, and that this disorder causes your child's achievements to lag behind his or her age and ability level. You'll find much more information on eligibility in Chapter 7.

- **Placements.** IDEA requires the school to offer a range of appropriate placement options. However, most children with learning disabilities will be placed in a regular classroom or perhaps in a special day class, unless they have additional, serious conditions that make a more restrictive placement appropriate. You might be happy to have your child mainstreamed in a regular classroom, but you'll have to make sure that classroom is appropriate for your child. Placements are covered in Chapter 8.
- **Techniques and methodologies.** Children with learning disabilities need different educational strategies than children with physical disabilities. Methodologies for helping children with learning disabilities tend to focus on basic learning skills, such as reading, spelling, calculating, memory, and processing. Classroom strategies—such as placing your child's seat away from distractions or arranging for someone to take notes for your child—can also be effective. Methodologies are covered in Chapter 5.

Harassment

Student bullying and harassment have increased significantly over the last ten years, and students in special education have not been spared. There are several issues you should be aware regarding student harassment and bullying:

The states and federal government are enacting laws that identify bullying as a problem and establish procedures for dealing with it. As of 2013, 49 states have antibullying laws (Montana, as of early 2014, is the only state with no such law).

State laws include those that require school districts to have antibullying policies; for example, Maryland's antibullying law states that each county board must establish a policy "prohibiting bullying, harassment, and intimidation" in consultation with parents, school staff, school volunteers, students, and members of the community. (Md. Code Ann., Educ. § 7-424.1(c).)

States define what constitutes bullying. North Carolina's law provides that bullying or harassing behavior includes "acts reasonably perceived as being motivated by any actual or perceived differentiating characteristic, such as race, color, religion, ancestry, national origin, gender, socioeconomic status, academic status, gender identity, physical appearance, sexual orientation, or mental, physical, developmental, or sensory disability, or by association with a person who has or is perceived to have one or more of these characteristics." (N.C. Gen. Stat. § 115C-407.15(a).)

States also create responsibilities for school districts to take specific action to identify bullying and establish procedures for taking appropriate action against the perpetrators of bullying. For example, in Massachusetts, the law requires that, after receiving a report that bullying occurred, the school principal or a designee must promptly conduct an investigation. If the school staff determines that bullying or retaliation has occurred, the staff member must take appropriate disciplinary action, notify the parents or guardians of a perpetrator, notify the parents or guardians of the victim, and notify the local law enforcement agency if the staff member believes that criminal charges may be pursued against a perpetrator. Also, to the extent consistent with state and federal law, the school must notify the parents of the victim of the action taken to prevent any further acts of bullying or retaliation. (Mass. Adv. Legis. Serv. Ch. No. 71.37O(g).)

States also have requirements for training, preventive education, monitoring, and reporting.

Bullying and harassment can be particularly serious for students with disabilities, who may be less equipped than others to understand and deal effectively with bullying. In August 2013, the U.S. Department of Education issued guidance on bullying ("USOSEP Dear Colleague: Bullying of Students with Disabilities") to ensure that students with disabilities who are subject to bullying continue to receive free appropriate public education (FAPE) under the Individuals with Disabilities Education Act (IDEA).

It is important to stress here that bullying, in addition to being deleterious for a child, can directly impact whether he or she can benefit from education and therefore be provided a "free appropriate public education."

If your child is facing harassment or bullying, it is crucial to:
- secure up-to-date information about the harassment itself
- have an updated assessment to detail the impact of that harassment, and
- have an IEP meeting to develop very specific goals and procedures for ending the bullying but also to discuss a process for dealing immediately and effectively with ongoing bullying.

Your child's IEP should include who will be responsible for identifying and responding to the bullying, what supportive services will be available for your child, what procedures will be in place to deal with the perpetrators, and, perhaps as important, a clear and strong school training process whereby staff and students are trained in recognizing and understanding bullying.

There are increasing numbers of lawsuits by students who have suffered emotional reactions to bullying and even have committed suicide. In one case, a student was harassed daily until, sadly, he killed himself. The school district where the bullying occurred is being sued for $20 million for failure to supervise.

Getting Started

Y ou may have noticed very early on that your child was not meeting certain developmental milestones. Or perhaps a teacher, pediatrician, or friend pointed something out to you. The recognition may come as a surprise or even a shock. What does this mean for your child's immediate educational experience? What does it mean for the future? Will your child now be labeled as learning disabled? Will the learning disability lead to psychological, behavioral, or other problems? How can you help your child succeed—in school and beyond?

The process you are about to embark on can be hard and frustrating. There may be times when school personnel don't seem sensitive, caring, or knowledgeable about your child. Your child's difficulties may seem to persist—or even get worse. At times, the problems may seem insurmountable. There may be a teacher shortage, insufficient school funds, or ineffective program options. For all your preparation, you may feel like you're getting nowhere.

You may ask yourself why this happened to your family. But if you plan, organize, and persevere, if you take small, daily steps (rather than try to solve the whole problem in one day), you will help your child. You may not make the school experience perfect, or even always tolerable, but your child will benefit from your efforts.

Whether you, your child's teacher, or another professional first discovers your child's learning problems, your school district has a clear legal responsibility under IDEA to ensure that all children with special education needs are identified, located, and evaluated. (See Chapter 2 for more on the school district's obligations.) Usually, this means that your child's teacher, school principal, or school psychologist will contact you, mention areas of initial concern, and perhaps suggest a meeting to discuss these concerns. The school will then likely recommend an evaluation by a specialist in your child's disability. And if your district does not take the initiative, this chapter will help you get things started. Having your child evaluated is the first major step in the special education process and ultimately the development of an IEP. (Chapter 6 discusses evaluations in detail.)

SKIP AHEAD

If your child has already been found eligible for special education or you have had experience with the IEP process, you can skip "First Steps," below. Even if you have been through the IEP process, however, be sure to read the discussions about how to gather and manage your child's records and keep track of deadlines. Even the most seasoned veterans of the IEP process will find these organizational strategies valuable.

First Steps

What's the first thing you should do if you believe your child is eligible for special education? This section provides some suggestions on how to get started. Keep in mind that although most children with learning disabilities experience difficulties at an early age, some do not run into real trouble until they are in junior or even senior high school.

Eligibility of Young Children (Ages Three to Five)

If your child is between the ages of three and five and is not yet enrolled in school, contact your local school district if you believe your child has a learning disability. Your child may be entitled to services under IDEA even before starting school. For example, a child with speech delays may be eligible for special instruction that focuses on language acquisition. To be eligible, your child must be experiencing developmental delays in physical, cognitive, communication, social, emotional, or adaptive development. (20 U.S.C. § 1401(3)(B).) If your child is found eligible, the IDEA rules and IEP procedures outlined in this book will apply.

Recognize Your Child's Special Learning Needs

It is very common for parents to realize that their child has unique needs but have no idea how those needs can be addressed in the educational process. It may be that your child's problems can be isolated and addressed fairly easily, or the problems may be more serious. But don't assume the worst; let the information you gather determine how serious the problem is and what you should do about it.

As any parent of a child with learning disabilities can tell you, there are lots of different learning disabilities that manifest in a wide variety of ways. Of all the categories of disability recognized by special education law, learning disabilities may be the hardest to define—even though children with learning disabilities make up the largest part of the special education population. (In 2006, the U.S. Department of Education found that more than 6.5 million children with disabilities, including more than 2.6 million with specific learning disabilities, were reentering special education in the United States.) The learning disability category includes lots of apples and oranges—dyslexia, writing or calculating difficulties, memory problems, processing problems, letter or number reversals, spelling mistakes, language difficulties, and organizational problems.

Instead of trying to diagnose your child's precise disability, focus instead on his or her needs: Does your child have trouble with comprehension, struggle with basic math concepts, have handwriting problems, or have difficulty remembering, understanding, and following spoken instructions? Here are some other behaviors or difficulties that might indicate a learning disability (Chapter 3 explains in more detail some of the signs of a possible learning disability):

- delays in developmental areas, such as language or fine motor skills (for example, your child can't use scissors, tie his or her shoes, or write letters accurately)
- difficulties processing or retaining information, such as understanding simple instructions, or problems with short- or long-term memory
- trouble with organization, planning, and being on time (such as missing deadlines or failing to hand in homework)
- social or emotional problems (including difficulty making friends or inappropriate emotional responses to events)
- trouble sleeping, eating, or getting along with the family
- sustained difficulties in paying attention or staying focused

- inappropriate or hyperactive behavior, or
- delays in physical milestones or other physiological difficulties, such as hearing or vision loss, poor coordination, difficulties with mobility, or handwriting problems.

Take notes on anything you can remember that might relate to these kinds of behaviors, delays, or difficulties. Don't worry at this stage about what might be "causing" these difficulties or what the proper term for your child's condition might be. Instead, focus on how your child's problems are manifesting themselves in daily life and in the classroom. Look at how your child performs basic tasks, at home and at school.

Keep in mind that the above list of difficulties is not identical to the more specific and formal list of conditions that may qualify your child for special education (see Chapter 7). At this stage, your child may or may not qualify for special education, and may or may not have a learning disability. Right now, you should be less concerned about the specific eligibility category than with identifying those behaviors that raise red flags for you. Certainly some of those behaviors may indicate a learning disability, but further evaluation and testing is almost always required to be sure. (See Chapter 6 for more information on evaluations.)

Don't Let Your Fears Hold You Back

Try to think clearly about your child's problems, even though you may feel some emotional upheaval or fear. You may feel anxious about the future. You may worry that you have done something wrong. These feelings are normal. Almost everyone who has had a child with a learning disability has felt exactly as you do right now.

The trick is to acknowledge your fears without letting them get in your way. No parent wants his or her child to face extra obstacles in life, but refusing to recognize potential problems won't make them go away. There is only one way to begin to get your child the help necessary to be successful—and that's to recognize which subjects, tasks, and behaviors present problems. Once you know where the problems lie, you can then figure out ways to address those problems effectively.

A child who is currently having difficulty in school will not automatically qualify for or be placed in special education. There may be interim steps or non-special-education solutions for your child. Those steps are discussed below.

As you begin to collect your thoughts, recollections, and observations about your child, you may also want to contact the school principal to request information about special education.

FORM

A sample letter requesting information on special education is below; a blank downloadable copy is available on this book's Companion Page on www.nolo.com. See Chapter 16 for the link.

A True Learning Disability or Something Else?

Because learning disabilities can be hard to pin down, the category is sometimes used as a catch-all classification—one in which children are sometimes improperly placed. Many experts believe that the number of children categorized as "learning disabled" would diminish significantly if children were taught to read properly. In California, for example, there was a time when reading was taught using a "whole language" approach rather than a phonics-based system. Many children who later ended up in special education simply never learned to read (and not because of any learning disability).

IDEA, as amended in 2004, states that a child will not qualify for special education if the key factor in his or her reading difficulties is "lack of appropriate instruction in reading." (20 U.S.C. § 1414(b)(5).) It remains to be seen how school districts will interpret this language or what methods they will use to separate those whose reading difficulties are caused by learning disabilities from those whose difficulties stem from instructional problems.

You should talk to your child's teacher to find out whether other children in your child's age group are having similar difficulties. Those problems might be due to the way the children were taught rather than the way they learn.

Request for Information on Special Education

Date: _February 20, 20xx_

To: _Ronald Pearl, Principal_

Mesa Verde Elementary School

123 San Pablo Avenue

San Francisco, CA 94110

Re: _Amber Jones, student in 2nd grade class_

of Cynthia Rodriguez

I am writing to you because my child is experiencing difficulties in school. I understand there is a special process for evaluating a child and determining eligibility for special education programs and services. Please send me any written information you have about that process. Please also send me information about how I can contact other parents and local support groups involved in special education.

Thank you very much for your kind assistance. I look forward to talking with you further about special education.

Sincerely,

Mary Jones

Mary Jones

243 Ocean Avenue

San Francisco, CA 94110

Phones: 555-1234 (home); 555-2678 (work)

> **TIP**
>
> **Get into the habit of writing.** You can always request information about special education by calling the school principal, who is likely to either provide you the information or refer you to the district's special education administrator. But the best approach is to make your request in writing. A letter is more formal, won't be forgotten as easily as a phone call, and creates a record of your contact with the school district.

Make a Formal Request to Start the Special Education Process

You can formally ask to begin the process of special education evaluation at any time. To start:

- Call your school and ask for the name and phone number of the special education administrator.
- Call the special education administrator and ask about the eligibility evaluation process in the district.
- Follow up your phone call with a written request (and keep a copy for your records).

> **TIP**
>
> **One letter or many—it's up to you.** A sample letter making a formal request to start the special education process and conduct an evaluation is below; a blank downloadable copy is available on this book's Companion Page on www.nolo.com. See Chapter 16 for the link. Other sample letters in this chapter make other requests. You can combine some or all of these requests into one letter, if you wish.

Gather Information

Whether you plan to begin the formal evaluation process right away or wait a bit, you should start gathering information on your child and his or her learning problem. Here are a few good ways to start.

Request to Begin Special Education Process and Evaluation

Date: _February 20, 20xx_

To: _Ronald Pearl, Principal_

Mesa Verde Elementary School

123 San Pablo Avenue

San Francisco, CA 94110

Re: _Amber Jones, student in 2nd grade class_

of Cynthia Rodriguez

I am writing to you because my child is experiencing difficulties in school. _As I mentioned to you over the phone, she is way behind in reading_ [or other specific difficulties your child is exhibiting].

I am formally requesting that the school immediately begin its special education process, including initial evaluation for eligibility. I understand that you will send me an evaluation plan that explains the tests that may be given to my child. Because I realize the evaluation can take some time, I would appreciate receiving the evaluation plan within ten days. Once you receive my approval for the evaluation, please let me know when the evaluation will be scheduled.

I would also appreciate any other information you have regarding the evaluation process, how eligibility is determined, and general IEP procedures.

Thank you very much for your kind assistance. I look forward to working with you and your staff.

Sincerely,

Mary Jones

Mary Jones

243 Ocean Avenue

San Francisco, CA 94110

Phones: 555-1234 (home); 555-2678 (work)

Talk to Your Child's Teachers

Find out what your child's teachers think is going on and whether they can recommend any possible solutions. Here are a few specific questions to ask:

- What are the teacher's observations? What are the most outstanding and obvious problems and how serious are they? Does your child have a problem with math, reading, or broader cognitive issues (processing information or memory lags)? Does the problem have social or emotional manifestations?
- Does the teacher think that some adjustments in the classroom—such as extra attention from a teacher or aide, after-school tutoring, or measures to address behavioral problems—might help?
- What activities or strategies might be useful at home? Do you need to spend more time on homework, focusing on certain subject matters?
- Has the teacher consulted any other school staff? If so, what are their observations, conclusions, and recommendations?
- Does the teacher believe the difficulties are serious and require more formal, special education involvement? If so, why, and what are the next steps?
- Are there any specific signs of a learning disability, such as difficulty processing information, trouble understanding instructions or cues, reversing letters or numbers, inability to concentrate, trouble sitting still, or problems expressing thoughts?

If you and the school agree to go ahead with interim, non-special-education steps, be sure to monitor your child's progress closely so you can determine whether they are working. Chapter 8 provides suggestions about tracking your child's progress.

Talk to Your Child's Pediatrician

Your child may have an organic or medical problem. While your pediatrician may not be an expert in special education, he or she can discuss your child's developmental growth (or lack of it); health-related matters that affect the educational experience; and other cognitive, physical, linguistic, and emotional factors that might affect special education eligibility and solutions. There are pediatricians who specialize in treating children with learning disabilities—if your own doctor doesn't know much about the subject, consider getting a referral to someone who does.

Talk With Other Parents

Talk to parents in your area, particularly those whose children have learning disabilities. Find out what experiences they've had and how they determined something was amiss. The local PTA should have information on parents with special education children, and most school districts have advisory committees of parents with children in special education. Call the school principal to find out more.

 RELATED TOPIC

Chapter 15 explains how to find or start a parents' group. Appendix B has information on various national special education support groups. A blank downloadable copy is available on this book's Companion Page on www.nolo.com. See Chapter 16 for the link.

Do Some Research

Look for written materials on special education, particularly for children with learning disabilities. A wealth of information is available online and in print. As you look into these resources, you'll see that they approach learning disabilities from very different perspectives. For example, this book focuses on how to navigate the special education process and develop positive and effective IEPs for your child. Other books focus more exclusively on the reasons for and nature of learning disabilities or provide significant detail on particular educational strategies for children with learning disabilities.

There is an ever-growing number of websites with general and disability-specific information. Here are two of my favorite sites:

- National Center for Learning Disabilities—www.ncld.org, and
- Learning Disabilities Association of America—www.ldaamerica.org.

There are also many information-rich sites for specific learning disabilities, such as the Attention Deficit Disorder Association, at www.add.org.

Learning Disability Support Organizations

Appendix B on this book's Companion Page on nolo.com provides more detail on organizations devoted specifically to learning disabilities. (See Chapter 16 for the link.) Because learning disabilities are such a large part of the special education world, there are a lot of excellent and helpful groups out there.

Obtain Your Child's School Records

As part of your information gathering, you must find out what is in your child's school file and what effect that information will have on the IEP process. You'll need this information to assess the severity of your child's difficulties and the possible need for special education. If your child is found eligible for special education, reviewing the school file will help you determine which services and programs may be appropriate.

Whether you are new at this or have been through many IEPs, whether you anticipate a major change in your child's educational program or no change at all, and even if you're not sure you want your child in special education in the first place, you should secure copies of your child's school file on a yearly basis. New information is usually added each year.

While the contents of your child's file may vary, here are some things you're likely to find:

- report cards and other progress reports
- medical data (immunization records, health reports)
- attendance records
- disciplinary reports
- testing data
- evaluations and other testing material
- teacher comments and other observations, and
- pictures of your child (it's fun to see the kindergarten picture, the second grade picture with the missing teeth, and so on).

Your Right to See Your Child's School File

You have a legal right to inspect and review any education records relating to your child. If your child is already in the special education

Request for Child's School File

Date: _March 3, 20xx_

To: _Ronald Pearl, Principal_

Mesa Verde Elementary School

123 San Pablo Ave.

San Francisco, CA 94110

Re: _Amber Jones, student in second-grade class_

of Cynthia Rodriguez

I would like a copy of my child's file, including all tests, reports, evaluations, grades, notes by teachers or other staff members, memoranda, photographs—in short, *everything* in my child's school file. I understand I have a right to these files under

IDEA, specifically 20 U.S.C. § 1415(b)(1) [or the Family

Educational Rights and Privacy Act (FERPA) (20 U.S.C. § 1232 (g))

if your child has not yet been found eligible for special education].

I would greatly appreciate having these files within the next five days. I would be happy to pick them up. I will call you to discuss how and when I will get the copies.

Thank you for your kind assistance.

Sincerely,

Mary Jones

Mary Jones

243 Ocean Ave.

San Francisco, CA 94110

Phones: 555-1234 (home); 555-2678 (work)

system, you have this right under IDEA. (20 U.S.C. § 1415(b)(1).) If your child has not yet been found eligible for special education, you still have a legal right to view the file under the Family Educational Rights and Privacy Act (FERPA). (20 U.S.C. § 1232 (g).) FERPA is a federal statute. The purposes of FERPA are twofold: to ensure that parents have access to their children's educational records and to protect the privacy rights of parents and children by limiting access to these records without parental consent. FERPA applies to all agencies and institutions that receive federal funds, including elementary and secondary schools, colleges, and universities. State law may also provide a right to your child's file, separate from IDEA or FERPA rights. Call your state department of education or your school district for information on your state's rules—including how you must make the request and how much time the school has to provide you with the file.

How to Get Copies of Your Child's File

When you ask to see your child's school file, put your request in writing and ask for everything. Send the written request to the administrator in your school district who is responsible for special education. That may be the school principal or a person in your district's central office. The site principal should be able to refer you to the appropriate person.

FORM

A sample letter requesting your child's school file is above; a blank downloadable copy is available on this book's Companion Page on www.nolo.com. See Chapter 16 for the link.

IDEA requires your child's school to grant your request without unnecessary delay and before any IEP meeting. The school must send you the file within 45 days, although it can and should send it more quickly. (IDEA regulations at 34 C.F.R. § 300.613(a).) FERPA includes the same 45-day deadline.

If you have any problem getting a copy of your child's school file in a timely manner, you can call and write the appropriate administrator, indicating that the law requires the school to provide the records without "unnecessary delay."

If the principal or administrator does not respond to your request, contact the school district superintendent and your state department of education. Failing to give you your child's records is a violation of the law. Chapter 13 covers procedures for handling legal violations by your district.

TIP

Some states have tighter deadlines. Your state special education law may give schools a shorter deadline to provide copies of your child's record than the 45-day limit imposed by IDEA. California schools, for example, must provide copies of the record within five days of a parent's request. Get a copy of your state's special education laws from your department of education early on so you know your rights—and cite the law when you request your child's file.

Cost of Getting Files

IDEA regulations allow the school to charge you a fee for copying your child's records, as long as the fee "does not effectively prevent (you) from exercising (your) right to inspect and review those records." (IDEA regulations at 34 C.F.R. § 300.617.) This means that you cannot be charged an excessively high fee—or any fee at all if you can show you cannot afford it. In addition, the school cannot charge a fee for searching and retrieving records.

If your child is not in special education, any fee for records might violate the Rehabilitation Act of 1973 (29 U.S.C. § 794) and the federal Freedom of Information Act. At least one court (*Tallman v. Cheboygan Area Schools*, 454 N.W.2d 171 (Mich. App. 1990)) has said that charging a fee for search and retrieval would violate the Freedom of Information Act.

While some districts can be uncooperative about providing free copies of your child's file, others provide them as a matter of course. If your district charges you for searching and retrieving the file or charges you when you can't afford to pay a fee, write a letter to your administrator, citing IDEA regulation 34 C.F.R. § 300.617.

Request for Reduction or Waiver of Fee Charged for Child's School File

Date: March 20, 20xx

To: Ronald Pearl, Principal
    Mesa Verde Elementary School
    123 San Pablo Avenue
    San Francisco, CA 94110

Re: Amber Jones, student in 2nd grade class of Cynthia Rodriguez

On March 3, 20xx I requested copies of everything in my child's school file. Your secretary called me on March 19, 20xx and stated that there would be a fee for the copies [or an excessive fee or a fee for searching and retrieving]. IDEA specifically states that you cannot charge a fee if it prevents me from exercising my right to inspect and review my child's file. I am on a fixed income and I cannot afford the fee you are charging.

[or: IDEA prohibits you from charging such a high fee. A fee of 15¢ a copy seems fair, not $1 a copy]

[or: IDEA specifically prohibits you from charging a fee for searching for and retrieving the files]

Therefore, I would appreciate it if you would send me copies, at no cost, at once. Thank you for your kind attention to this matter.

Mary Jones
Mary Jones
243 Ocean Avenue
San Francisco, CA 94110
Phones: 555-1234 (home); 555-2678 (work)

What to Look for in Your Child's School File

Items that you are likely to find in your child's file are listed at the beginning of this section. As you review those documents, look for any information about your child's performance and needs, as well as the opinions of teachers and other professionals. Make sure you ask for everything, even if some items seem unimportant—you never know what you'll find buried in the file.

Always Get Copies

IDEA allows you to review your child's school file *and* receive copies. (34 C.F.R. § 300.613.) These are two different rights—and you should exercise them both. You should always secure actual copies of your child's file. If you can, you should also go to the school and review the original file, just to make sure the school district gave you everything.

Amending Your Child's File

You have the right to request that any false, inaccurate, or misleading information, or information that violates the privacy or other rights of your child, be amended or removed from your child's school file. (34 C.F.R. §§ 300.618–621.)

Your child's file is confidential and any "personally identifiable data, information, and records collected or maintained" must be protected. Your school district also has to provide you with a list of the "types and locations" of those files. (34 C.F.R. §§ 300.610, 616.)

If the school refuses to amend or remove the information, you have the right to a due process hearing on the issue. (See Chapter 12.)

FORM
A sample request to amend the child's school file is below; a blank downloadable copy is available on this book's Companion Page on www.nolo. com. See Chapter 16 for the link.

Start an IEP Binder

Many parents have found a simple three-ring binder with clearly labeled sections to be an invaluable organizing tool. A binder allows you to keep everything in one convenient location—from report cards to test results to IEP forms.

Include every important item in your IEP binder. What's an important item? Anything that contains substantive information about your child or procedural information concerning how and when things happen in the IEP process. While certain items can probably go into a file drawer, if you have any doubt, add them to your binder.

Use the Forms in This Book

Nearly two dozen sample forms, checklists, and letters appear throughout this book, with copies in Appendix E on this book's Companion Page on nolo.com (see Chapter 16 for the link). You can simply print the relevant forms and insert them into your IEP binder—either as a separate section or in one of the major sections listed below. The IEP blueprint (discussed in Chapter 5) is one key document you should include as a separate section in your binder. Another is the IEP Material Organizer Form (discussed in Chapter 10), which you'll use to highlight key information in your binder and easily access your materials during the IEP meeting. These and other forms have space for far more information than you'll be ready to provide right now. That's okay. You're just getting started. It's perfectly fine to leave many of the form sections blank. You can fill them in later, as you read through this book and get into the IEP process.

Listed below are some of the most important materials for your binder. Make as many sections as necessary to help you easily locate the information you'll need throughout the IEP process.

Your Child's File and Relevant School Materials

Your child's school records will play a key role in the IEP meeting, in developing the IEP itself, and possibly at any due process mediation or hearing. When you get copies of your child's file (including report cards, attendance and disciplinary records, evaluations and testing data, and teacher comments), review the documents carefully and put important items in your binder.

Request to Amend Child's School File

Date: <u>April 2, 20xx</u>

To: <u>Ronald Pearl, Principal</u>
<u>Mesa Verde Elementary School</u>
<u>123 San Pablo Avenue</u>
<u>San Francisco, CA 94110</u>

Re: <u>Amber Jones, student in 2nd grade class</u>
<u>of Cynthia Rodriguez</u>

I recently reviewed a copy of my child's file and would like to have a portion of the file amended, specifically:

<u>The memorandum from the school psychologist, Ms. Taylor,</u>
<u>stating that my child had severe emotional problems, is</u>
<u>inaccurate and inappropriate because Ms. Taylor did no testing</u>
<u>and only observed my child briefly. This is insufficient to support</u>
<u>the conclusion she reached.</u>

IDEA gives me the right to request that all information that is "inaccurate or misleading or violates the privacy or other rights of [my] child" be amended. (34 C.F.R. § 300.618.) I feel that this is just such a case and, therefore, request that you rectify the situation immediately.

Please notify me in writing as soon as possible of your decision regarding this matter. Thank you.

Sincerely,

Mary Jones

<u>Mary Jones</u>
<u>243 Ocean Avenue</u>
<u>San Francisco, CA 94110</u>
<u>Phones: 555-1234 (home); 555-2678 (work)</u>

You can put everything in one large section of your binder labeled "school records," or you can divide the material into several sections. You'll probably have an easier time locating the information if you break it down into categories.

In addition to your child's file, your binder should contain other relevant school materials, such as:

- evaluations completed by the school
- samples of your child's work
- notes from your child's teacher and other staff members
- correspondence to and from the school
- past IEPs
- your notes and information on available programs and services, including the qualifications of particular teachers or service providers within the school district (Chapter 8 discusses how to develop information on available school options), and
- forms and informational materials sent to you by the school district, such as the school's IEP form and copies of key statutes and regulations on special education. (As mentioned earlier, the school is required by IDEA to provide you with a copy of federal and state statutes and regulations.)

TIP

Always get a copy of the school's IEP form. Whether you're new to the IEP process or you've been through it before, be sure to get a copy of the current local IEP form (this varies from district to district) and any school guidelines on the IEP process. Keep the form and related materials in your binder. (You can find an example of an IEP form on this book's Companion Page on www.nolo.com. See Chapter 16 for the link.)

Your Child's Health and Medical Records

Your child's school file will probably include some medical information, such as the results of hearing or vision tests done at school. Be sure your binder includes these documents, as well as medical records and important letters from your child's pediatrician and other health professionals.

> **Binder Versus File Drawer**
>
> As your child progresses in school, your binder could quickly become unwieldy. Consider developing a new one each year. You can keep a file drawer or box of dated materials—for example, "2007 evaluation" or "2008 report cards." In your binder, you should keep only materials that are relevant to the current IEP year.

Independent Evaluations

As explained in Chapter 8, an independent evaluation may be the most important document supporting what you want for your child. You'll definitely want to keep a copy of all evaluations in your binder.

Information on Programs and Services Outside the School District

If you're exploring private programs or service options, such as a specialized school for children with learning disabilities, be sure to keep the details in your binder, including suggestions made by other parents, school brochures, and notes of your conversations and visits. (Chapter 8 explains how to develop information on programs and services outside of your school district.)

Special Education Contacts

You'll want to have a list of the names, mailing addresses, phone and fax numbers, and email addresses of people you deal with on a regular basis, such as your child's teacher, the district's special education administrator, your child's physician, the school nurse, staff members who provide related services, parents or parent groups, and the like.

Keep this list of contacts in a prominent place in front of your binder. Also, keep a copy with you, in case you need to phone or write any of your contacts when you're away from home.

FORM

A sample Special Education Contacts form is below; a blank copy is available on this book's Companion Page on www.nolo.com. See Chapter 16 for the link. Print as many copies as you need.

Articles and Other Information on Your Child's Learning Disability

Your binder should include copies of articles or other printed materials about your child's disability. There's no need to keep everything you find; just make copies of the most informative and helpful materials. That way, you'll have an authoritative reference on hand if a school representative questions what you want for your child. ("According to an article I read, multisensory approaches can be very effective for children with dyslexia; I have a copy right here, if you'd like to take a look.") The articles will also remind you of good ideas for the blueprint and IEP.

Key Legal Requirements

As you immerse yourself in the details of your child's situation and needs, you'll find it helpful to refer now and then to "the letter of the law"—the precise language the law uses to define or explain the issues you're dealing with. Doing so will help you remain focused on what you can, and can't, expect to achieve. And incidentally, it doesn't hurt to refer to specific legal language at an IEP meeting—it shows you know your stuff and have a working knowledge of IDEA. Here are some key IDEA requirements; you may want to add more that relate specifically to the issues that affect your child:

- **The definition of your child's disability:** A "specific learning disability" is a "disorder in one or more of the basic psychological processes involved in understanding or in using language, spoken or written, that may manifest itself in the imperfect ability to listen, think, speak, read, write, spell or to do mathematical calculations…." (34 C.F.R. § 300.8(c)(10).)

- **Related services:** "Transportation and such developmental, corrective, and other supportive services as required to assist a child with a disability to benefit from special education…." (34 C.F.R. § 300.34(a).)
- **Least restrictive environment:** "Special classes, separate schooling or other removal of children with disabilities from the regular educational environment occurs only if the nature or severity of the disability is such that education in regular classes with the use of supplementary aids and services cannot be achieved satisfactorily." (34 C.F.R. § 300.114(a)(2)(ii).)

There are hundreds of such IDEA regulations—other important areas are assessments (34 C.F.R. §§ 300.301–320); IEPs (34 C.F.R. §§ 300.320–328), and procedural rights (34 C.F.R. §§ 300.500–520). If you anticipate specific disagreements with your school district, look for regulations that cover those issues, too.

IEP Journal

The importance of keeping a record of all conversations, visits, and information-gathering activities, whether on the phone or in person, cannot be overemphasized. To help you remember who said what (and when), start an IEP journal. For every important conversation or incident, make a note of:

- the date and time of the conversation or meeting
- the names and positions of everyone who participated in the discussion, such as your child's teacher, other school staff, the special education administrator, your pediatrician, or another parent
- what was said by whom (this is really important), and
- any necessary follow-up actions (for example, a person to call or documents to provide to the school or evaluator).

You'll want to fill in your IEP journal just as soon as possible after a conversation or meeting has ended. The longer you wait, the more likely you are to forget important details or confuse dates, times, and statements or promises made. Don't be shy about taking notes when you meet or talk with someone. To establish written verification of what you've been told, send a confirming letter soon after your conversation. Confirming letters are covered in the following section.

Special Education Contacts

Name, Address, Phone and Fax Numbers, and Email Address

School Staff

School: Lewis Elementary, 123 Rose St., Chicago, 60611; 555-1234

(main phone), 555-5678 (fax)

David Werner, Principal, 555-9876, DWE@aol.com

Charlene Hanson, District Special Ed. Administrator, 4111 Main, Chicago, 60611

555-4201 (phone), 555-7451 (fax), chsed @dusd.edu

Thayer Walker, Carrie's teacher, 567 Elm Ave., Chicago, 60611

555-0111 (classroom), 555-0114 (home)

Dr. Judy Goffy, school psychologist, 555-4333 (phone), drjg@aol.com

Outside Professionals

Dr. Hugh Maloney, independent evaluator, 780 Spruce Lane, Chicago

60612, 555-5169 (phone), 555-5170 (fax), drhm @compuserv.com

Martha Brown, tutor, 2229 Franklin, Chicago, 60612, 555-1490

Other Parents

Kevin Jones (son Robert in Carrie's class), 7 Plainview Dr., Chicago, 60614

555-5115, kj@aol.com

Melaney Harper, District Community Advisory Chair, 764 Rockly, Chicago

60610, 555-7777 (phone), 555-9299 (fax)

Support Groups

Chicago Learning Disabilities Association (contact: Mark Kelso), 775 Kelly Rd.

Chicago, 60610, 555-6226 (phone), 555-7890 (fax), chldas@aol.com

State Department of Education

Special Ed. Office (contact: Dr. Lea Casper), State Department of Education

88 Capitol Row, Springfield, 61614, 217-555-8888 (phone)

217-555-9999 (fax), ilsped@worldnet.att.net

Other

Dr. Joan Landman, Carrie's pediatrician, 32 Ashford Rd., Chicago, 60611

555-2222 (phone), 555-0987 (fax)

Illinois Special Ed. Advocates (Steve Mill, Esq.), 642 Mill Dr., Chicago, 60611

555-4511(phone), 555-8709 (fax), spedatt@netcom.com

FORM

A sample IEP journal page is below; a blank copy is available on this book's Companion Page on www.nolo.com. See Chapter 16 for the link. Make several copies and keep a few with you—for example, if you make phone calls from work. You can use the Class Visitation Checklist in Chapter 8 to keep detailed notes on your visits to school programs.

IEP Journal

Date: _11/3/xx_____ **Time:** _____4:30_____ **a.m./p.m.**

Action: ☒ Phone call _201-555-0105_ ☐ Meeting _____

☐ Other: _____

Person(s) Contacted: _Dr. P. Brin (Sp. Ed. Administrator)_____

Notes: _I explained that Steve is having problems in reading,_

composition, and spelling, plus some social difficulties.

___I said Steve needs an aide._____

___Dr. B: "We can't do that now; wait until the IEP."_____

___I said we need IEP at once._____

___Dr. B: "We just had one; can't schedule another for at least_

_____two months."_____

Confirming Letters

Confirming what someone has said to you provides some proof of that conversation. A confirming letter can provide useful evidence—of what was said, by whom, and when—for an IEP meeting or a due process hearing.

To be sure the school district receives confirming letters, send them certified mail, return receipt requested.

EXAMPLE: Your son needs a good deal of one-on-one help. You want a qualified aide to work with him on reading, math, and spelling at least half of the school day. Your child's teacher tells you during a classroom visit that he agrees that your son needs one-on-one help for much of the day. In addition, the special education administrator admits to you that the amount of aide time your son is currently receiving is not enough. You note both of these conversations in your IEP journal and send the administrator a confirming letter. Later, at the IEP meeting, the administrator balks at providing your son with more aide time. Your confirming letter will be quite helpful in establishing that both your son's teacher and the school administrator told you your son needs more aide time.

Sample Confirming Letter

Date: May 14, 20xx

To: Salvador Hale, Special Education Administrator
Coconut County School District
1003 South Dogwood Drive
Oshkosh, WI 50000

Re: Rodney Brown, 4th grader at Woodrow Wilson School

I appreciated the chance to speak with you yesterday regarding Rodney's current problems with reading comprehension. I agree with your comment that he needs a one-on-one aide for at least half of the day. I look forward to our IEP meeting next week and resolving Rodney's current difficulties in school.

Sincerely,

Martin Brown
Martin Brown
145 Splitleaf Lane
Oshkosh, WI 50000
Phones: 555-4545 (home); 555-2500 (work)

Keep Track of Deadlines

A large part of your organizational chores will involve tracking and meeting the various deadlines in the IEP process. This section explains the yearly IEP cycle and shows you how to stay on top of your deadlines.

The Yearly IEP Cycle

To really get organized, you'll need to know when things happen in the IEP cycle. Once your child is evaluated and found eligible for special education, the yearly IEP process will involve three broad considerations:

- Review—how are things currently going?
- Reassess—what additional information is needed?
- Rebuild—will the program be the same next year or should it be changed?

IDEA requires that an IEP be in place before your child begins the school year. (20 U.S.C. § 1414(d)(2)(A).) To develop a complete initial IEP, you'll need to gather information, deal with evaluations, prove that your child is eligible for special education, prepare for the IEP meeting, attend the IEP meeting, and work out any disagreements you might have with the school. This means you'll have to start planning well in advance to make sure everything gets done in time.

The best way to think about the IEP cycle is to start from your final goal—an IEP in place by the start of the school year—and work backward.

Finish Before Summer

To make sure that all special education issues are resolved before the new school year begins, you will want an IEP meeting in the spring of the previous year. This will give you time to resolve any disputes before the next school year starts. Because school personnel are usually gone during the summer, plan for the IEP meeting in May—or better yet, April—in case there is a dispute that has to be resolved through due process.

Request Your Meeting During the Winter

To ensure that your child's IEP meeting takes place in the spring, put the school district on notice by submitting a written request in February or March stating that you want the annual IEP meeting in April or May.

Begin Planning in the Fall

You'll need to be well-prepared for the spring IEP meeting. Don't start collecting information a few weeks or even a month or two in advance. You'll need much more time than that. Start in the fall or early winter of the preceding year.

> **TIP**
>
> **Keep in touch with your child's teacher.** It's crucial to monitor your child's progress throughout the school year. Talk regularly with your child's teacher, and spend some time in the classroom, if possible. By keeping in touch with the school, you'll be able to assess how your child's reading, writing, and other goals are being met. This will also give you the opportunity to identify problems early on that might require an immediate IEP. Chapter 8 gives advice on keeping tabs on your child's progress.

The Cycle Isn't Set in Stone

Let's say you've just discovered that your child's problems in school might require special education. It's October. You didn't participate in the IEP cycle the previous year because it wasn't an issue. You'd prefer not to wait until the spring to have an IEP meeting to develop a plan for the following year, because your child would lose almost a whole year of school. Or, you went through the IEP cycle the previous year, but the current program is not working. It's November, and you don't want to wait until spring for a new program. What do you do?

Don't wait until spring to raise issues that need immediate attention. Start gathering information, and request an assessment and IEP meeting ASAP. Any time you need an immediate IEP meeting, you should request one.

> (!) **CAUTION**
>
> **Annual midyear IEP meetings aren't a good idea.** Many students' annual IEP meetings take place in December or January. While you can request an IEP meeting at any time, and should when there is an immediate concern, it is generally not a good idea to have your yearly IEP in the middle of the school year. If it is, you'll be making decisions too far in advance of the next school year. The easiest way to get back on schedule is to indicate at the midyear IEP meeting that you want another one at the end of the school year, preferably in April or May. Follow up your request with a confirming letter.

A Sample Year in the Life of Your Child's IEP

Let us assume you are planning for the school year that begins in the fall of 2015. Ideally, by starting your preparation a year ahead of time, in the fall of 2014, you will have enough time without rushing or facing last-minute problems.

Step One: Information Gathering—Fall (September–December)

No matter how many times you have been through the special education process, you should take some time in the fall to gather information and develop a sense of what your child's program should be. Here are some tasks you'll want to accomplish:

- Talk to teachers, school staff, and other parents.
- Request copies of your child's school records.
- Request an evaluation of your child as needed (see Chapter 6).
- Begin drafting your child's blueprint (see Chapter 5).
- Schedule visits to your child's class or other programs you think might be viable (see Chapter 8).
- Gather other information such as letters from your pediatrician and your child's tutor (see Chapter 8).

Step Two: Evaluation—Winter (January and February)

After the first few months of school, the key issues for your child should begin to crystallize for you. You will know either that your child needs to be in special education or, if he or she is already eligible for special education, which programmatic components make sense. Now is the time to assess the information you have or need to make a strong case for eligibility and/or the program and services you want for your child. Here are some steps to take:

- Assess the current information in your child's record and decide whether it supports your IEP goals for your child.
- Monitor the progress your child is making under the current program.
- Complete additional evaluations, if you need more supporting information (discussed in Chapters 6 and 8). Depending on who will be doing any additional evaluations and how busy their calendars are, you may need to schedule them earlier in the year.
- Continue developing your child's IEP blueprint (see Chapter 5).

Step Three: IEP Preparation and IEP Meeting—Spring (March–May)

Spring is the time to work toward getting an IEP program in place for your child. This may be the most labor intensive time of the whole cycle. Some of the things you'll need to do are:

- Finalize your child's IEP blueprint of program and service needs (see Chapter 5).
- Draft your goals for your child's IEP program (see Chapter 9).
- Prepare for the IEP meeting and invite participants who will speak on your child's behalf (see Chapter 10).
- Attend the IEP meeting (see Chapter 11).

Step Four: Dispute Resolution—Spring-Summer (June–August)

If you did not reach an agreement with the school administrators on your child's IEP program, then you can go to a due process mediation or hearing. (See Chapter 12 for more information.) It is important to complete this process before the beginning of the new year.

Step Five: School Begins—Fall (September)

You've been through your first (or another) IEP cycle. You'll want to monitor your child's progress in school and see if the IEP program is working. Remember: If it's not, you can request another IEP meeting and try to come up with some changes that make sense.

Keep a Monthly Calendar

It is vitally important to keep a written calendar that includes the details of IEP tasks (such as drafting goals) and events (such as evaluations, school visits, and the IEP meeting).

Write down these details on some type of month-at-a-glance calendar (your own or the form provided here), including dates on which:

- you were told things would happen—for example, "Scott's school file should be mailed today"
- you need to schedule a meeting—for example, "Request IEP meeting no later than today"
- you need to call or meet with someone, such as a teacher, a pediatrician, or another parent, or
- you need to start or complete a particular task, such as develop an IEP blueprint.

FORM

A sample Monthly IEP Calendar is below; a blank downloadable copy is available on this book's Companion Page on www.nolo.com. See Chapter 16 for the link. Make copies of this for each month of the year.

Track Your Child's Progress

Whether your child is just entering special education or already has an IEP in place, it's vitally important that you keep track of his or her progress in school. Gauging how well your child is doing will help you in several ways:

- It will provide you with a basis for comparing one semester or year to the next, and one subject to the next. If you don't keep close tabs on your child's progress, you won't know whether he or she is improving or getting worse, whether certain subjects are posing more difficulty than others as time goes by, or whether a particular classroom, service, or teaching methodology is having a positive effect.

- It will help you make your case for eligibility. If your child is not yet in the special education system, you can use the materials you gather to show that your child's academic achievement is not what it should be, or that certain subjects are posing particular difficulty.

- It will help you draft effective goals. When you sit down with the IEP team to write goals for your child, you will know exactly what subjects give him or her trouble—and where he or she needs to work especially hard to see improvement. This will help you tailor the goals to your child's particular needs. (See Chapter 9 for more on goals.)

- It will help you argue for a particular placement or service. If your child is not making appropriate progress, you can argue that the current placement or related services need to be changed. Keeping track of how your child is doing in every subject will give you the information you need to evaluate your child's educational program.

- It will help you develop a positive relationship with your child's teacher. Most teachers welcome parents who want to play an active role in their child's education, as long as the parents are respectful of the teacher's time and experience. By keeping in touch with your child's teacher and weighing in on issues of special concern, you'll help the teacher do a better job educating your child. And there's a lot that parents can learn from teachers, too—including which teaching methods might be appropriate, or what exercises or activities you can do at home to reinforce classroom lessons.

Get into the habit of reviewing all of your child's homework, classroom assignments, tests, and teacher reports. (Be sure to keep any that seem to really illustrate your child's difficulties or successes for your IEP binder.) Plan to visit your child's classroom often—volunteer your time, serve as a class parent, or participate in planned activities for

Monthly IEP Calendar

Month and Year: Oct 20xx

1	2	3	4 call teacher re: math problems	5	6	7
8	9	10 written req. for access	11	12	13 meet w/ sp. ed. support group	14
15	16	17	18	19 call Am Lrg. Disab. Assoc. #: math resources	20	21
22	23	24 visit class 10:30	25 meet w/ Mary son in same class	26	27 follow up phone call re: eval request	28
29	30	31				

parents. This will give you a chance to see how your child does in the classroom environment.

Talk to the teacher to set up a reasonable schedule for a brief update or conversation about your child. Remember, most teachers have more work to do than they have hours to do it in, so don't expect to hear from the teacher every day or every week. Instead, ask for some communication twice a month or so, on a day and time that's convenient. Some teachers find it easiest to send parents a brief email report of their child's progress; others would rather have a phone conversation. (If the teacher prefers a conversation, make sure to take notes.)

Create a section in your IEP binder for documents relating to your child's progress. Save copies of written updates from the teacher and samples of your child's schoolwork here. For more information on keeping track of your child's progress with an existing IEP, see Chapter 8.

Calendaring a Due Process Request

When Congress reauthorized IDEA in 2004, it added a requirement that you must file for a due process hearing within two years of when you knew of the dispute, unless your state has a different time period. See Chapter 12 for more detail. It is a good idea to note the date when the dispute materialized for you—usually at an IEP meeting. Make this note on your yearly calendar as well as on a calendar you might check more frequently.

Developing Your Child's IEP Blueprint

A t some point in the IEP program, you'll need to describe in detail what you believe your child's educational program should look like, including the placement and support services your child needs. I call the specifics of this program a blueprint. Despite the fancy name, a blueprint is just a list of items or components that you want in your child's program.

Why create a blueprint? Primarily to help you be an effective advocate for your child. To convince others that your child needs particular services or assistance, you must first be able to articulate exactly what you want for your child and why it's appropriate.

There are a few other reasons for creating a blueprint:

- It forces you to be specific. For example, stating that your child needs help in reading is not as effective as saying that your child needs to work one-on-one with a reading specialist for one hour per day, four days per week.

- You'll know what documentation or evidence you will need to develop before the IEP meeting. For example, if your blueprint includes a one-on-one reading specialist one hour per day, four days per week, you'll need information from your child's school record and other supporting material—and perhaps people to speak at the IEP meeting—to justify this type of help.

- IDEA requires that the program fit the child, not the other way around. Just because your school district offers a particular class or program doesn't necessarily mean it's an appropriate placement for your child. For example, if your school has a special education class geared toward students who are developmentally disabled, that might not work for your child who has handwriting problems. A blueprint can help you determine what may be missing from the school's proposal.

- The blueprint serves as a standard against which you can evaluate your child's existing program and the options currently available to you.

- The blueprint provides you with a continual reference point as you talk with others about your child's needs and move toward the IEP meeting.

- The needs of a child with a learning disability can sometimes be hard to pin down. Making a blueprint will help you, your child, teachers, and aides home in on those needs and the educational strategies that will meet them most effectively.

The blueprint represents your ideal IEP program. It is your starting point. If you could be the special education administrator for your school district for one day, this is the IEP program you would design for your child.

You may think it's too early to draft a blueprint. Perhaps your child was just evaluated and found eligible for special education, but hasn't been in special education yet. Or maybe your child has been in special education for some time, but is scheduled for a new evaluation in another month. It's possible a new special education administrator will take over in the spring, with promises of new program options about which you know little. In any of these situations, you may think you don't have enough information to do a good job—and, in truth, there are always more facts you can gather. But you have to start sometime, and now is as good a time as any. Don't worry if your blueprint is skeletal or incomplete at first.

Even parents new to special education usually have some intuitive sense of what their children need—for example, help organizing their homework and assignments, extra work on handwriting or spelling, or strategies to control impulsive behavior. Take a moment to think about it; by the time you finish this chapter, you'll have the beginnings of a useful blueprint, not just vague notions of what might help (or what's going wrong). And as you use this book and gather more information on your child's needs, you'll be able to develop a more complete blueprint.

Begin at the End: Define Your Child's Needs

It's the first day of school in the upcoming school year. Close your eyes and picture what your child's classroom will look like. Is it a regular classroom, a special classroom for children with learning disabilities, or even a private school? Don't limit yourself—after all, you're imagining the best plan for your child. Is there an aide that helps your child? What subjects do they work on? How often does the aide work with your child and in what kind of setting—alone or with other children? How many students are in the class? Do they also have learning difficulties? Does your child have access to voice-recognition software, books on tape, a calculator, or other technological assistance? What classroom strategies do you want for your child—written instructions for assignments, rewards for good behavior, or opportunities to work with other children in a small group?

Sit down with a pad of paper and pen (or in front of your computer) and start to write out the ideal program and services for your child. Remember that your blueprint is your wish list for your ideal IEP. Don't dwell on the fact that you fought over the IEP last year or you're expecting a fight again. Don't draft your blueprint to follow the school district's program if you think it's not appropriate. This is your chance to detail exactly what you want for your child.

Preparing an IEP Blueprint

This section covers the seven key components of a blueprint, the items you want included in your child's IEP. You can use the blueprint to develop your IEP form, although the two documents won't be identical. (Chapter 11 explains how to do this.)

Some components are quite general, such as ideal classroom setting; others are very specific, such as a particular class or teaching method. Some of these components may not be relevant to your child's situation—feel free to skip any sections that don't apply. You may not have enough information to complete the entire blueprint now, especially if you've only just realized that your child is having trouble. As you learn more, you'll fill in the gaps.

As you develop the blueprint, be sure to make it as specific to your child's learning disability needs as possible. The fact that a specific item is not referred to in IDEA or is not "common" does not mean it cannot be in your blueprint and ultimately in your child's IEP. For example, IDEA does not refer to or require that a child with learning disabilities be provided the Lindamood-Bell program (a multisensory program that helps children understand phonics), but if your child needs that program, it should be on the blueprint.

An "Appropriate" Education

As you think about your child's needs, remember that while it's helpful to know what an ideal program and services for your child would look like, the law requires only that the district provide an *appropriate* education for your child. The precise meaning of an "appropriate" education is hard to pin down. When Congress passed the IDEA in 1975, it was concerned with providing an education that would help students with disabilities become independent. Educators, parents, and courts have come up with various additional definitions. Some see an "appropriate" education as one in which the student can progress from grade to grade (regardless of specific grades or academic achievement), others look to see if the child is provided a "basic floor of opportunity" to learn. Some see evidence of progress in meeting goals as proof that the program is appropriate, still others refer to an education "reasonably calculated to provide meaningful educational opportunities." Congress was concerned with providing an education that will help students with disabilities become "independent."

As you can see, none of these definitions provide the ultimate test or set of rules we all would like. That is why what is appropriate for your child must relate directly to his or her unique needs. A child who needs a one-on-one aide to work on math concepts or spelling to advance from "grade-to-grade" or have a "meaningful education" would be entitled to that aide. If he or she can advance or receive a meaningful education without that aide, the aide may not be required as part of an "appropriate" education. For another child, whose psychological complications require placement in a residential program in order for that child to have a "basic floor of opportunity," such a placement would be appropriate.

You should draft your ideal blueprint for your child and then examine that blueprint to make sure you can justify it to the IEP team as necessary for an "appropriate" education for your child.

One of my first clients was a deaf child whose parents could not communicate in sign language. We asked for and eventually got sign language classes for the parents as part of the child's IEP, even though

IDEA does not mention sign language classes for parents of deaf children. Remember, IDEA does not list every conceivable IEP item, because it recognizes that the IEP team needs the flexibility to include those items that meet the individual child's unique needs.

 FORM

A sample IEP Blueprint is below; a blank copy is available on this book's Companion Page on www.nolo.com. See Chapter 16 for the link. Be sure to put your blueprint draft into your binder, along with supporting information and documents. (See Chapter 4.)

Classroom Setting and Peer Needs

In this section, specify the type of classroom you'd like for your child, including the kinds of peers he or she should have. You may not have a good sense of all of these details right now. Start by putting general information in the blueprint (for example, that you want your child to be in a small, mainstreamed class, without any children who have serious behavioral problems). You'll fill in the details as you get more fully immersed in the process.

Specific items to address (when relevant) include:
- regular versus special education class
- partially or fully mainstreamed
- type of special education class (for example, for learning disabled students or students with language delays)
- number of children in the classroom
- ages and cognitive ranges of children in class
- kinds of students (with similar or dissimilar learning disabilities) and behaviors that might or might not be appropriate for your child—for example, a child with attention deficit disorder may need a classroom where other children do not act out, and
- language needs—for example, a child who has language processing problems or a delay may need to model children with higher language abilities.

IEP Blueprint

The IEP blueprint represents the ideal IEP for your child. Use it as a guide to make and record the educational desires you have for your child.

Areas of the IEP	Ideal Situation for Your Child
1. Classroom Setting and Peer Needs—issues to consider:	
☐ regular versus special education class	_____ _____
☐ partially of fully mainstreamed	_____
☐ type of special education class	_____
☒ number of children in the classroom	A class of no more than 10 students _____
☒ ages and cognitive ranges of children in class	Age range 9-10; same cognitive range as Mark
☒ kinds of students and behaviors that might or might not be appropriate for your child, and	No behaviorally troubled students No mixed "disability" class _____
☐ language similarities.	_____
2. Teacher and Staff Needs	
☒ number of teachers and aides	1 teacher; 1 full-time aide or 2 half-time aides
☒ teacher-pupil ratio	10:1 pupil-teacher ratio
☒ experience, training, and expertise of the teacher, and	Teacher with specific learning disability training, experience, credentials
☒ training and experience of aides.	Aide: previous experience working with L-D students
3. Curricula and Teaching Methodology—be specific. If you don't know what you do want, specify what you don't want.	Slingerland method Teaching strategies that include significant repetition _____

IEP Blueprint (continued)

Areas of the IEP	Ideal Situation for Your Child
4. Related Services—issues to consider:	
☒ specific needed services	1:1 aide two hours per day
☒ types of services	Speech and lang. therapy 3 times/week, 40 min. per session, 1:1
☒ frequency of services, and	30 minutes of psych. counseling once a week with psychologist experienced with children with learning disabilities and emotional overlay
☒ length of services.	A class of no more than 10 students
5. Identified Programs—specify known programs that you think would work for your child, and the school that offers them	Special day class (5th grade) for learning disabled at Washington School (Ms. Flanagan)
6. Goals—your child's academic and functional aims	Improve reading fluency and comprehension: Read three-paragraph story with 80% comprehension; complete reading within 10 minutes Improve peer relationships: Initiate five positive peer interactions/week
7. Classroom Environment and Other Features—issues to consider:	
☒ distance from home	No more than five miles and less than 30-minute bus ride to school
☐ transition plans for mainstreaming	

IEP Blueprint (continued)

Areas of the IEP	Ideal Situation for Your Child
☐ vocational needs	
☒ extracurricular and social needs, and	Involvement in after-school recreation and lunchtime sports activities
☒ environmental needs.	Small school (no more than 250 students); quiet classroom; protective environment (procedures to ensure students do not wander); acoustically treated classroom
	A class of no more than 10 students
8. **Transition Services**—higher education, independent living skills, job training; required before age 16.	Will learn the transportation system
	Will open a bank account
	Will learn how to keep track of daily expenses
	Will learn how to look for and apply for a job
9. **Involvement in the General Curriculum/Other**—to what extent will your child be involved in regular programs and curriculum, and what help will your child need to do it?	
☐ amount of time in regular education classroom (100%, 80%, none, etc.)	
☒ modification of general curriculum	Large-type materials
	Repeated review/drill
	1:1 aide to work on reading comprehension
☒ statewide assessment exams: Will your child take them? Will accommodations be necessary?	Assessments:
	Large-print versions
	Additional time to complete testing
	Supervised breaks within test sections

One of the more complex issues for parents of children with learning disabilities is how to balance the need for a program that will serve your child's unique needs against the importance of placement in a regular classroom. In many cases, your child's needs can be met in a regular classroom, but there are circumstances in which you may feel you have to choose one over the other.

At times, IDEA's goal of placing disabled children in a regular classroom (sometimes called mainstreaming or inclusion) must give way if a child needs to be placed in a more specialized program. There are pluses and minuses to each type of placement. A regular classroom placement offers your child the chance to be in a regular environment with children who don't have disabilities, to model their behavior, to work on standard curriculum and subject matter, to participate in sports and other extracurricular activities, and to benefit from all that a regular school environment provides, including the chance to be inspired by the challenges it poses. Conversely, a regular classroom may prove too difficult for some children with learning disabilities. The child may not be ready for the subject matter, may not have developed sufficient basic skills to be able to keep up, or may simply be overwhelmed by the size, activity, and amount of work in a regular classroom.

Placement in a special classroom may allow a child with learning disabilities to develop basic learning skills more efficiently and effectively, reduce the pressure on that child, allow a child to be with other children at the same level of development, and give the child a chance to work with staff that specialize in learning disabilities. Conversely, a special classroom may include too many different types of students and behaviors, may feel stigmatizing to the child (this issue may be particularly important to older children), and generally will not expose the child to all the characteristics and options of a regular classroom.

As you develop the classroom section of your blueprint, analyze the pluses and minuses of a regular or special day class and develop the blueprint accordingly.

Teacher and Staff Needs

Use this section to identify your child's needs concerning teachers and other classroom staff, such as:

- number of teachers and aides
- teacher-pupil ratio—for example, your child may require a ratio of no more than four students to one teacher (while this may be possible in a special day class, it won't be available in a regular class)
- experience, training, and expertise of the classroom teacher— regular education teachers may not always have special education experience or training in teaching children with learning disabilities
- experience, training, and expertise of the special education teacher—resource specialists are often used in class or for pull-out sessions to remediate learning disabilities. You want specialists who are experienced in dealing with your child's disability and the particular learning disability strategies and methodologies your child needs, and
- experience, training, and expertise of aides.

Curricula and Teaching Methodology

In this section, identify the curricula and teaching method or methods you feel are appropriate for your child. These might include both formal and informal methods for helping your child work on areas of difficulty. Teaching strategies and methodologies may range from simple exercises, day-to-day tactics, and plans used at school or home to improve reading, spelling, math, and language skills, to specific, named teaching programs and approaches.

Strategies and methodologies don't address only academic subjects. They might also include helping a learning disabled student organize his or her desk or showing a student with social anxiety how to take a time out, count to ten, or take a deep breath when faced with a difficult situation.

Multisensory Methodology

You may have already heard about multisensory methodology, a common approach to teaching children with learning disabilities. A multisensory approach uses a child's visual, auditory, and tactile-kinesthetic skills (that is, the child's sense of sight, hearing, and touch) to develop reading, language, spelling, and math skills. These methodologies often break learning tasks down into sequential steps, so the child can develop basic learning skills from the ground up. Multisensory approaches are often used for children with learning disabilities because they develop and encourage language acquisition and reading development.

Some well-known multisensory methodologies include:

- **Lindamood-Bell:** a sequencing program that helps children develop phonemic awareness and understand how sounds are developed—and, therefore, improve their reading, speech, and spelling skills.
- **Slingerland:** this methodology uses multisensory skills simultaneously to teach the rules and structure of the English language. Students build from the most simple level of language—the letter—to spelling, reading, writing, and oral language skills.
- **Wilson Reading System:** teaches word structure by focusing on spelling and decoding for students with language and reading difficulties.
- **The Spalding Method:** like Slingerland, Spalding uses an integrated, multisensory, and simultaneous approach to help students develop reading, writing, spelling, and oral language skills.
- **Orton-Gillingham:** using this simultaneous, sequential, and multisensory approach, students start by learning how letters look, sound, and feel, then move on to forming words and understanding written language.

RESOURCE

Find out more about teaching methodologies on the Internet. Start by searching the websites of the organizations listed on this book's Companion

Page on www.nolo.com, particularly www.ldonline.org. See Chapter 16 for the link. Also, check out the website of the Child Development Institute, at www. childdevelopmentinfo.com, which has lots of helpful information on strategies for students with learning disabilities. Or, go to your favorite search engine and plug in the name of a particular methodology, such as Slingerland or Lindamood-Bell.

You can also buy programs that will help your child spell, multiply, or read more easily. While these programs are usually not part of the IEP, you can use them to give your child some extra help. These programs might include books, tapes, and software about reading through phonics, developing better memory, mastering spelling, and so on. Check the websites listed above as well as national organizations such as the Learning Disabilities Association of America, at www .ldaamerica.org, for more information on available programs.

Strategies and Methodologies for Specific Learning Disabilities

In addition to the teaching methodologies mentioned above, there are teaching strategies, methods, and materials that educators often use to help children with a particular learning disability, such as dyslexia or auditory processing disorder. Some common ideas are listed here; you can find many more online.

- **ADD/ADHD:** a structured classroom and regular schedule; help with transitions during the school day (such as returning from recess or changing classrooms); help organizing thoughts and ideas for projects; rewards for positive behavior; breaks during the day for physical activity.
- **Dyscalculia:** allowing the student to use a calculator; using games to teach mathematical concepts; asking the student to explain a mathematical process orally; using concrete examples before moving to abstract ideas; asking the student to estimate an answer before beginning to solve a math problem.
- **Dysgraphia:** providing alternatives to writing (such as using a computer or giving oral presentations); giving extra time for writing assignments; allowing a student to use a spell-checker; varied writing assignments (for example, writing letters, a journal, lists, or reports on a topic of special interest to the

student); written handouts that allow the student space to write (for example, an outline of a lecture with space for notes or a worksheet with math problems and space to calculate the answers); allowing the student to use graph paper or heavily lined writing paper.

- **Dyslexia:** books on tape; assigning varied reading materials (such as magazines, newspapers, comics, and advertisements); allowing more time for homework and other assignments; phonics-based instruction and multisensory approaches.

- **Auditory Processing Disorder:** seating the child near the teacher; teaching that combines oral instruction with visual aids; asking the student to repeat information and instructions back to the teacher or aide before beginning an assignment; rhyming games; giving the student a note-taker; speech-language therapy.

- **Visual Processing Disorder:** large-print books, written materials, and other adaptations (such as enlarged projected materials); teaching that combines writing (on the blackboard or charts) with oral information; allowing the student to explain test answers orally; puzzles and other games that emphasize spatial relationships; allowing the student to use a ruler, highlighters, and graph paper.

Related Services

Include in your blueprint a detailed list of necessary services, specifying the type and amount to be provided (for example, how many sessions per week and how long each session will last). The law does not limit the kinds of related services that must be provided to a child with learning disabilities. Generally, a school district must provide a related service if it is necessary to ensure that your child benefits from his or her education or if your child needs such services to be in a regular classroom. Related services for a learning disabled child might include a one-on-one aide, speech therapy, physical therapy, transportation, and/or psychological services. (See Chapters 2 and 8 for more detailed discussions of related services.)

Does Your Child Have a Right to a Specific Methodology?

While IDEA does not require that a particular methodology or curriculum be included in the IEP and provided to your child, there is no prohibition against it. If a child needs a specific methodology to benefit from special education, then it is required; if not (or if you cannot prove it's necessary), the school district does not have to provide it.

Ultimately, your child's IEP goals will specify the key learning strategies in your child's IEP. They describe how your child will accomplish specific educational tasks. They may not name particular methodologies, but they do set forth the detailed, day-to-day activities that will help your child with his or her learning disability. If you can't get a particular methodology into the IEP, make sure that the written goals describe how you want your child to be taught.

Identified Programs

In Section 1 of the blueprint, you may have stated whether you want your child in a regular or special education classroom. If you know about a program in a particular school that you think would work best for your child, be it a regular classroom or a special education classroom, public or private, identify that program here.

Goals

IDEA used to refer to a child's "goals and objectives" (and some school representatives may continue to use these terms): Goals were long range in nature, while objectives were generally more specific, short-term benchmarks that would help a child achieve the broader goal. When Congress amended IDEA in 2004, however, it took out all references to objectives and benchmarks.

The law now refers to measurable annual goals, including "academic and functional goals" designed to meet the child's disability-related and other educational needs. (20 U.S.C. § 1414(d)(1)(A).) Because the statutory language is very general, it gives the IEP team a lot of latitude when coming up with goals—and nothing in the law prevents the team from using specific, concrete goals (much like the objectives that used to be required).

Examples of *goals* for students with learning disabilities include:

- improve reading comprehension or other academic skills, such as math, spelling, or writing
- improve social skills
- resolve a serious emotional difficulty that impedes school work
- improve fine or large motor skills
- develop greater language and speech skills
- develop independent living skills, or
- improve auditory or visual memory.

RELATED TOPIC

Chapter 9 discusses goals in detail, and explains how to write effective goals for children with learning disabilities.

Classroom Environment and Other Features

Use your blueprint to identify any other features of the program you want for your child, such as:

- distance from home
- transition plans for mainstreaming
- vocational needs
- extracurricular and social needs
- environmental needs—protective environment, small class, small campus, acoustically treated classroom, or the like
- computer programs and technological services that can help your child, and
- any plans you have for addressing your child's needs outside of school—for example, tutoring, helping your child with homework, helping organize assignments and school materials, or after-school activities to build coordination or social skills.

Involvement in the General Curriculum

In this section of the blueprint, you should describe the extent to which you want your child to be involved in regular school programs and curriculum. For example, if you want your child placed in a regular classroom using the regular curriculum, but your child will need some one-on-one time with an aide and some modifications to the regular classroom teaching methodologies, you should indicate that here.

You should also jot down any modifications you believe your child will need in order to take statewide assessment tests. As these tests become more common, school districts are having to accommodate children with disabilities—and the 2004 amendments to IDEA state that the IEP should include any modifications a child will need to participate in these tests. There are a variety of possible accommodations, but not all are available and allowed in every state and for every test. (See, for example, the test variations available to California's statewide assessments, as listed in the sample IEP form in Appendix D on this book's Companion Page on nolo.com (see Chapter 16 for the link). This is your blueprint, so you should list the accommodations that would best ensure that the assessments measure your child's ability, not the effects of his or her disability. Be warned, however, that this is an area where school districts don't have much flexibility to deviate from the state's rules about what is and is not allowed as an accommodation.

Other Sources of Information for the Blueprint

Your blueprint will be a work in progress. As you learn more about your child's needs (from professionals and others) and find out what services and programs are available, you can add to or change the information on your blueprint.

People who are trustworthy and know your child—such as other parents, your pediatrician, the classroom teacher, or a tutor—are excellent sources of information for your blueprint. Pose your question like this: "Terry is having some problems with reading (math, cognitive growth, language development, social issues, emotional conflicts, mobility, fine or gross motor activities, or whatever) and I'm wondering if I should look for a new program (or different related services). Do you have any suggestions of people I might talk to or programs or services I might consider?"

RELATED TOPIC

Chapter 8 contains important information about gathering facts, visiting school programs, and developing supportive material, such as an independent evaluation. This information will help you with your blueprint.

What's Next?

If you are new to special education, your next step is to learn about the evaluation and eligibility processes—how your child is evaluated and becomes eligible for special education. Read Chapters 6 and 7 carefully.

If you are not new to special education, your next step will depend on your child's situation. Your child may need an evaluation before the IEP meeting—if so, be sure to read Chapter 6. If your child does not need an immediate evaluation and has already been found eligible for special education, move on to Chapter 8.

Evaluations

E valuations are important tools that help you and the school district determine what your child's needs are and how they can be met. The school district will rely very heavily on the results of the evaluation in determining whether your child is eligible for special education and, if so, what the IEP will include.

CAUTION

Evaluations or assessments? This chapter covers evaluations—the tests and other information-gathering methods used to determine a child's eligibility for, and progress in, special education. Many advocates use the term "evaluations" interchangeably with the term "assessments," but they have different legal meanings. Under IDEA, assessments are the statewide tests that evaluate the progress of all schoolchildren (not just those in special education) toward meeting various academic and other standards. Don't worry if your school district or a teacher refers to eligibility testing as an "assessment"; just make sure you understand how they are using the term.

Evaluations are observations, reports, and tests that provide specific information about your child's cognitive, academic, linguistic, social, and emotional status. Evaluations describe your child's current developmental levels—how he or she reads, perceives information, processes information, calculates, remembers things, performs physical tasks, relates to other children, and takes in, expresses, and understands language.

Because evaluations will determine your child's eligibility for special education and provide information on which programs and strategies might be helpful to your child, they should be completed before any educational decisions are made. Ideally, the evaluation report will support what you want included in the IEP, as set out in your blueprint. (See Chapter 5.) For example, if you feel your child should be placed in a regular classroom where distractions are minimized (in a seat near the front of the class, for example), or if your child has difficulties with handwriting and needs to take oral rather than written tests, your chances of getting these accommodations are increased if the evaluation report makes these recommendations.

Special Education Evaluations Versus General Assessments

Most (if not all) states require schools to administer a variety of tests to measure how children are doing in school and whether they are meeting certain state standards. These tests—often called general assessments—measure a child's mastery of a specific subject matter, such as American history or algebra. Most children also take tests to graduate from high school and qualify for college. While special education evaluations often measure similar abilities or aptitudes, they are intended to be used for a different purpose: to determine whether a child is eligible for special education and which special education services will be helpful to a particular child.

Since 1997, IDEA has required schools to include special education children in state- and district-wide assessments, with appropriate accommodations for the child's unique needs. When IDEA was amended in 2004, Congress added language stating that children with disabilities must be provided with "appropriate accommodations and alternative assessments" if necessary. Any alternative assessments given must be aligned with state content standards—that is, they must be related to any state rules regarding required subject areas for testing. (20 U.S.C. § 1412(a)(16).)

Not all of these tests are sensitive to special education test takers, however. For example, California requires high school seniors to pass an "exit exam" before they graduate, but the State Board of Education has generally ignored the needs of special education students and failed to make appropriate exit exam accommodations or modifications. The state was sued for this oversight, but a settlement was reached in 2008 that does not exempt special education students from taking exit exams in order to graduate. You should carefully review any state or district tests in which your child participates to make sure that the test is appropriate and that your child receives any accommodations necessary to take the test.

This chapter explains:
- when evaluations are done
- how an evaluation plan is developed
- how to evaluate tests, including the tests often used for children with suspected learning disabilities, and
- how to review, change, or challenge an evaluation.

When Evaluations Are Done

There are two kinds of evaluations: an initial eligibility evaluation to determine whether your child qualifies for special education services and subsequent or follow-up evaluations to get up-to-date information on your child's status and progress. (20 U.S.C. § 1414(a).) While evaluations can generally be done at almost any time in your child's school year or even school career, the initial evaluation must be done *before* your child can be found eligible for special education services.

The Evaluation Process, Step by Step

Here is how an evaluation typically proceeds:

1. You request an evaluation or the school identifies your child as possibly needing special education. (See Chapters 2 and 4.)

2. The school presents you with a written evaluation plan listing all testing to be done on your child. This plan should focus on identifying your child's strengths and weaknesses and pinpointing possible learning and other disabilities.

3. You approve the evaluation plan (or ask that certain tests or evaluation tools be added and/or others eliminated).

4. You meet with the evaluator to discuss areas where your child seems to be having problems, based on your personal observations, physician reports, and the like. You can also discuss any concerns you have about the evaluation. IDEA does not require this meeting, but I recommend it.

5. The school evaluates your child.

6. You receive a copy of the school's report.

7. You schedule independent evaluations if necessary. (See Chapter 8.)

8. You attend the IEP eligibility meeting or, if your child is already in special education, the yearly IEP meeting (see Chapter 11), where the evaluation results are discussed.

While the school district has a duty to identify and evaluate all children who may be in need of special education (referred to as the district's "child find" responsibility) (20 U.S.C. § 1412(a)(3)), you don't have to wait for your school district to act. If you suspect your child needs help, contact your school right away to request an evaluation.

FORM

You can find a sample Request to Begin Special Education Process and Evaluation in Chapter 4; a blank downloadable copy is available on this book's Companion Page on www.nolo.com. See Chapter 16 for the link.

Once your child is found eligible for special education, he or she must be evaluated at least every three years, or more frequently if you or a teacher requests it. You have a right to have your child reevaluated at least once a year; if you want more frequent reevaluations, you will need the school district's consent. (20 U.S.C. § 1414(a)(2).) There's more about reevaluations at the end of this chapter.

Your Child May Have Other Needs

When your child is "suspected" of having a learning disability, the evaluation process must necessarily focus on that concern, but not to the exclusion of other possible problems. A child with a specific learning disability may have other needs and therefore other potential areas of eligibility for programs and services. Remember that your child can and must be evaluated in all areas of suspected disability or need. See Chapter 7 regarding IDEA's criteria for determining whether a child has a specific learning disability.

IDEA requires the school district to complete your child's first evaluation and determine whether your child is eligible for special education within **60 days** of receiving your consent to do the evaluation. And that's **60 calendar days**, not business or school days—weekends and holidays count toward the 60-day deadline. If your state has its own time frame for the initial evaluation and determination of eligibility, then that deadline will apply rather than the 60 days specified by IDEA. (20 U.S.C. § 1414(a)(1)(C)(i)(I).) Remember, your school is required to provide you with an explanation of all applicable special education laws, whether federal or state.

If you "repeatedly" fail or refuse to "produce" your child for the evaluation, then the school district will not be required to meet the 60-day deadline. If your child changes school districts before the previous district has made an eligibility determination, the new district has a responsibility to make "sufficient progress" in meeting the 60-day deadline, but will not necessarily be bound to it. (20 U.S.C. § 1414(a)(1)(C)(ii).)

> **CAUTION**
>
> **Don't take no for an answer.** Not all teachers are experienced at recognizing learning disabilities. If you suspect that your child has a learning disability, insist on an evaluation, even if the school is resistant. School representatives may try to convince you that your child is just having a normal developmental delay, or that an "evaluation"—usually just the teacher's impressions of your child—doesn't point to a learning disability. This may be the case, but the only way to know for sure is to have your child evaluated.

The Evaluation Plan

Before an evaluation can begin, the school district must give you a written plan listing all testing procedures that will be used to evaluate your child (including the specific tests that will be administered).

Evaluations will test for intellectual, cognitive, academic, linguistic, social, and emotional status, including how your child reads, perceives information, processes information, calculates, remembers things, performs physical tasks, relates to other children, and takes in, expresses, and understands language.

Evaluation plans will vary from child to child and from learning disability to learning disability.

Developing the Evaluation Plan

Evaluation plans can be drawn up by a group of people, usually including the parents, the child (if appropriate), a regular education teacher, a representative of the school district, someone who can interpret the instructional implications of the evaluation results, and, at the discretion of the school or parents, other individuals who have knowledge or special expertise regarding the child. (20 U.S.C. § 1414(c).) In reality, however, evaluation plans are usually developed by the school district and then given to you.

This group is not legally required to meet. If it does decide to meet, it must:

- review any existing data, including evaluations and information you provide
- review current classroom-based evaluations and observations (by teachers and related services providers), and
- based on these materials and input from the child's parents, identify any additional information necessary to determine whether the child has a qualifying disability (or in the case of a reevaluation, whether the child continues to require special education); the child's present levels of performance and educational needs; and whether any changes should be made to the child's current educational program and services. (20 U.S.C. § 1414(c).)

Should Your Child Be Evaluated at All?

Some parents resist having their children evaluated because they do not want their child in special education, they believe that testing will categorize their child in ways that are harmful, or they think that their child will be set apart from the rest of the school or from regular education. While these are understandable positions, you must weigh them against the importance of finding out as much as you can about your child's needs and how they can be addressed. Because parents can exercise a lot of control over the evaluation process, the opportunity to learn more about your child should outweigh your emotional reluctance.

This planning process is your first chance to make sure that the evaluation is broad enough to give the evaluator a complete picture of your child's strengths and weaknesses. The best way to ensure that you are included from the beginning of the planning process is to call and write your special education administrator to formally request that you be involved in any evaluation planning (keep a copy of your letter for your records). Be sure to give yourself a reminder by including this step on your planning calendar. (See Chapter 4.)

The Relationship Between Evaluations and Eligibility for Special Education

Your child's initial evaluation will determine whether he or she is eligible for special education. Of course, you will want an evaluation that is thorough, fair, and informative about your child's ability and needs. And if you believe that your child needs special education services, you will also want the results to clearly demonstrate your child's eligibility.

As discussed in Chapter 7, your child is eligible for special education based on a specific learning disability if he or she has a disorder that has sufficient impact on his or her education in one of the following areas: listening, thinking, expressing and understanding language, reading, writing, spelling, or math. As you go through the evaluation process, remember that your child will have to meet this definition in order to qualify for special education.

Ignoring these eligibility requirements until the evaluation process is underway—or completed—may doom your plan to secure services for your child. You do not want to proceed with the evaluations until you know which findings will support eligibility (and which will not). Armed with this information, you can maximize the chances that your child will be found eligible.

Legal Requirements for Evaluations

IDEA guarantees every child certain rights in the evaluation process. An evaluation must:

- use a variety of tests, tools, and strategies to gather information about your child
- not be racially or culturally discriminatory
- be given in your child's native language or communication mode (such as sign language if your child is deaf or hard of hearing)
- validly determine your child's status—that is, it must include the right test(s) for your child's suspected areas of disability
- be administered by trained and knowledgeable personnel, in accordance with the instructions provided by the producer of the tests
- not be used only to determine intelligence
- if your child has impaired speaking or sensory skills, accurately reflect your child's aptitude or achievement level—not just your child's impairment
- evaluate your child in "all areas of suspected disability," including health, vision, hearing, social and emotional status, general intelligence, academic performance, communicative status, motor abilities, behavior, and cognitive, physical, and developmental abilities, and
- provide relevant information that will help determine your child's educational needs. (20 U.S.C. § 1414(b).)

In addition, the process must include other material about your child, such as information you provide (a doctor's letter or a statement of your observations, for example), current classroom assessments and observations (such as objective tests or subjective teacher reports), and observations by other professionals. (20 U.S.C. § 1414(c)(1).)

The Evaluation Plan Document

At the end of this planning process, your district will come up with a written document listing the formal tests and other tools that will be used to evaluate your child, including observation, interviews, and careful analysis of how your child functions.

While school districts use different evaluation plan forms or templates, the plan document must include:

- named tests and other tools (such as observations, interviews, or evaluations)
- a section where you can request additional tests or other methods of evaluation, and
- a place for you to indicate your approval or disapproval, and space for you to sign and date the plan.

Later on in this chapter, we discuss how to evaluate the plan, and include a list of items you might want added to the evaluation.

Analyzing the Tests

Usually, a person who is associated with your school district and who knows something about learning disabilities will determine which tests are to be given to your child. There's a very good chance that this person will also administer or supervise the evaluations. How will you know if the proposed tests are appropriate for your child?

You'll need to do some homework to find out what the tests measure, how their results are reported, and, most important, whether they're appropriate for your child. The information in this section will help you get started.

Gathering Information

Your best sources of information are people familiar with special education testing generally and the specific tests proposed for your child. These might include your child's teacher, the district's evaluator, other parents, and your pediatrician. You might also talk to independent special education evaluators you've worked with, school special education personnel you trust, or a private learning disability consultant (more likely to be available in more heavily populated areas). Get in touch with organizations that specialize in your child's learning disability, such as the Council for Exceptional Children or a state association for learning disabilities. You will note specific references throughout this chapter to various organizations and websites that can provide lots of valuable evaluation information and help you locate a learning disability expert.

> **RELATED TOPIC**
> Chapter 8 discusses independent evaluations. Appendix B provides a list of advocacy, parent, and disability organizations you might consider contacting for information on different types of evaluations and learning disability consultants. Appendix B also references books on testing and evaluations. The appendixes are available on this book's Companion Page on www.nolo.com. See Chapter 16 for the link.

Here's what you want to find out:
- Whether the proposed tests are appropriate to evaluate your child's suspected learning disabilities.
- What the tests generally measure, such as general cognitive skills, language abilities, memory, math, or reading.
- Whether the results of the tests are expressed in numeric scores, descriptive statements about your child's performance, or both.
- How the results are evaluated—for example, will your child score in a certain percentile ("Mary is in the 88th percentile") or will your child be given a different result ("Mary scored at the second grade level"). IDEA used to require a severe discrepancy between a child's ability and performance as part of its eligibility requirements for children with learning disabilities, but the amendments of 2004 no longer require states to use this discrepancy model. So even though the numerical results of any test will be important to help you and the school district understand your child's challenges and needs, they may not be used to determine eligibility. (See Chapter 7 for more on this important change.)

- Whether the test results will provide a solid basis for specific recommendations about classroom strategies, teaching methods, and services and programs for your child.
- How the tests are administered—for example, are they timed? Are they oral or written?
- Who will do the evaluation and what specific expertise, training, and experience he or she has in administering these particular tests.

The Ever-Changing World of Learning Disability Evaluations

Testing, particularly testing for learning disabilities, is complicated and, at times, controversial. While we want and need objective information, we don't want to lose sight of our children as individuals rather than numbers. Educators and even legislators are constantly rethinking how testing should be used to evaluate eligibility for special education. Some argue that we should move away from traditional assessments for learning disabilities because they are designed to measure discrepancies between ability and achievement—which can happen only after the child has failed. There will likely be continued focus on alternative methods to identify children with learning disabilities at an earlier age, so they can receive assistance before they fall behind.

Although IDEA used to require that a child show a severe discrepancy between achievement and ability in order to be found eligible for special education, the 2004 amendments no longer require states to use this discrepancy standard. As of 2008, there has appeared to be little change in how states determine what constitutes a specific learning disability. This is not surprising, since Congress made it a discretionary matter for each state to decide whether or not to continue using the "severe discrepancy" standard. (See Chapter 7 for more on eligibility requirements.)

Tests for Identifying and Evaluating Learning Disabilities

To make sure your child's evaluation will be effective and appropriate, you'll need to know about the specific tests used to identify learning disabilities. Tests for learning disabilities tend to be more objective in nature than tests for other types of disabilities—the results will usually be expressed in terms of a percentile, grade level, or other numerical scale. In contrast, evaluations used for children with emotional difficulties, for example, often involve evaluating behavior, mood, and relationships, and the results cannot always be reduced to "numbers." (As discussed in more detail in Chapter 7, on eligibility, reliance on tests with numeric results has its benefits and drawbacks.) The sections that follow divide specific evaluation tools into categories based on what they test (intelligence, perception, language, and so on). You'll note that some of the tests cover a wide variety of areas.

The sections that follow do not include every test for learning disabilities; there are a variety of tools out there. Don't be surprised if the tests seem to melt into a detailed and somewhat confusing muddle of numbers and phrases, or if you find it difficult to compare the areas covered by these tests—IQ, perception, language, and so on—with the language in IDEA that defines learning disabilities. You will learn more about the tests as you read this chapter, do research, and talk to education specialists.

Even experts in learning disabilities—who often have years of experience with these tests—sometimes get bogged down in the numbers and technical language. If you get confused or discouraged, remember these tips:

- A lot of people—even those who work in the field of education— are confused by the multitude of tests. Don't be intimidated by test terminology; if you're confused, chances are good that you're not alone.
- Ask what the test is called, why it is being given, and what all the numbers and phrases mean. If the answer isn't clear, ask again. When the evaluator or school administrator uses a term

like "short-term auditory memory," "abstract thinking," or "aphasia," ask him or her to explain the concept in language that you can understand. I know I have to think for a moment (or longer) to remember what "sequential processing," "simultaneous processing," and "spatial memory" are.

- Find out how the test results are recorded—for example, as a percentage score, a "stanine" score (a rating on a scale of 1 through 9), or a chronological score.
- If a number of tests will be given that seem to assess similar skills or functions, find out why. What are the differences between the tests, if any? Is there a reason for giving multiple tests? How does one judge the results of these tests, particularly if they reach different conclusions about the same learning abilities?

Finding Out More About Tests for Learning Disabilities

You can find lots of resources on the many tests for learning disabilities on the Internet; just type the test name into your favorite search engine. Here are some websites you might find especially useful:

- www.parentpals.com
- www.ldonline.org (the website of Learning Disabilities Online)
- www.nichcy.org (publications available from the National Dissemination Center for Children With Disabilities).

If you don't have Web access, your local library should have a number of useful books on learning disabilities and learning disability evaluation. Also ask your school district special education administrator for written information on the subject.

Ask the school evaluator, other parents, and your pediatrician about tests for learning disabilities. You might also want to check the website for your state's department of education. These sites often provide other information about learning disabilities, including links to resources within the state department of education. See Appendix B on this book's Companion Page on nolo.com (you'll find the link on Chapter 16) for a list of organizations that can provide information about the many tests used in special education.

Intelligence Tests

Intelligence tests or IQ tests provide an overall sense of your child's intellectual capabilities and cognitive development. But they are controversial—IDEA 2004 reflects Congress's uncertainty about their value. See "IQ Tests Are Controversial," below. Your child's score will be used, along with other information, to determine whether your child is eligible for special education based on a learning disability. (See Chapter 7 for more on eligibility.) Each of these tests has a number of subtests that assess more specific areas, such as short-term memory and vocabulary.

Here are some IQ tests commonly used for children with learning disabilities:

- **Stanford-Binet:** for individuals from age two to adult, this test measures short-term memory and various areas of quantitative, visual, and abstract reasoning.

- **Kaufman Assessment Battery for Children (KABC):** for children age three to 18, the KABC tests both achievement and intelligence (problem-solving rather than factual knowledge); a good test of a child's memory.

- **Wechsler Intelligence Scales for Children, 3rd Edition (often referred to as WISC-III):** the WISC-III is often the preferred IQ test. It is used to measure intellectual development and giftedness, and to uncover learning disabilities and developmental delays. The test is divided into Verbal and Performance scales, which measure a child's arithmetic, vocabulary, short-term memory, factual information, comprehension, attention to visual details, and abstract and concrete reasoning skills. The Wechsler scores tend to be in the 60–130 standard score range, with a percentile finding ranging from "very superior" to "mentally impaired."

Other important tests, particularly for measuring cognitive development—memory, understanding of concepts, problem-solving and general knowledge—are:

- Battelle Developmental Inventory (assesses motor ability, cognitive levels, and social behavior)
- Bayley Scales of Infant and Toddler Development (evaluates behavior and motor skills), and

- McCarthy Scales of Children's Abilities (tests general verbal, perceptual, and memory IQ).

These three tests are generally used for younger children.

IQ Tests Are Controversial

The use of intelligence or other standardized tests to measure a child's ability is controversial. Compelling arguments have been made that IQ tests do not fully measure native intelligence, but instead reflect certain biases as well as environmental influences on a child. Many tests have been criticized for failing to account for cultural and linguistic differences. For example, the cultural differences between some white and African American children are not reflected in certain tests.

Some tests have been the subject of pitched court battles. In one federal case, *Larry P. v. Riles*, 793 F.2d 969 (9th Cir. 1984), the court found that IQ tests discriminate against African Americans. Other tests identify a disproportionate number of racial minorities as needing special education. Since the 2004 amendments to IDEA, IQ tests have been even more disfavored as a method of determining special education eligibility.

At a broader level, many educators and advocates have raised concerns about how heavily schools rely on testing and have questioned whether standardized tests accurately measure ability or achievement. As more and more states require students to take a variety of tests before they can graduate, these questions become increasingly more important.

For what it's worth, statisticians tell us that the "average" range of intelligence, as measured by IQ test scores, is 90–109. One can only wonder how Beethoven, Woody Guthrie, or Rosa Parks might have scored on IQ tests. I wouldn't be surprised if their scores were quite high, but if not, would we question their native intelligence? IQ tests play an important role in the IEP process for children with learning disabilities, but your child's abilities and potential cannot—and should not—be reduced to a test score.

> ## Test Scatter
>
> IQ tests generally have subtests, and there may be a marked difference—
> called "scatter"—in your child's subtest scores. For example, a child may
> score very high on a subtest that evaluates reading comprehension, but
> very low on a subtest that looks at the child's understanding of spatial
> relationships. Your child's IQ score will be an average of these different
> subtest scores, which may not reflect his or her true potential and problems.
> A wide scatter indicates that your child has marked areas of strength and
> weakness. This is why it's very important to find out how your child scored
> on the subtests.

Assessments for ADD/ADHD

Testing for ADD/ADHD is less technical and formulaic than most
tests used for learning disabilities. If you suspect your child has ADD/
ADHD, you should have his or her pediatrician do a thorough medical
exam. Observational checklists and teacher and parent rating scales are
also often used to determine whether there is ADD/ADHD. These tests
are exactly what they sound like—the teacher or parent observes the
child and notes whether particular behaviors are present. The Conners'
Parent Rating Scales, the Conners' Teacher Rating Scales, and the Child
Behavior Checklist are several observational assessment tools that are
frequently used for determining ADD/ADHD.

Tests for Perception Abilities

Children with learning disabilities may have difficulties (or strengths)
in auditory (listening) or visual (seeing) perception. As part of any
evaluation of perception, your child should have hearing and vision tests
to find out whether hearing loss or poor eyesight is part of the problem.

Some tests used to determine whether a student has difficulties
processing language (as opposed to a hearing loss) are the Test of
Auditory Perceptual Skills, which assesses auditory memory for
numbers, words, and sentences, and the Goldman-Fristoe-Woodcock

Test of Auditory Discrimination, which assesses the child's ability to distinguish sounds.

Two tests sometimes used to assess visual perception problems are the Bender Visual-Motor Gestalt Test and the Developmental Test of Visual-Motor Integration (in which, among other things, the child is shown designs on a card and is asked to reproduce those shapes).

Academic/Psychoeducational Tests

These tests measure your child's skill level in specific classroom areas, such as reading, math, writing, and spelling:

- **Kaufman Test of Educational Achievement,** which assesses decoding skills as well as spelling, reading comprehension, and math skills.
- **Wechsler Individual Achievement Test,** which assesses some of the same areas as the Kaufman and also oral and written expression and listening comprehension.
- **Woodcock-Johnson Psychoeducational Battery and Peabody Individual Achievement Test,** which assesses science and social studies comprehension, as well as reading and math skills.
- **Test of Written Language (TOWL),** which measures writing ability, including capitalization, punctuation, spelling, vocabulary, syntax, grammar, and story composition.

Language

Language evaluation involves many different areas, including a child's ability to produce and express language through sound, and to receive, understand, and express information.

Some of the more well-known language tests are the Test of Early Language Development (TELD), the Peabody Picture Vocabulary Test (PPVT), the Test for Auditory Comprehension of Language (TACL), and the Sequenced Inventory of Communication Development (SICD). The Clinical Evaluation of Language Fundamentals (CELF) is also a highly respected evaluation tool for language. These tests measure, among other things, whether a child understands the words spoken (auditory processing), how to speak, and how to use words in sentences that convey the child's intended meaning.

CAUTION

Make sure you have the right test edition. There are a wide variety of tests used to determine whether a child has a learning disability. Many of these tests have been revised over the years, and now exist in several different versions. Make sure that the tests given to your child are the most recent editions. Some tests designate the edition or revision in the title (for example, the WISC-III is the 3rd edition of the Wechsler).

Testing Children With Limited English Proficiency

The 2004 amendments to IDEA recognize an important change in American demographics: that the "limited English proficient population is the fastest growing in our Nation." (20 U.S.C. § 1400(c)(11).) To address this issue, Congress has created rules about the assessment of children with limited English proficiency. The district must administer evaluations in the child's native language, so that the tests will yield "accurate information on what the child knows and can do academically, developmentally, and functionally." (20 U.S.C. § 1414(b)(3).) Tests and evaluations that don't take this issue into consideration will not be considered "appropriate."

These protections also apply to deaf and hard of hearing children who may not be proficient in English. Many of these children not only have a different native language—American Sign Language, or ASL—but also use an entirely unique communication mode—visual or sign language.

Approving, Rejecting, or Changing the Evaluation Plan

IDEA requires the school district to get your permission before it can evaluate your child. Your consent must be "informed," which means that you must understand fully what you are consenting to. If you don't give permission, the school district can still seek to evaluate your child, but it will have to go to due process and get an order from the judge allowing it to proceed. If the school district doesn't force the issue, however, then it is not obligated to provide special education or hold an IEP meeting. (20 U.S.C. § 1414(a)(1).)

IDEA allows a teacher or specialist to "screen" children to determine appropriate teaching strategies "for curriculum implementation" without parental permission; such screenings are not considered evaluations to which you must consent. While this rule seems like a sensible way to let teachers do their jobs, it may be hard to tell the difference between a screening and a full-fledged evaluation. You should certainly ask teachers and the special education administrator to give you detailed information on any such screenings they conduct. Then, if the school tries to use screening information during eligibility discussions at an IEP meeting, you can object that this information is not supposed to be part of the eligibility process. (20 U.S.C. § 1414(a)(1)(E).)

If your child is already in special education and you refuse to allow further evaluation, your child retains the right to his or her current program and services, but the district can take you to due process to get approval to reevaluate your child over your objections. (See Chapter 12 for more on due process.)

If you have concerns about the plan submitted to you, you have every right to ask for changes. IDEA specifies that the process should include evaluations and information provided by:

- the parents
- classroom-based, local, or state assessments
- classroom observations, and
- observations by teachers and related services providers.

(20 U.S.C. § 1414(c); 34 C.F.R. § 300.305(a)(1)(i)–(iii).)

You can request that specific tests be administered to your child or that certain information be used to evaluate your child and included as part of the report. This information might include a formal interview with you, a review of your child's schoolwork, a teacher's observations, or a pediatrician's report. Be as specific as possible in your request. For example, if your child has limited fine motor skills and problems with handwriting, ask the evaluator to analyze handwriting samples.

Now is the time to make sure that the plan is appropriate and complete. Before you approve the plan, consider whether it should include any of the following:

- teacher and parent reports
- information from experts specializing in your child's learning disability
- specific tests you want included
- interviews with you and others who know your child well
- letters from a family doctor or counselor
- daily or weekly school reports or diaries, and
- other evidence of school performance, including work samples.

Include a Parent Interview

It is very important to include a parent interview in the evaluation. The interview gives the evaluator valuable information about your child, much of which may not be available through formal tests—your observations and understanding from living with your child provide a wealth of information. A parent interview also gives you a chance to meet with the evaluator and make sure that he or she understands your concerns (and includes them in the report).

TIP

What "other information" should be included in the plan? By this time, you have probably gathered information about your child—secured the school file and talked to teachers, other parents, or experts—and developed some sense of the key issues. You should also have some ideas about your child's learning difficulties and, therefore, what the evaluations should be testing. Be sure to take a look at your blueprint, no matter how incomplete it may be. Also look at Chapter 7, particularly its discussion of IDEA's criteria for determining the existence of a specific learning disability.

Approving or Rejecting the Plan

If you want changes in the evaluation plan, call and write your school district. Explain that you are exercising your right under IDEA (20 U.S.C. § 1414) to request that additional materials be added to your child's plan and/or items be taken out.

Ultimately, you must sign the plan and indicate whether you accept or reject it. Signing the plan need not be an all or nothing proposition. You can:

- accept the plan
- accept the plan on condition, or
- reject the plan.

Accepting the Plan

If you accept the plan as submitted to you, mark the appropriate box— most evaluation plans have approval and disapproval boxes—sign and date the plan, and return it to the school district. If there is no acceptance box, write "plan accepted," sign and date the plan, and return it. Be sure to make a photocopy of the plan and add it to your IEP binder.

IDEA requires that you give "informed" consent, which means you understand what you are consenting to. Therefore your district cannot expect you to agree to a plan describing tests that you do not understand. You have a right to be told what is being done and why. Only then can you give an "informed" consent to the evaluation.

Your consent to the evaluation cannot be used or construed as consent for a specific plan for special education and related services. You have the right to separately consent to or contest those items. (34 C.F.R. § 300.300(a)(1)(ii).)

The district can proceed without your approval of a reevaluation provided they prove they could not secure the consent. However, they must show that they have made "reasonable efforts" to obtain your consent and you have failed to respond. (34 C.F.R. § 300.300(c)(2).)

Accepting the Plan on Condition

There are two reasons why you might accept the plan with a condition. First, you might accept the tests proposed, but want additional tests administered or additional information considered. Second, you might not want certain proposed tests administered to your child—perhaps you believe that they aren't reliable or that they test for a problem that your child doesn't have.

Whatever the reason, indicate your partial acceptance of the plan on the form as follows:

> I approve only of the following tests:
>
> Wrat, Kaufman
>
> and/or want the following included as part of my child's evaluation plan:
>
> an interview with my child's pediatrician
>
> and my child's tutor.
>
> Date: March 1, 20xx
>
> Signature: *Jan Stevens*

Rejecting the Plan

You have every right to reject the plan and force the evaluator or school district to work with you to come up with an acceptable plan. Your reasons for rejecting the plan will usually fall into one or more of the following categories:

- the tests are not appropriate
- you want additional tests and materials as part of the evaluation, or
- the evaluator is not qualified.

Note, however, that if you reject the initial evaluation, the school district cannot then be found in violation of the law that requires they provide your child with a "free appropriate public education." In addition, when you reject the initial evaluation, the district is not required to hold an IEP meeting. (34 C.F.R. § 300.300(a)(3).)

Evaluating the Evaluator

Your child's evaluation must be "administered by trained and knowledgeable personnel in accordance with any instructions provided by the producer of the tests." (20 U.S.C. § 1414(b)(3).) How can you judge the qualifications of the evaluator? Here are some guidelines:

- Make sure the evaluator has specific knowledge about, and expertise in, learning disability evaluations.
- Ask the special education administrator for the credentials of the evaluator. If the administrator refuses, assert your right to know under IDEA.
- Ask other parents and your child's teacher what they know about the evaluator.
- If you are working with an independent evaluator (see Chapter 8), ask if he or she knows the school's evaluator.
- If possible, meet with the evaluator prior to the testing (discussed below).

To reject the plan, check the disapproval box, sign and date the form, and return it to the school district. If there is no box, write "evaluation plan rejected," sign and date the form, and return it. Keep a copy.

If the plan is not clear or does not give you enough room for your objections, you should attach a letter to the plan. A sample letter is below. Use this as a model and adjust it depending on your specific situation.

After you submit your rejection (partial or complete) of the plan, the evaluator or school district will probably attempt to come up with a plan that meets your approval. If the district feels the original plan was appropriate, it has the right to proceed to mediation or a due process hearing to force the issue, although this is not frequently done. (See Chapter 12.) If the school district does not agree to your changes, you have the right to refuse your consent and/or go to due process yourself for a ruling on your requested changes.

Can the District Force the Evaluation Against Your Wishes?

While it is not common, districts do have the right to compel a child to be evaluated (either for the first time or a reevaluation) even if the parents reject the evaluation plan. In such cases the district is required to initiate and succeed at a due process hearing (see Chapter 12 on due process hearings). While the IDEA statutes and regulations do not tell us what a district must prove in order to convince the hearing officer to order the evaluation without parental consent, hearing officers are generally going to look for specific evidence proving that unless the child is evaluated, there will be negative educational consequences for the child. (34 C.F.R. § 300.300(a)(3).)

Meet With the Evaluator

After you accept the plan proposed by the school district, the evaluator will contact you to schedule the testing of your child. Now is the time to think ahead. In a few months, when you are at the IEP meeting planning your child's IEP program, the school district will pay the most attention to the evaluation done by its own evaluator. Therefore, you will want to take some time to establish a positive relationship with the evaluator before testing begins.

A good relationship is one in which the parties don't have preconceived ideas about each other or view each other with hostility. Try to put aside any negative comments you might have heard about the evaluator from other people (or any bad experiences you've had in the past). Start with the assumption (or new attitude) that the evaluator is there to help your child get an appropriate education. Of course, this may not be easy. The evaluator may not be easy to talk to or may be put off by parents who want to play an active role in the process. No matter what attitude the evaluator adopts, try to remain rational and pleasant.

Letter Rejecting Evaluation Plan

Date: December 14, 20xx

To: Carolyn Ames, Administrator, Special Education
Central Valley School District
456 Main Street
Centerville, MI 47000

Re: Evaluation Plan for Michael Kreeskind

I am in receipt of the November 21, 20xx evaluation plan for my son Michael. I give my permission for you to administer the Vineland, PPVT-III, and Wechsler (WISC-III) tests, but not the rest of the ones on your list. I have investigated them and feel they are too unreliable.

In addition, I am formally requesting, pursuant to 20 U.S.C. § 1414 (a) and (b), that the plan reflect the following:

- that the evaluator will meet with me and my husband to review Michael's entire history and will include the issues raised during that meeting in the report, and

- that the evaluator will review samples of Michael's work and letters from professionals who have observed Michael.

I have one final concern. I have reviewed the credentials of Brett Forrest, the evaluator selected by the district to evaluate Michael. I am concerned that Mr. Forrest has no prior experience evaluating children with specific or suspected learning disabilities. Specifically, I do not believe he is trained or knowledgeable about the specific tests to be administered, as required under IDEA 20 U.S.C. § 1414(b)(3)(A)(iv). Therefore, I do not approve of the assigned evaluator, Brett Forrest, and request that an appropriate one be assigned, and that proof of the evaluator's qualifications be provided to us.

Thank you very much.

Michelle Kreeskind

Michelle Kreeskind
8 Rock Road
Centerville, MI 47000
Phones: 555-9876 (home); 555-5450 (work)

Reality Check: The Evaluator Works for the School District

While you should assume that the evaluator wants to develop a good and appropriate educational plan for your child, don't lose sight of the fact that the evaluator is an employee of the school district. Some evaluators know exactly what a school district can provide and will tailor their reports accordingly, rather than prepare a report based on what a child truly needs.

On the other hand, just because the report doesn't support what you want, it doesn't necessarily follow that the evaluator is acting against your child's best interests. The conclusions may be well reasoned and supported by the data. Be objective. Are the recommendations consistent with or contrary to what you know about your child? If you conclude that the evaluator is biased against you, request a new one. Remember, you always have the right to an outside or independent evaluation. (See Chapter 8.)

Your job is to educate the evaluator about your child. The evaluator will have test results to evaluate and reports to read, but he or she doesn't live with your child. To the extent possible, help the evaluator see your child from your perspective, particularly as it relates to the academic programs and services you feel are necessary for your child. Ideally, you want the report to recommend eligibility and the program and services you want for your child as articulated in your blueprint (in Chapter 5).

So how do you get your points across? If possible, meet with the evaluator before the testing is done (another reason why including a parental interview in the plan is so important). The law doesn't require an evaluator to meet with you (unless that's part of the evaluation plan), but the law does not prohibit it, either. Call up and ask for an appointment. Say that you'd appreciate the chance to talk, are not familiar with all the tests, would like to find out how they are used, and would just feel a lot better if you could meet for ten or 15 minutes. If the evaluator cannot meet with you, ask for a brief phone consultation or send a letter expressing your concerns.

Whether you meet in person, talk on the phone, or state your concerns in a letter, you'll want to be clear and objective about:

- **Eligibility evaluation.** Let the evaluator know the specific problems your child is having in school, the material you have documenting those problems, and why you believe those problems qualify your child for special education.

EXAMPLE: "Daniel has had a terrible time with reading. He's only in the second grade, but he is way behind. His teacher agrees—I have some notes of my conversation with her from last October. I could provide you with a copy of them if that would help. I'd greatly appreciate it if you could focus on Daniel's reading problem in your assessment."

- **Eligibility criteria language.** While discussing the assessment, be sure that the evaluator understands that you want him or her to specifically address your child's eligibility for special education based on learning disability. In Chapter 7, we discuss the criteria for eligibility, including the key regulatory language that the evaluator should use. For example, the regulations include language about whether or not a child has "achieved adequately" given his or her age. So, you want the evaluator to specifically and clearly address whether or not your child has "achieved adequately," for his or her age.
- **IEP program evaluation.** If your child is already in special education or is likely to be found eligible, let the evaluator know of the IEP program components you believe are important.

EXAMPLES:

"Noah needs a small, highly structured class with minimal distractions."

"Kayla needs a lot of work with reading, reading comprehension, and language skills. I would like you to evaluate the reports done by her doctor, her teacher, and the classroom aide, and address their suggestions in your recommendations section."

Letter Requesting Evaluation Report

Date: _November 3, 20xx_

To: _Harvey Smith, Evaluation Team_

Pine Hills Elementary School

234 Lincoln Road

Boston, MA 02000

Re: _Robin Griffin, student in Sean Jordan's_

1st grade class

I appreciate your involvement in my child's evaluation and look forward to your report. Would you please:

1. Send me a copy of a draft of your report before you finalize it. As you can imagine, the process can be overwhelming for parents. It would be most helpful to me to see your report, because the proposed tests are complicated and I need time to analyze the results.

2. Send me your final report at least four weeks before the IEP meeting.

Again, thank you for your kind assistance.

Sincerely,

Lee Griffin

Lee Griffin

23 Hillcrest Road

Boston, MA 02000

Phones: 555-4321 (home); 555-9876 (work)

Be careful about how specific you get. The evaluator may think you're trying to take over and might not appreciate being told exactly what to include in the report. For example, coming right out with "Please recommend that Megan have a full-time, one-on-one aide" or "Please write that Connor should be placed in the learning disability program at Center School" may be a little too direct. You may need to be a bit less specific, such as "The teacher wrote that Megan can't learn to read without constant one-on-one attention. Would you please address that need in your report?" Remember, your blueprint is a good guide here.

Don't be disappointed if the evaluator doesn't fully or even partially agree with what you are requesting. The best you can do is to be clear about your child's problem, what you feel your child needs, and what materials support your conclusions. Ultimately, if the evaluator does not address your concerns and you have good evidence to support them, the value of the school's evaluation may be diminished.

Reviewing the Report

After your child is evaluated, the evaluator will issue a report. Some issue their reports in two stages: a draft report and a final report. Ask the evaluator how and when the report will be issued. Ideally, the evaluator will write a draft report that you can review before the final report is issued prior to the IEP meeting. Ask to see a draft report, but don't be surprised if your request is rejected. IDEA does not require your school district to show you a draft of the report.

Even if the evaluator will issue only one version of the report, it is imperative that you see it before the IEP meeting. IDEA requires the school district to give you a copy of the report and of information documenting eligibility. (20 U.S.C. § 1414(b)(4)(B).)

If the district is unwilling to show you the report before the meeting, simply indicate (in writing) that you won't agree to an IEP meeting date until you receive the report. Of course, the district might not care too much about postponing the IEP meeting, so you might also say that holding the IEP meeting before you have the chance to see the report will require additional meetings and use up more district resources.

By asking to see the report (preferably a draft of the report) ahead of time, you let the school district know that you plan to carefully review the evaluator's work. This will help you keep a sense of control over the process and prepare for the IEP meeting. It will also keep you from wasting valuable time poring over the report at the IEP meeting.

FORM

A sample letter requesting the report is included here; a blank downloadable copy is available on this book's Companion Page on www.nolo. com. See Chapter 16 for the link.

If you disagree with anything in the draft report or feel something is missing, ask the evaluator to make a change or add the missing information. Be prepared to point to material outside the report that supports your point of view.

If the evaluator won't make the changes—or sends you only the final version—what can you do if you disagree with the final report? You can reject it. While you can express your disagreement before the IEP, it might be a better strategy to wait for the meeting and prepare your counterarguments with the evidence you have, including existing material and your independent evaluation (if any).

TIP

Don't forget independent evaluations. Remember that you have the right to have your child evaluated by someone outside of the school district, often referred to as a private or independent evaluation. Such independent evaluations are tremendously valuable when you disagree with the school district's evaluation. The independent evaluator can analyze the district's evaluation in detail and point out any shortcomings. See Chapter 8 for more information on independent evaluations.

Reevaluations

In addition to the right to an initial eligibility evaluation, IDEA also gives your child the right to periodic reevaluations. Your child must be reevaluated at least once every three years or when the school district determines that there is need for improved academic and functional performance. In addition, you, the school district, or your child's teacher can request a reevaluation once a year—and if you make this request, the school district must grant it.

You do not have a unilateral right to more than one reevaluation per year, however: The school district will have to consent to any additional yearly reevaluations. (20 U.S.C. § 1414(a)(2).) While it is certainly true that a student can be overevaluated, which can tax both your child's and the school district's stamina, there may simply be times when a second or third evaluation in one year is necessary. For example, if your child isn't progressing as you expected, teachers are raising concerns, IEP goals seem way out of reach, or for any other reason a significant change is necessary, it's probably time for a reevaluation. If you find yourself in this situation, put your request to the school district in writing, noting as specifically as possible why additional information is needed and why the current evaluation is not adequate, complete, or up to date.

Final Evaluations

A final evaluation is not required when your child's special education terminates. However, when those services end, the school district must provide you with a "summary" of your child's "academic achievement and functional performance" as well as "recommendations" regarding your child's "postsecondary goals." (34 C.F.R. § 300.305(e).)

Eligibility

Determining your child's eligibility for special education is a two-step procedure. First, your child is evaluated. Next, the IEP team meets to determine whether your child qualifies for special education. This IEP meeting is different from the IEP meeting where your child's annual academic program is developed, although they may be combined.

Eligibility, like evaluations, IEP meetings, and other aspects of the special education process, is bound by the requirements of IDEA. And like those other procedures, it can be a source of disagreement between parents and a school district.

 RELATED TOPIC

If your child has already been found eligible for special education, skip ahead to Chapter 8. If your child hasn't yet been found eligible and you haven't read the chapter on evaluations, read Chapter 6 before reading this chapter. Your child will be found eligible for special education only if the evaluation demonstrates that he or she meets the criteria explained in this chapter. Therefore, you must keep the eligibility requirements in mind as you prepare for the evaluation. Similarly, you must consider what types of tests and analyses might demonstrate a qualifying condition as you learn about eligibility requirements.

Your child may be found eligible for special education based on any of a number of disabling conditions listed in IDEA. To qualify on the basis of a learning disability, your child must meet very specific eligibility requirements. These requirements are fairly technical; if you find yourself in a muddle, remember these tips:

- **Take it slowly.** Some of the qualifying conditions have multilayered definitions. Don't try to take it in all at once. Breaking a definition down into manageable parts will help you figure out what evidence you need to show that your child meets all of the eligibility requirements.
- **You're not a specialist in learning disabilities and you don't have to become one.** Don't be put off by some of the complicated terminology. For now, you need a basic understanding of your child's condition and how it affects his or her educational experience.

Ask your pediatrician, the school nurse, or the evaluator. Contact other parents and local or national learning disability support or advocacy organizations, (Chapter 15 discusses parent organizations, and the appendix lists useful resources.)

- **Focus on key portions of each definition.** Pay attention to words such as "specific" or "significant." These are clues that a minor disability may not qualify your child for special education. A child who doesn't fall under one of the delineated conditions may fit into the catchall category, "other health impairment." A child who does not ultimately qualify as learning disabled may be eligible under other special education categories.

- **The IEP team has flexibility in finding eligibility.** There are no hard and fast rules that determine eligibility—there is not a list that the IEP team checks off and then concludes, "Voila, Peter is qualified" or "Sorry but Jean does not meet the specific qualification list." IDEA gives the IEP team a good deal of leeway to find eligibility (or not). In doing their evaluation, the IEP team will receive and interpret a variety of information from many different individuals.

- **Your input is important.** The IEP team must draw upon information from a variety of sources, including parental input when determining eligibility. (20 U.S.C. § 1414(d)(3)(A).) You can, and should, use this opportunity to make sure that the IEP team understands and considers every aspect of your child's disability, not just test scores.

- **Keep up with legal changes.** As you'll learn in this chapter, Congress changed the eligibility rules for children with learning disabilities when it amended IDEA in 2004. To stay on top of current interpretations of the rules, you'll want to stay in touch with advocacy groups for updates on how the eligibility process is evolving. See Appendix B on this book's Companion Page on nolo.com for a list of organizations. (See Chapter 16 for the link.)

This chapter covers:

- The general requirements your child must meet to be eligible for special education.

- The more detailed (and often more confusing) criteria used to determine special education eligibility based on a learning disability.

Eligibility Is Not an Annual Event

Once your child is found eligible for special education, he or she won't need to requalify each year. There are only three situations in which your child's eligibility might have to be determined again:

- Your child dropped out of special education and wants to reenter.
- You or school district representatives propose a change from one eligibility category to another (for example, if it becomes apparent that your child's difficulties in school are related to ADD/ADHD rather than a specific learning disability as defined by IDEA).
- There is evidence that your child no longer qualifies for special education (for example, your older child's reading disability has been remediated to the point where he or she is reading at grade level and doing well in school). Reevaluation is not required if your child's eligibility status changes because he or she graduates from high school with a regular diploma or exceeds the age of eligibility (22 years old). (20 U.S.C. § 1414(c)(5)(B).)

- The IEP eligibility meeting: the meeting where the IEP team decides whether your child qualifies for special education.
- Your options if your child is not found eligible.

Eligibility Requirements: Generally

In order to qualify for special education, your child must meet two distinct eligibility requirements: (1) He or she must have a disabling condition, as defined in IDEA, and (2) The impact of that condition must create a need for special education. In other words, it is not enough to show that your child has a disability—you must also show that your child's disability is causing enough problems to warrant special education help.

This section covers these general requirements. The following section discusses the special rules that apply to children with learning disabilities.

As you will see, this is complicated stuff, and at first you may feel overwhelmed. But keep your head up—you can do this—and remember that the process also feels complicated for the folks on the other side of the IEP table.

IDEA provides a list of disabling conditions that qualify a child between the ages of three and 22 for special education, including:

- hearing impairments, including deafness
- speech or language impairments, such as stuttering or other speech production difficulties
- visual impairments, including blindness
- multiple disabilities, such as mental retardation-blindness
- deaf-blindness
- orthopedic impairments caused by congenital anomalies, such as a club foot
- orthopedic impairments caused by diseases, such as polio
- orthopedic impairments caused by other conditions, such as cerebral palsy
- specific learning disabilities
- emotional disturbance (see "Emotional Disturbance as a Disabling Condition," below)
- autism
- traumatic brain injury
- mental retardation, and
- other health impairments that affect a child's strength, vitality, or alertness, such as a heart condition, rheumatic fever, nephritis, asthma, sickle cell anemia, hemophilia, epilepsy, lead poisoning, leukemia, diabetes, Attention Deficit Disorder (ADD), and Attention Deficit Hyperactivity Disorder (ADHD).

As you prepare for the eligibility process, understand that IDEA uses many terms that are open to a variety of interpretations. For example, there's no precise definition of a "disabling condition," or the limits for "educational performance," or even an "education." Neither you nor the school district can consult a table or a list that will tell you whether a child with a learning disability or an emotional problem qualifies for special education.

A Word About Labels

This list of disability categories asks you to define your child as "this" or "that." Labeling is one of the difficult and unpleasant parts of the IEP process. Many people feel that labels are unnecessary, even harmful—and from a psychological perspective, they may be right. From a legal perspective, however, your child must fit into one of these categories to be found eligible for special education. If you can, focus on the specifics of your child's condition rather than the label. Remember, your goal is to secure an appropriate education for your child; proving that your child qualifies for special education under one of the eligibility categories is part of the process.

It is important, however, to acknowledge the label for the purpose of meeting the eligibility criteria while making sure your child does not become defined by that label. For example, Brent has dyslexia, which causes him some significant problems in school and qualifies him for special education. But Brent is also a terrific center on the basketball team, he hates to clean up his room, at times he frustrates and worries his parents, he has a good heart, and, most importantly, he is quite determined to make his way in the world. These are the qualities that define him.

As you go through this chapter keep in mind the following:

- Carefully read the definition of the "disabling condition" that applies to your child (these conditions are explained in the IDEA regulations at 34 C.F.R. § 300.8). What is required for your child to qualify? For example, most definitions require that the condition cause an "adverse effect," but the definitions for "specific learning disability" do not.
- The terms "adversely affect" and "education" are not defined. Is an education merely grades or test scores, or is it more, such as

learning how to make friends, develop independent living skills, and gain greater control over anger or anxiety? Over the years, courts have provided some guidelines: While the law doesn't require the school to maximize a child's potential, the child is entitled to a full educational opportunity, and one that allows the child to develop self-sufficiency and academic advancement. Whether a program provides a meaningful benefit should be evaluated in relation to the child's potential.

You can find this list at 20 U.S.C. § 1401(3) and 34 C.F.R. § 300.8. You'll see that the eligibility criteria for each of the listed disabilities are slightly different.

We'll focus on eligibility for learning disabilities later in this chapter.

Adverse Effect

It is not enough to show that your child has a disabling condition; you must also demonstrate that your child's disability has an adverse effect on his or her educational performance. Proving this adverse effect will be the crux of your eligibility work.

IDEA does not say how "adverse effect" is measured, but your child's grades, test scores, and classroom or other behavior will provide important evidence of adverse effect. While grades can most directly show whether a disabling condition is adversely affecting educational performance or achievement, they don't tell the whole eligibility story. A parent can (and should) argue that a child who receives As, Bs, or Cs but cannot read at age level, has trouble processing language, or has great difficulty with writing is not benefiting from his or her education, and that the child's disability is therefore directly affecting educational performance, regardless of grades.

If your child is getting passing grades, you will need to make the connection between your child's disability and school performance in some other way. Factors to consider (other than grades) include:

- limited progress—for example, little or no improvement in reading, math, or spelling even though the teacher does not fail your child; high school students might have significant difficulty in social studies, geometry, or English

- difficulties in cognitive areas, such as mastering basic concepts, memory, or language skills—forgetting to turn in homework, trouble with reading comprehension, or difficulty grasping abstract concepts might demonstrate these problems
- discrepancy between performance and ability—for example, the child is developmentally and chronologically ten years old, but reads at a six-year-old's level; your eighth grader has an above-average IQ but is performing at the sixth grade level on math and spelling tests
- evidence of emotional, behavioral, or social difficulties, or
- physical difficulties, such as handwriting or hearing problems.

The IEP team has a lot of discretion in determining whether your child is eligible for special education. If your child has passing grades, the team may need to exercise that discretion to find that a disability has adversely affected his or her educational performance in other ways.

Traumatic Brain Injury

Children who have had a traumatic brain injury (TBI) may be eligible for special education (34 C.F.R. § 300.8(c)(12).) The regulations define a TBI as an "acquired injury to the brain caused by an external force, resulting in total or partial functional disability or psychosocial impairment" and "adversely [affecting] a child's educational performance." TBI applies to injuries that impair at least one of the following: memory; attention; reasoning; abstract thinking; judgment; problem-solving; sensory, perceptual, and motor abilities; psychosocial behavior; physical functions; information processing; and speech.

The regulation states that a TBI does *not* apply to brain injuries that are "congenital or degenerative or to brain injuries caused by birth trauma." This exclusion seems odd. First, IDEA generally is concerned with the consequences, not the cause, of the disability. Second, there's no explanation for excluding these three injuries, when they too can result in the impairments listed. The exclusion suggests a rigid distinction not fully related to the reality of a child's disability and the conditions that affect the child's ability to learn.

The Flexible Concept of "Eligibility"

As you have seen, IDEA is often less than crystal clear in terms of what conditions it covers and what it requires of school districts. In addition, state laws that parallel IDEA have their own definitions and scope. For example:

- Maine's law states that "educational performance" means more than "academic knowledge" but also the "cultivation of skills and behaviors needed to succeed generally in life." These include nonacademic areas such as self-direction, practical problem solving, collaboration, and flexibility. Clearly, these go way beyond the traditional notion of academic activities as the sole definition of an education. (*Mr. and Mrs. I. v. Maine School Administrative Dist. No. 55*, 2005 WL 1389135.)

- In another case, the court noted that although the student had no "academic" needs or problems, her education was "adversely affected" because depression, distractibility, and suicidal thoughts affected her attendance and emotional state. (*NG v. District of Columbia*, 556 F.Supp.2d 11 (D. D.C, 2008).)

- The state of Arkansas defines "adverse effect" to include an impact on "affective, behavioral and physical characteristics," further enforcing the view that an "education" is not just grades.

- Although an "emotional disturbance" can be a disabling condition, the line between emotional problems and social maladjustment (which is not legally disabling) is not easy to draw. In *Springer v. Fairfax County School Board*, 134 F.3d. 659 (4th Cir. 1998) the court noted that the population targeted by the emotional disturbance category can be a "wild and unruly bunch.... adolescence is, almost by definition, a time of social maladjustment." If emotional disturbance included a "bad conduct" definition, then almost every teenage student would meet the eligibility criteria. On the other hand, some courts have sided with the *Mr. and Mrs. I. v. Maine* court, discussed above, which noted that a student who is anxious, sad, or being teased and not relating to peers can qualify. The line between a social maladjustment and a qualifying "emotional disturbance" will depend on the specific evidence and, frankly, on how the judge views social norms.

Emotional Disturbance as a Disabling Condition

A child who has an "emotional disturbance" (this is the term now used by IDEA) qualifies for special education. Although this term can conjure up images of bizarre behavior and institutionalization, children with a wide range of emotional difficulties can qualify for special education in this category. When you look at the actual defining language in IDEA, you'll see that it encompasses issues that might affect most human beings at some point in their lives, and certainly could arise for children who might have a learning disability. Some children with learning disabilities, especially those who do not receive support and services, may have difficulties with peers and/or teachers, have trouble sleeping and eating, or experience fears and anxieties as a result of the consequences of the learning disability. For example, it would not be surprising if a child with a learning disability didn't want to go to school and seemed to feel sick a lot of the time.

IDEA defines an emotional disturbance as a condition that has existed over a long period of time to a marked degree and adversely affects your child's educational performance (20 U.S.C. § 1401(3)(A), 34 C.F.R. § 300.8(c)(4).) The regulations don't specify how long "over a long period of time" must be. Nor do they define "to a marked degree," or what is needed to show that the disturbance "adversely affects" a child's educational performance. The first two requirements are not part of the eligibility requirements for other disabling conditions. The disturbance results in:

- an inability to learn that is not explained by intellectual, sensory, or health factors
- an inability to build or maintain satisfactory interpersonal relationships with peers and teachers
- inappropriate behaviors or feelings under normal circumstances (for example, extreme frustration, anger, or aggression over minor setbacks or disagreements)
- a general pervasive mood of unhappiness or depression, or
- a tendency to develop physical symptoms or fears associated with personal or school problems (for example, a child might get a stomachache before tests or oral reports).

> ### Emotional Disturbance as a Disabling Condition, continued
>
> A child who is only socially maladjusted will not qualify for special education, although a child who is emotionally disturbed can also be socially maladjusted. A child with a learning disability may also have some of the characteristics listed above but not qualify as having an "emotional disturbance" under IDEA. The IEP team still can (and should) address those emotional difficulties in the IEP by developing goals and providing services to meet those emotional needs. In this situation, you want to treat the emotional difficulties as part of the learning disability. Rather than label the behaviors as an "emotional disturbance," simply have the IEP team address them as one of many aspects of your child's learning disability. For example, the IEP might describe how the teacher, teacher's aide, school counselor, and written goals will address your child's fears about taking written tests, or how they will assist your child in dealing with peers who in class make fun of his or her difficulties.

Eligibility Standards for Children With Learning Disabilities

Proving that your child is eligible for special education because of a learning disability is a two-step process. First, you must show that your child has a qualifying "specific learning disability." Second, you must show that the disability affects your child's ability to benefit from his or her education.

The learning disability regulations are at 34 C.F.R. § 300.8(c)(10) and 34 C.F.R §§ 300.307–311.

Step One: Identifying a "Specific Learning Disability"

IDEA's Definition

Here is IDEA's definition: "Specific learning disability means a disorder in one or more of the basic psychological processes involved in understanding or in using language, spoken or written, that may manifest itself in the imperfect ability to listen, think speak, read, write, spell, or to do mathematical calculations." (34 C.F.R. § 300.8(c)(10)(i).)

What does this mean? The two key elements are the disorder and the effect of the disorder on the child's ability to communicate and learn. "Disorder" is a fairly broad term—think of it as a "problem." So, if your child has a problem that affects his or her ability to read, listen, think, write, speak, spell, or do math, your child might have a specific learning disability.

Examples of Qualifying Conditions

IDEA also lists certain specific conditions, "such as perceptual disabilities, brain injury, minimal brain dysfunction, dyslexia, and developmental aphasia." (34 C.F.R. § 300.8(c)(10)(i).)

These specific areas may qualify your child for the learning disability category. If you feel that any of these conditions might be affecting your child's ability to learn, discuss this with your child's doctor or assessor.

Conditions That Do Not Qualify

Under IDEA, a specific learning disability does not include learning problems that are "primarily the result of visual, hearing, or motor disabilities, of mental retardation, of emotional disturbance, or of environmental, cultural, or economic disadvantage." (34 C.F.R. § 300.8(c)(10)(ii).)

The line between what qualifies under 34 C.F.R. § 300.8(c)(10)(i) and what does not under 34 C.F.R. § 300.8(c)(10)(ii) is vague, at best. For example, a "perceptual disability" could be a qualifying condition, but not when it is the result of a "visual" disability. If your child's difficulties seem to ride this line, make a concerted effort to use the language that will qualify. For example, if your child has difficulty reading, your supporting documentation should describe the condition in terms of a "perceptual disability" and not in terms of a problem with vision.

The regulations further state that a child will not qualify for special education if the "determinant factor" is either lack of appropriate instruction in reading or math, or limited English proficiency. (34 C.F.R. § 300.306(b).) If your child has not received appropriate instruction in reading or math, or has limited English proficiency, you will need to show that the main thing affecting your child's performance is not these factors but an actual "disorder in one more of the basic psychological processes involved in understanding or in using language."

State and Federal Definitions of Learning Disabilities

Many states have their own definitions of learning disabilities. For example, West Virginia law defines learning disabilities as "a heterogeneous group of disorders manifested by significant deficits in the acquisition and use of listening, speaking, reading, writing, reasoning, or mathematical abilities." Minnesota defines a learning disability more simply as a "severe underachievement."

As discussed in Chapter 2, states are allowed to enact special education laws that give children more protections and rights than the IDEA. State law, however, cannot take away rights the IDEA provides—no matter what your state law says, your child is always entitled to the protections and requirements of the IDEA.

As a general rule, state laws defining a learning disability tend to be more complicated and detailed than the IDEA. School districts often use state law definitions, but you can rely on IDEA if your state's law is too confusing or complicated. If you think your state law on learning disability eligibility violates IDEA (that is, it is more restrictive or less protective of your child), you should contact your state department of education and the U.S. Department of Education and Office of Civil Rights. (You can find contact information through the United States Department of Education website, at www.ed.gov.) Also, make sure you have the most recent version of your state's law—states may have changed their rules after the 2004 amendments to IDEA.

Documenting the Condition

Your supporting documentation must specifically discuss your child's learning disability, as defined by IDEA. If possible, use the qualifying language from the regulations (in 34 C.F.R. § 300.8(c)(10)(i)) and try not to use the language that will not qualify your child (in 34 C.F.R. § 300.8(c)(10)(ii)). If appropriate, your supporting documentation should refer to any tests that support proof of the condition. Include any conclusions as well—for example, "Sarah has significant difficulty with addition and subtraction and has not demonstrated an ability to read consistent with her age and abilities."

No Requirement to Prove Adverse Effect

Most eligibility conditions require proof that the disabling condition "adversely affects a child's educational performance." However, adverse effect is not required to show the existence of a learning disability. Instead, a learning disability requires the proof of other specific factors. We discuss these requirements in "Step Two," below.

Step Two: Showing the Effect of a Learning Disability

If you have established that your child has a specific learning disability, you must then show that the learning disability results in a need for special education. Having a "disorder" (or problem) is not merely enough. If your child can function adequately in school without special education services or programs, it is not likely he or she will meet this second step of the eligibility requirement.

The IEP team determines eligibility, and you must provide the IEP team with as much proof as possible that special education is necessary for your child.

IDEA provides specific (though not always clear) guidelines about how the IEP team must prove and document a child's need. We discuss these in the sections that follow. You can find the relevant regulations at C.F.R. §§ 300.307 and 300.309. To make the most impact, your supporting documentation should use as much qualifying language as possible. We'll show you how.

Adequate Achievement

The regulations of IDEA 2004 offer a method of determining whether or not a child's learning disability requires special education. This method focuses on the relative achievement of the child and basically asks, "Is the child achieving as he or she should be for his age and grade?"

The regulation that covers this part of the eligibility process is found at 34 C.F.R. § 300.309(a). It is a detailed, sometimes vague, and not easily mastered regulation. Read the text of the regulation in the box below. Then we'll break it down part by part.

The first part—§ 300.309(a)(1)

The first part of this regulation tells the IEP team to consider the achievement of the child in several skill areas. Can the child speak, write, read, and do math adequately for his or her age or grade? Again, we note that here the issue isn't whether the child has a disorder but rather what effect the disorder has on the child's education.

Your supporting documents should discuss your child's struggles in these areas. They should specify whether or not your child is achieving like other children his or her age. If your state administers tests that determine the grade level at which your child is achieving, and your child is testing below his or her actual grade level, discuss those tests as well.

The regulation also requires that this lack of achievement occur even though the child has received appropriate "learning experiences and instruction." This ensures that eligibility won't be granted "merely" because of poor teaching. If you can show that your child has received appropriate instruction, then certainly discuss this in your supporting documents. However, the school district is in the best position to prove this point and you should approach this part of the process prepared to ask the district to do so.

If your school district contends that the problem is due entirely to a bad "learning experience," ask the school district to prove it specifically and in consideration of the No Child Left Behind law, which requires that teachers be appropriately and fully trained. Also, ask the district to show that your child's difficulties would not exist if he or she had received appropriate learning experiences and instruction.

The language of this regulation is broad and somewhat imprecise. (What does "achieve adequately" mean exactly?) Some courts have ruled that if a child is receiving average grades he or she is "achieving adequately." On the other hand, numerous courts and the U.S. Department of Education have stated clearly that a student who is making sufficient "academic" progress may still be eligible for special education. For example, a student who does well in class but has a speech and language impairment can qualify for nonacademic reasons—the inability to relate to peers, for example. It appears that some decision makers will view a student's grades as the only means for determining eligibility, whereas others will look beyond grades. Contact your state department of education and your local advocacy group for assistance in preparing to prove to your school district that your child is not achieving adequately. See Appendix B on this book's Companion Page on nolo.com for contact information. You'll find a link in Chapter 16.

Use the language of the regulation in a way that allows the IEP team to find that your child belongs in special education. Present your supporting documentation using the terms of the law as much as possible and, where appropriate, refer to any test results that support your conclusion. Here is an example:

EXAMPLE: Bill has had significant and long-standing difficulties in achieving adequately in the areas of spelling, reading, writing, and math. His work is not consistent with his age or native abilities and intelligence. Our testing shows in detail that he has difficulties in oral expression, reading comprehension, and mathematical problem solving even though he has been provided learning experiences and instruction appropriate for his age. We believe that Bill qualifies for special education as a learning disabled student and, moreover, is in significant need of such services. If he is not found eligible, we have very significant concerns about his ability to benefit from his education, develop the skills he is capable of developing, and being able to become a fully independent and productive adult.

The Text of the Regulation: 34 C.F.R. § 300.309(a)

Here we give you the verbatim text of the regulation that describes how an IEP team determines whether or not a learning disability has a significant impact on a child's education. We explain this regulation in the main text on the previous and next pages.

The regulation states that IEP team may determine that a child has a specific learning disability, if:

(1) The child does not achieve adequately for the child's age or to meet State-approved grade-level standards in one or more of the following areas, when provided with learning experiences and instruction appropriate for the child's age or State-approved grade-level standards:

(i) Oral expression.

(ii) Listening comprehension.

(iii) Written expression.

(iv) Basic reading skill.

(v) Reading fluency skills.

(vi) Reading comprehension.

(vii) Mathematics calculation.

(viii) Mathematics problem solving.

(2)(i) The child does not make sufficient progress to meet age or State-approved grade-level standards in one or more of the areas identified in paragraph (a)(1) of this section when using a process based on the child's response to scientific, research-based intervention; or

(ii) The child exhibits a pattern of strengths and weaknesses in performance, achievement, or both, relative to age, State-approved grade level standards, or intellectual development, that is determined by the group to be relevant to the identification of a specific learning disability, using appropriate assessments, consistent with §§ 300.304 and 300.305; and

(3) The group determines that its findings under paragraphs (a)(1) and (2) of this section are not primarily the result of—

(i) A visual, hearing, or motor disability;

(ii) Mental retardation;

(iii) Emotional disturbance;

(iv) Cultural factors;

(v) Environmental or economic disadvantage; or

(vi) Limited English proficiency.

The second part—§ 300.309(a)(2)

The second part of 34 C.F.R. § 300.309(a) provides detail as to how to prove the effect or impact of the learning disability on your child.

Despite the confusing combination of words, phrases, and directives, this part of the regulation basically states that the lack of adequate achievement can be shown by either (1) "the child's response to scientific, research-based intervention," or (2) a pattern of strengths and weaknesses that the IEP team determines to be the result of a learning disability.

How do you deal with this requirement in your supporting documents? First, you try not to get too frustrated—remember, you can do this. Then you do the following:

- Decide which words fit best with your child's situation. For example, if your child was not provided with "scientific, research-based intervention," then don't use that part. Use language from the next paragraph to describe how your child "exhibits a pattern" of weaknesses.
- Look to the key phrases: "sufficient progress" and "exhibits a pattern of strengths and weaknesses." Highlight those phrases that apply to your child and use them forcefully in your supporting documents to explain why your child requires special education.
- Find out from your school district whether it has intervention that is "scientific, research-based." If it does, get the details.
- Contact your state department of education and advocacy groups to find out what information they have that explains these requirements. (See Appendix B on this book's Companion Page on nolo.com for contact information.)
- Keep in mind that while it is your responsibility to be prepared to prove all of the elements of a learning disability, it's the responsibility of your school district to explain to you how it interprets and applies these regulations. For example, does the school district have some rules or policies about what constitutes "achieving adequately" or making "sufficient progress"?

The third part—34 C.F.R. § 300.309(a)(3)

Finally, the IEP team must also find that the child's condition is not primarily a result of a visual, hearing or motor disability, mental retardation, emotional disturbance, cultural factors, environmental or economic disadvantages, or limited English proficiency.

If your child has any of these conditions, then the condition alone will not prevent him or her from qualifying under the learning disability category. He or she cannot qualify as learning disabled solely on the basis of any of the conditions listed in 34 C.F.R. § 300.309(a)(3). However, your child can have one or more of the conditions listed in the regulation and still qualify as long as the specific requirements of learning disability eligibility are met. Be sure to discuss this with your doctor or assessor to understand what these conditions mean and to learn how they are different from a learning disability.

Severe Discrepancy

Prior to the reauthorization of IDEA in 2004, a child would qualify as learning disabled if, among other things, there was a "severe discrepancy" between "intellectual ability and achievement." Many states developed very complex mathematical formulas for determining whether that "severe discrepancy" existed. See Appendix C on this book's Companion Page on nolo.com for a detailed discussion of severe discrepancy methods. You'll find the link in Chapter 16.

The U.S. Congress and the U.S. Department of Education now send a clear message to the states: The states "(m)ust not require the use of a severe discrepancy" formula in determining learning disability eligibility. (34 C.F.R. § 300.307(a)(1).) Congress notes that the severe discrepancy method can delay intervention until there is proof of failure, which may make remediation difficult or impossible. (This is sometimes referred to as the "wait to fail" model.) Congress has also weighed in on the IQ tests used to measure severe discrepancy, stating that they exacerbate the delay and have little "instructional relevance."

Note that IDEA does not prohibit the use of the severe discrepancy method; it just says that the states can't require its use. In 2007, the U.S. Department of Education reaffirmed the new "severe discrepancy" rule, which provides that states can, but do not have to, use the severe discrepancy model. Though a state cannot require a school district to use the severe discrepancy model, the district can use it if it so chooses. This gives school districts a broad range of options for determining whether a student qualifies as a learning disabled student.

Determining Learning Disability: Eligibility & Numbers

As you probably already know, many of the assessment tools used in education to determine a child's potential disability involve objective information in the form of test scores (for example, a specific number, a percentile or a percentage on a standard assessment test). These numbers are important for two reasons: in many cases they will be the basis for a determination of eligibility and they also provide data that can tell you a good deal about your child's status.

Some states use very complicated numeric evaluations to determine a child's learning disabled eligibility. For example, see Appendix C, "The Severe Discrepancy Model," on this book's Companion Page on nolo.com to read California's law on how to use the severe discrepancy model to find a child eligible as learning disabled (you'll find the link in Chapter 16). The subsection is complex, difficult to understand, and often makes it hard for parents to prepare for an eligibility IEP. When you are faced with a state with laws like California or a school district that uses only objective tests to determine learning disability eligibility, there are several things you should do.

First, tell the district that any "severe discrepancy" model (which usually relies on numeric findings) can no longer be required (34 C.F.R. § 300.307(a)(1). The federal regulation actually declares that states "must not require the use of the severe discrepancy" formula in determining a learning disability.

Second, rely on the federal regulation for determining learning disability eligibility (34 C.F.R. § 300.309), as discussed above. This regulation does not use or require any particular kind of assessment tool/test.

Third, know that IDEA requires that a determination of eligibility be based on a consideration drawn from "a variety of sources, including aptitude and achievement tests, parent input, and teacher recommendations...." (34 C.F.R. § 300.306(c)(i).)

Also, states with language like California's may have further ways to find a child eligible as learning disabled. For example, right after the byzantine subsection on finding severe discrepancy (in Appendix C, as mentioned above), California law provides that the IEP team may find that a severe discrepancy exists even if standardized tests don't show it, as long as the team writes a report following certain guidelines.

> ### Determining Learning Disability:
> ### Eligibility & Numbers (continued)
>
> You can remind the IEP team that your child is not a set of numbers and there are many ways to prove a learning disability based on observations, anecdotes, schoolwork, and so on. Do not hesitate to inform your district at the beginning of this process that you want to know what specific rules apply to finding learning disability eligibility. If they use a "numbers-based" system, inform them that under the IDEA you will want to discuss other evidence of your child's learning disability.

You should find out exactly what your state makes of these laws. Contact your state department of education and/or advocacy group and specifically ask: (1) Did your state have a "severe discrepancy" standard before 2004 (probably yes)? and (2) if so, has the state replaced it with something else? Specifically, is the state replacing it with the language found in IDEA regulation 34 C.F.R. § 300.309 (discussed above)?

Scientific, Research-Based Intervention and Research-Based Procedures

While IDEA discourages the use of the "severe discrepancy" model, it now encourages school districts to use "research-based procedures" and a process of determining eligibility "based on the child's response to scientific, research-based intervention." (34 C.F.R. § 300.307(a)(2) and (3).)

As you can see, the language used in these sections of the 2004 reauthorization of IDEA is broad and vague. We still don't fully know how this language affects the eligibility process. Pay close attention to the way your school district determines eligibility. Stay in touch with your state department of education and national organizations, such as the Learning Disabilities Association of America (see Appendix B on this book's Companion Page on nolo.com) to find out how these eligibility rules are being interpreted and implemented. Everyone in the special education field, including school personnel, is trying to figure out what this language means and how to apply it when making eligibility decisions.

Use IDEA's Key Phrases

All of all your supporting documents—whether letters, reports, assessments—should strongly and clearly make the case for eligibility by using the phrases and terms found in IDEA and its regulations. Your supporting documents provide evidence that your child qualifies for special education because he or she meets the meaning of those key phrases.

Request that your assessor, doctor, and tutor use this key language when they describe your child's learning difficulties.

Try to get used to saying these phrases in conversation so that they come easily to you in the IEP meeting or when you ask that certain information be included in the IEP. For example, "I'm glad we're talking about Sue's difficulty achieving adequately in reading. I'd like to add that to the IEP addendum."

Throughout this chapter we provided examples of language that will bolster your efforts at establishing eligibility. We recommend that you keep a list of the phrases that might apply to your child.

Here are a few phrases you might use in your supporting documents. Tailor the sentences to your child's situation—we've underlined the key words you should include. Add more phrases to this list, as appropriate for your child.

- My child has a <u>specific learning disability</u>.
- My child has <u>a disorder that manifests in the imperfect ability to read and do mathematical calculations</u>.
- My child's problems are <u>not primarily the result of visual, hearing, or motor disabilities, of mental retardation, of emotional disturbance, or of environmental, cultural, or economic disadvantage</u>.
- My child's problems are <u>not due to lack of appropriate instruction in reading or math, or limited English proficiency</u>.
- My child shows <u>a pattern of weakness in her achievement in reading comprehension compared to other children her age</u>.
- My child's disorder is causing her to <u>not achieve adequately for her age and grade</u>.

Use Supporting Documents to Prove Your Case

In general, aim to document that your child meets the requirements of these regulations by showing his or her difficulties in every way you can. Include critical facts that show he or she is struggling—for example, below-average grades, low test scores, or evidence that your child is not developing basic skills.

Remember that the IEP team has discretion in determining whether your child qualifies as learning disabled. The requirements are not mathematically precise or so clear that an easy checklist can be developed, so do your best to describe your child's problems fully and persuasively.

Finally, be sure to check with your state department of education, your school district, as well as local advocacy groups to find out what state-specific policies or laws clarify the eligibility process in your area.

Preparing for the IEP Eligibility Meeting

After your child is evaluated, the school district will schedule an IEP meeting to discuss your child's eligibility for special education. The IEP program meeting—when you and the school district hammer out the components of your child's IEP—must be held within 30 days after your child is found eligible for special education. Depending on the circumstances of your case, your school district may hold off scheduling the IEP program meeting until after your child is found eligible. But if it seems likely that your child will be found eligible, the school district may schedule the IEP program meeting to immediately follow the eligibility meeting.

RELATED TOPIC

The strategies for a successful IEP eligibility meeting and a successful IEP program meeting are the same. To prepare for the IEP eligibility meeting—or the possibility of a joint IEP eligibility and program meeting—review Chapters 10 and 11.

To prepare for the eligibility meeting, follow these tips:

- **Get a copy of your child's school file.** If you don't already have a copy, see Chapter 4.
- **Get copies of all school evaluations.** Evaluations are covered in Chapter 6.
- **Find out the school district's position.** If the evaluation report recommends eligibility, call the special education administrator and ask if the district will agree with that recommendation. If the answer is yes, ask whether the IEP program meeting will be held right after the eligibility meeting. If the report is not clear about eligibility, call the administrator and ask what the district's position is on your child's eligibility. If the evaluation recommends against eligibility, be prepared to show that your child is eligible. Here are a few suggestions:
  - *Review the school file and evaluation report.* Cull out information that supports your child's eligibility, such as test results, grades, and teacher comments.
  - *Organize all other reports and written material that support your position on eligibility.* Observations from teachers and teachers' aides are especially important. Ask anyone who has observed your child and agrees that he or she should be in special education to attend the IEP eligibility meeting. If a key person cannot attend, ask for a letter or written observation report.
  - *Consider an independent evaluation.* An independent evaluation may be necessary if the school district's report concludes that your child is not eligible for special education. Even if your child is found eligible, you may disagree with the school's recommendations regarding services and programs—many times these are spelled out in the school district's evaluation report. The independent evaluator is often your strongest and most qualified supporter for eligibility and the components of the IEP. See Chapter 8 for more on independent evaluations.
- **Get organized.** Organize all of your documentation before the eligibility meeting, so you can find what you need right away.

- **Do your homework.** Be prepared to discuss your state's criteria for eligibility based on a learning disability.

RELATED TOPIC

Chapter 8 provides tips that will help you organize existing material—and develop new information—to make your case at an IEP eligibility or program meeting. Chapter 8 also discusses how to use an independent evaluator.

Attending the Eligibility Meeting

Many of the procedures and strategies used at the IEP eligibility meeting are similar to those used at an IEP program meeting. Chapters 10 and 11 explain how to prepare for, and make your points at, an IEP meeting. This section highlights some issues that are particularly important for eligibility meetings.

Who Should Attend?

For a child with a learning disability, the IEP team must include the parent, the child's regular teacher (or a regular classroom teacher qualified to teach a child of that age, if the child has no regular teacher or has not yet reached school age), and at least one person qualified to conduct individual diagnostic examinations of children, such as a school psychologist, speech-language pathologist, or remedial reading teacher.

You may want to ask others to attend, however, especially if you anticipate a fight over eligibility or don't know the district's position. Such people might include:
- an independent evaluator
- teachers who have worked with your child
- other professionals who know your child, and
- an expert who can explain evaluations and how your child meets your state's eligibility requirements, particularly if you must show a severe discrepancy.

Whether you decide to ask any of these people to attend the IEP eligibility meeting may depend on their availability, the strength of their point of view, and cost. Sometimes, a letter from your pediatrician or another professional might be just as effective (and certainly less expensive) than paying the expert to attend in person. As a general rule, do not pay someone to attend the IEP eligibility meeting unless you are certain that there will be a disagreement and you'll need that person to argue your side. In most eligibility disputes, an independent evaluator will be your most effective witness.

Preparing Your Participants

Make sure your participants are prepared to:
- describe who they are, their training, and how they know your child
- discuss their conclusions about your child's eligibility for special education and the basis for those conclusions—such as observation, long-term relationship with your child, or testing
- contradict any material concluding that your child is not eligible for special education
- prove that your child has a severe discrepancy, if required by your state's rules, and
- present their findings within the context of the IDEA requirements, using as many of the key phrases as possible. Your written documentation should do the same. See "Use IDEA's Key Phrases," in the previous section.

Submitting Your Eligibility Material

As you prepare for the IEP eligibility meeting and gather material that supports your child's eligibility (such as an independent evaluation), you will have to decide whether to show your material to the school district before the meeting.

You are not legally required to do so, but consider the kind of relationship you want to have with the school district. If you ask for the school district's evaluation in advance, it's only fair to offer the district a copy of yours. Granted, you will give the school a chance to prepare a rebuttal. On the other hand, if you submit an independent evaluation or other material at the IEP meeting, the school may ask to reschedule the meeting in order to review your material. In the long run, your best bet is to treat the school district as you want to be treated. If you have favorable material that the school district hasn't seen, submit it in advance or at least call the administrator and ask if the school wants your information ahead of time.

Remember that the material the IEP team considers can be drawn from a "variety of sources," including aptitude and achievement tests, parental input, and teacher recommendations. (34 C.F.R. § 300.306(c) (1)(i).) Moreover, there is no prohibition of materials not listed in the law. For example, if you have a letter from a doctor, a report from a private school or tutor, or any useful observation from anyone, you can and should include them for the eligibility team to consider.

Meeting Procedures

An IEP eligibility meeting generally proceeds as follows:
- general introductions
- review of school material
- review of any material you want to introduce, and
- discussion of whether and on what basis your child qualifies for special education.

In deciding whether your child is eligible, the team must draw upon a variety of sources, including aptitude and achievement tests, parent input, teacher recommendations, physical conditions, social or cultural background, and adaptive behavior. The group's evaluation must also include observation of the child's academic performance in a regular classroom setting (or, for children who are not in school, in an appropriate environment for a child of that age). (34 C.F.R. § 300.310.) The team is required to carefully consider and document all of this information.

The team also has to document its eligibility findings in a written report, which must include the following information:

- whether the child has a specific learning disability
- the basis for making the determination
- relevant behavior noted during observation of the child
- the relationship of that behavior to the child's academic functioning
- any educationally relevant medical findings
- whether there is a severe discrepancy between achievement and ability that is not correctable without special education and related services
- the effects of environmental, cultural, or economic disadvantage, and
- the effects of a visual, hearing, or motor disability, mental retardation, emotional disturbance, or limited English proficiency on the child's achievement level.

Each team member must state, in writing, whether the report reflects his or her conclusions. If it does not, the team member must submit a separate statement of his or her conclusions. You are entitled to copies of all evaluation reports and documentation of any recommendations regarding eligibility. (34 C.F.R. § 300.311(a) and (b).)

Outcome of Meeting

If the school district determines that your child is eligible for special education, then it will proceed to the IEP program meeting—either immediately after the eligibility meeting or at some later date. If the school district finds that your child is not eligible for special education, see "If Your Child Is Not Found Eligible for Special Education," below.

Joint IEP Eligibility/Program Meeting

The school district may combine the IEP eligibility and program meetings into one. In such a situation, your child is found eligible for special education, then the IEP team shifts gears and immediately begins to develop the IEP program: goals, program, placement, services, and the like.

Request for Joint IEP Eligibility/Program Meeting

Date: _March 10, 20xx_

To: _Valerie Sheridan_

McKinley Unified School District

1345 South Drive

Topeka, KS 00000

Re: _Grace Lee, 4th grade student_

at Eisenhower School

I believe there is sufficient information for us to discuss both my child's eligibility for special education and the specifics of my child's IEP at the same meeting. I would appreciate it if you would plan enough time to discuss both of those important items at the _April 14, 20xx_ IEP meeting. I would also like to see any and all reports and other written material that you will be introducing at the IEP meeting, at least two weeks before the meeting.

Thanks in advance for your help. I look forward to hearing from you soon.

Sincerely,

Albert Lee

Albert Lee

78 Elm Drive

Topeka, KS 00078

Phones: 555-1111 (home); 555-2222 (work)

Holding one meeting may save you time and scheduling headaches, but it also requires you to do a lot of up-front preparation. If you're not ready to discuss the IEP program at the IEP eligibility meeting, ask for another meeting to give yourself time to prepare.

On the other hand, if you'd like to combine the meetings (assuming your child is found eligible), ask the school district to do so. Make your request well ahead of the scheduled eligibility meeting, so you and the school district will have enough time to prepare.

 FORM

A sample Request for Joint IEP Eligibility/Program Meeting is above; a blank downloadable copy is available on this book's Companion Page on www. nolo.com. See Chapter 16 for the link.

If Your Child Is Not Found Eligible for Special Education

You may attend the IEP eligibility meeting, point out significant information that supports your child's eligibility, and argue your points in a manner worthy of Clarence Darrow, all to no avail. What then? You have two options.

Exercise Your Due Process Rights

"Due process" is your right to take any dispute you have with your child's district—whether a disagreement about an assessment, eligibility, or any part of the IEP—to a neutral third party to help you resolve your dispute. Due process is covered in Chapter 12.

Seek Eligibility Under Section 504 of the Rehabilitation Act

Section 504 of the federal Rehabilitation Act (29 U.S.C. § 794) is a disability rights law entirely separate from IDEA. It requires all agencies that receive federal financial assistance to provide "access" to individuals with disabilities. Historically, Section 504 has been used to require public agencies to install wheelchair-accessible ramps, accessible restrooms, and other building features, and to provide interpreters at meetings. Section 504 also requires school districts to ensure that children with disabilities are provided access to educational programs and services through interpreters, notetakers, readers, and the like.

Your child may be entitled to assistance under Section 504 even if he or she is not eligible under IDEA. The first step in the process is to refer your child for Section 504 services—this simply means asking the school to consider your child's eligibility under Section 504. Some school districts automatically consider children who are found ineligible under IDEA for Section 504 services; if yours does not, request—in writing—that it do so.

Once a child has been referred, the school will evaluate eligibility. It will look at:

- whether the child has a physical or mental impairment
- whether the child's impairment substantially limits the child's "major life activities," including learning, and
- what types of accommodations the child needs in order to receive a free, appropriate public education.

If your child is found eligible for help under Section 504, the school must develop a written plan describing the modifications, accommodations, and services your child will receive. Like an IEP, the Section 504 plan must be individually tailored to meet your child's needs. Many schools have developed a standard form for Section 504 plans; ask your school if it has one.

Because Section 504 tries to achieve the same result as IDEA—to give children the help they need to succeed in school—many of the tips and strategies described in this book will be useful to you as you develop a Section 504 plan for your child. The eligibility, procedural, and other requirements of Section 504 are different from IDEA's requirements, however. Because this book focuses on the IEP process, you'll need to get more information on Section 504 if you decide to proceed.

RESOURCE

Need more information on Section 504? Contact the U.S. Department of Education, Office of Civil Rights (www.ed.gov/about/offices/list/ocr/index.html); your school district; your local community advisory committee; or one of the disability groups listed in Appendix B. You can find a copy of the Section 504 regulations in Appendix A. The appendixes are available on this book's Companion Page on www.nolo.com. See Chapter 16 for the link.

Gathering Information and Evidence

Once your child is found eligible for special education, the IEP team must decide what types of instruction and assistance your child will receive. This is where the promise of special education is fulfilled or broken—the specifics of the IEP plan will spell out exactly what help your child will get to overcome his or her learning disability.

Your role in this process is vital—after all, no matter how kind and professional your child's teachers and school administrators may be, they are not going to understand your child as you do, nor will they likely have the time or energy to explore options as fully and passionately as you will. It is therefore vital that you do some legwork to find out what's available, decide what would be most effective for your child, and present your findings persuasively to the IEP team. This chapter will help you meet these challenges.

By now, you should have a copy of your child's school file (see Chapter 4) and the school district's evaluation report (see Chapter 6). You should also have developed a rudimentary IEP blueprint for your child (see Chapter 5). In addition, you may have spoken to other parents, your child's teacher and classroom aide, your child's pediatrician, and others who have information about your child's learning disability and needs. In other words, you probably have a mountain of available information—and you may not know exactly how you can put it to use.

The key to a successful IEP meeting is developing and presenting information that supports your child's need for a particular program and class, services, and teaching methods. This chapter shows you how to:

- review your child's school file and the school district's evaluation report
- track your child's current progress in school
- look into available special education programs, services, and methodologies—both within and outside of the school district— that may be appropriate for your child
- figure out whether available programs and services fit your child's education needs and whether you need additional information to make your case, and

- make a list of other materials you might generate to support your position, such as an independent evaluation, a statement from your child's teacher, or a statement from your child's pediatrician or other professional.

RELATED TOPIC

Chapter 10 provides a system for organizing all of your materials—positive and negative—to best make your case at your child's IEP meeting.

Analyze the School District's Information

Your first step in preparing for the IEP program meeting is to figure out what position the school will probably take and whether you can use any of the school district's own documents and statements to show that your child needs a particular program. Start by reviewing all of the information you've received from the school district. As you look over your child's school file, evaluation report, and other items, there are several issues to consider.

Read Between the Lines

Can you figure out what position the school district will take simply by reading your child's file and evaluation report? For example, if the school district's materials say "Matteo needs to be placed in a regular classroom with one hour a day of extra assistance to work on his reading" or "Henry needs speech therapy twice a week," you'll know exactly where the district stands.

Sometimes, you need to look for less direct statements, such as "Henry has difficulty understanding instructions given by the teacher" or "No matter how often I tell him about the homework, Henry does not follow through." Comments like these clue you in to how the district is thinking about your child. The statements in the example show that the district recognizes that your child is having trouble with basic learning processes, notably possible auditory processing or sequential thinking problems.

Where to Look for the School District's Position

You can find the school district's position in a variety of material. It is most likely to come up in an evaluation report, but you may also come across the school district's position in a letter, teacher report, or memo, or another written item in your child's file. Your child's teacher, the school evaluator, or another district employee may even have stated the school district's position in a conversation.

 RELATED TOPIC

If a school district employee says something to you that supports your position, be sure to send a confirming letter. (See Chapter 4.)

Sources of the School District's Information

It's important to figure out who is saying what in the school district's material. These speakers are the district's experts—and their opinions will greatly influence the IEP process. Specifically, you'll want to know each person's:

- name and position—for example, a teacher, teacher's aide, counselor, evaluator, or learning disability or resource specialist
- training and expertise, and
- first-hand experience with your child.

Clearly, the most persuasive opinions come from those who know your child and have experience dealing with children who have learning disabilities. On the other hand, it may be easier to challenge the opinions of someone who hasn't taught or evaluated your child, has very few years of experience, or has no special expertise in learning disabilities.

Make sure to figure out which school personnel (for example, a classroom teacher, school psychologist, reading specialist, or speech/language therapist) have the most experience and training in your child's particular type of learning disability.

Keeping Track of the School District's Statements

Once you've reviewed all of the information available from the school district, make a chart like the one below to highlight key elements of your child's program (see your blueprint), whether the school district agrees or disagrees with your position, and where in the school district's materials the issue is addressed. Note where the school district data supports or opposes your position and where you have gaps that need to be filled—little or no information to show that a particular program or service is necessary for your child to receive an appropriate education. Finally, note the source of the information—was it in writing or did someone say it to you?

Changing a Report or Evaluation

If there is something in your child's school file or the evaluation report that is inaccurate or harmful to your child, find out whether the school district is willing to change the statement. Start with a phone call. For example:

"Hello Mr. Altman, I'm Von Williams's father. I read your report and I appreciate your help in evaluating Von's needs. I did want to ask you a question. You say on page 4 that Von does not need help with his reading comprehension. Did you review the report by Von's teacher, which states that he does need one-on-one reading help?"

To make a formal request for a change, see Chapter 4 (changing something in a school file) and Chapter 6 (changing a draft evaluation report).

Key Elements for Child's Program

Child: R. Boston

Date: June 1, 20xx

Desired IEP Components	District Material	District Position
Placement in regular class	4-4-xx Evaluation	Disagrees, p. 14
1:1 aide for regular class	4-4-xx Evaluation	No position
	3-12-xx Biweekly Teacher Report	Teacher agrees
LD Curricula	2-4-xx Teacher Report	Teacher responds to parents Qs about LD
LD Methodology	Evaluation of Dr. Jones	No position yet
LD Strategies	Evaluation of Dr. Jones	No position yet
Adaptive Physical Ed	5-2-xx Adaptive P.E. Evaluation	Disagrees (but see comment on p. 5)

Chart Your Child's Progress

As you prepare for an IEP program meeting, take some time to learn how your child is currently doing in school—in regular or special education. At the IEP meeting, you'll want to be able to describe exactly how your child is doing in the current program, what your child's strengths and weaknesses are, and what additional help your child needs. Pay special attention to those areas most likely affected by your child's learning disability (such as reading, spelling, language, or calculations).

Here are a few ways to get current information about your child:

- Ask the teacher(s), teacher's aide, and service provider for periodic reports focusing on key areas of need for your child—reading, behavior, language development, social interaction, physical mobility, and the like.
- Ask the teacher(s) for samples and reports of your child's work.
- Visit your child's class.
- Set up periodic meetings with your child's teacher(s). If your child already has an IEP, ask the teacher whether the current IEP goals are being met.

EXAMPLE: One of your child's current IEP goals is to read a three-paragraph story and demonstrate 80% comprehension by answering questions. First, ask the teacher whether your child can read a three-paragraph story. Then ask about your child's reading comprehension level. If it's not up to 80%, where is it: 60%? 40%? 20%?

To organize this material, you can create a chart for your child's teacher to update your child's progress regularly (once a month, for example) in key areas such as math, reading, behavior, and motor development, as well as emotional and psychological issues and self-help skills. Do remember that teachers have a remarkable amount of paperwork to complete—try to be sensitive to the teacher's time when you consider how often you want to receive a written report. If the teacher can email reports to you, that might make the process easier.

Progress Chart

Student: Micah Jacobs

Class: Ms. Frank's 3rd Grade

Date: February 23, 20xx

Key Goals	Current status	Comments
Math	Progressing appropriately? ☒ yes ☐ no	On schedule to complete goals.
Reading	Progressing appropriately? ☒ yes ☐ no	On schedule to complete goals. Needs to improve reading fluidity.
Writing	Progressing appropriately? ☒ yes ☐ no	On schedule to complete goals.
Spelling	Progressing appropriately? ☐ yes ☒ no	Reversals continue to be problem.
Social-Behavior	Progressing appropriately? ☐ yes ☒ no	Still problems with focus; hard time not teasing others.
Language development	Progressing appropriately? ☒ yes ☐ no	On schedule, but some problems going from specific to general.
Motor development	Progressing appropriately? ☒ yes ☐ no	Small motor problems affecting handwriting.
Other	Progressing appropriately? ☒ yes ☐ no	When struggling with spelling and handwriting, seems to feel high level of stress.

FORM

A sample Progress Chart is above; a downloadable copy is available on this book's Companion Page on www.nolo.com. See Chapter 16 for the link. You can tailor this chart to your child's particular goals. This form will help you track your child's general progress, as well as whether your child is meeting the IEP goals. (See Chapter 9 for more details on developing goals.)

Explore Available School Programs

To prepare for the IEP program meeting, you will want to gather information about your child's existing program and other programs that may be appropriate for your child. By finding out what's available, you'll have a better sense of what the best approach for your child might be.

Program possibilities include:

- placement in a regular classroom, perhaps with support services (such as a one-on-one aide, classroom accommodations such as seating in the front of the room, speech/language therapy, occupational therapy for small motor/handwriting difficulties)— ask about local options, including your child's neighborhood school
- placement in a classroom specifically designed for children with learning disabilities, difficulties with communication, or other disabling conditions—ask about special day classes at your neighborhood school, nearby schools, or other schools in the area, or
- placement in a specialized program, such as a private school or residential program—ask about the existence and location of any such programs (these more restrictive options won't be appropriate for many children with learning disabilities).

For students with learning disabilities, there may be some kind of "pull-out" program that includes a small group of students and one staff person with some expertise in learning disabilities. This person may be a resource specialist (RSP), aide, or LD teacher. Many students with learning disabilities receive specific services—special help in or out of the regular classroom—but are not in a special classroom or separate program. As you read through this chapter, remember that your child's

IEP program and services might include anything from a little extra help in a regular classroom to placement in a special school.

When you gather information, explore every possible option—even those programs or services that don't seem to offer exactly what your child needs. Even if the program and services aren't right for your child, you'll have more information about what's out there. And you'll be able to respond effectively to any discussions about those programs and services at the IEP meeting. For example, if the school district recommends that your child use or attend one of these programs, you can respond, "With all due respect, I visited that classroom for children with learning disabilities and it is inappropriate for my child for the following reasons…."

Ask About Available Programs and Services

Contact your child's teacher, the school evaluator, the district special education administrator, other parents, your PTA, and local community advisory committee. Ask about programs and services for children with learning disabilities within your district.

Don't be surprised if the school administrator (or even the classroom teacher) is reluctant to tell you about programs. You may hear, for example, "It's way too early to be looking at programs for next year, Mr. and Mrs. Gough. We've just started this year." Or, "Let's wait until the IEP team meets and goals are drafted. Then we can talk about programs."

While school personnel may have reasons for making assertions like these, you have every right to find out about available program options. Emphasize that you are not looking to change programs or force an early IEP decision—you are merely trying to gather information. You might respond, "I appreciate what you are saying, Ms. Casey, but it will really be helpful to me and my child to get started as soon as possible, so we can plan ahead. I am not looking for a change in programs or for a commitment on your part. Is there some reason why I shouldn't be gathering information about programs in the district?"

If the administrator steadfastly refuses to let you visit programs, put your concerns in writing.

FORM
A sample Program Visitation Request Letter is below; a download-able copy is available on this book's Companion Page on www.nolo.com. See Chapter 16 for the link.

If the administrator still refuses your request, don't give up. Indicate that you understand the concerns but feel that you cannot make a decision about placement without some basic information about available programs. Make it clear that you are more than willing to visit programs again after the IEP meeting.

If you get nowhere, contact the administrator's superior. If that fails, contact your school board of education. If you don't make any progress, you can file a complaint with your state department of education or other appropriate educational agency, as discussed in Chapter 13. The complaint might not be processed until after the date set for the IEP meeting. If this happens, you'll have to decide whether to postpone the IEP meeting or ask (at the IEP meeting) to see the programs after the meeting. In that case, you may not be ready to sign the IEP at the meeting. (See Chapter 11 for more information on signing the IEP.)

When to Visit Programs

Ideally, you will want to visit programs in the fall of the school year. While it may seem logical to visit right before the IEP meeting, checking out possible program options earlier offers these advantages:

- The sooner you see a particular program, the sooner you'll have a sense of whether or not it is appropriate for your child.
- If you can't decide whether a program is a good fit for your child, there will be time for others, such as an independent evaluator, to take a look and give you an opinion.
- You'll have time to visit a program more than once (and you should, if it's necessary).

Visit Programs

The best way to find out what a particular school or program has to offer is to spend some time there. However, while school administrators may be willing to provide you with some information about existing programs, they may be reluctant for you to actually visit a program before the IEP meeting. Although the IEP team might not know which program will best meet your child's needs until after you have the IEP meeting, nothing in IDEA prevents you from visiting potential programs before the meeting, as long as your requests are reasonable.

"If the Law Doesn't Require It, We Don't Have to Do It"

Some school administrators will take the position that they don't have to do anything unless it is expressly required by IDEA. For example, because IDEA does not expressly state that a parent can visit programs at a specific time, some administrators will take the position that you have no legal right to visit before the IEP—and, therefore, that you can't do it. Technically, the administrator is correct that the IDEA doesn't require such visits, but that doesn't mean that the school can't allow you to visit. The fact that something is not required by law does not mean that it is not permitted.

It is reasonable and fair for you to visit available school programs. As a parent or guardian, a tax-paying citizen, and a member of the community in which your child's school district is located, you have the same right of access to school programs as anyone else (and your school's policy probably provides for this type of access). For the school district to deny a reasonable request is itself unreasonable, and you should approach the situation that way. Ultimately, the school will have to explain and justify its decision. And while there are certainly exceptions, most people want to be fair and reasonable. Your best strategy is to avoid getting tangled up in a debate about what "the law" requires or allows. Instead, simply approach the situation with the point of view that your request is reasonable and should be granted. This strategy usually works (and if it doesn't, the school district will end up looking bad for refusing your reasonable request).

Program Visitation Request Letter

Date: _November 6, 20xx_

To: _Mr. Carlos Avila, Special Education Administrator_

Carlson Unified School District

8709 Fourth Street

Helena, MT 00087

Re: _Elizabeth Moore_

I am writing to request permission to visit programs in the District that might be appropriate future placements for my daughter, Elizabeth. I appreciate the concerns you have, and I realize that you can't know for sure which programs are appropriate until after the IEP meeting. Nonetheless, I think it would be very helpful for me to see existing programs so I can be a more effective member of the IEP team. I do not feel I can make an informed IEP decision without seeing, firsthand, all possible options. I want to assure you that I understand that by giving me the names of existing programs, you are not stating an opinion as to their appropriateness for my child.

I assure you that I will abide by all rules and regulations for parental visits. If those rules and regulations are in writing, please send me a copy.

Thanks in advance for your help. I hope to hear from you soon.

Sincerely,

Arnette Moore

Arnette Moore

87 Mission Road

Helena, MT 00087

Phones: 555-3334 (home); 555-4455 (work)

Visitation Guidelines

The purpose of your visits is to gather information. As you plan your visits, keep these tips in mind:

- Ask to visit all program options.
- Follow the policies and rules established by the school district, site administrator, and teacher.
- If an independent evaluator or other professional will attend the IEP meeting, have that person join you. Be sure to inform the school district ahead of time.
- Do not ask for any personal information about the students, such as names of individual children. A teacher should not give you this information. You can (and should) talk with any parents you know who have children in the programs.
- Find out as many details as possible about each program or class, using the same information you use in your blueprint (see Chapter 5):
  - student description (number of students in the program; students' disabilities, age, cognitive range, and language range)
  - staff description (details on teachers and aides)
  - teacher-student instruction (teacher-to-class, small group, or individual instruction)
  - curricula, methodology, and other teaching strategies used
  - classroom environment (behavior problems, noise level, number of teachers and teacher aides, and how much time teacher aides spend in class)
  - related services (how many children leave the class to go to another program and how often; how many children receive related services—such as help from a one-on-one aide—in the class), and
  - any other comments you have on the program.

IDEA does not require the teacher to provide you with this information, so make sure to ask for it in a pleasant, matter-of-fact way. If the teacher balks, indicate that the information you seek is important and noncontroversial, and should be made available.

Class Visitation Checklist

Date: _9/11/xx_   Time: _9:00-10:15 a.m._

School: _Jefferson School, Chicago_

Class: _3rd Grade Special Day Class for Learning Disabled (Teacher: Sue Avery)_

Student Description:

Total students: _17_   Gender range: _12 boys; 5 girls_

Age range: _7 - 10 (ten kids are nine or younger; seven ten-year-olds)_

Cognitive range: _"Wide range; probably from pre-K through 5th grade skills,"_
says S. Avery (teacher).

Language/communication range: _Two students with hearing impairment; two_
other students with delayed communication skills (1st grade level).

Disability range: _12 students have specific learning disability, three are retarded,_
borderline one has emotional disturbance, and one autistic-like behavior.

Behavioral range: _Five students acting out throughout class, four other_
students constantly demanding of teacher. Two students sent to principal
because of behavior. Rest of class generally cooperative, quiet.

Other observations: _Overall impression was of a class of children with varied_
needs and behavior, which made it difficult for the teacher to focus on any one
group of children for very long.

Staff Descriptions:

Teachers: _Sue Avery has four years' experience working with learning disabled_
children. She was generally very patient with students (less so with the
behaviorally troubled children), but she seemed easily distracted.

Class Visitation Checklist, continued

Aids: In class two hours per day; worked with all children, no one child more than few minutes. Seemed mostly to superficially check in with students, but not provide any sustained 1:1 help. Aide has no specific training working with learning disabled children.

Other observations: Neither teacher nor aide seemed fully comfortable with curriculum, particularly given varied needs of students. Both were very nice to students.

Curricula/Classroom Strategies:

Curricula: "Using Mathematics" (Book 2) for math, teacher-developed materials for spelling, and "Project Explore" for science lessons.

Strategies: Teacher/aide when working 1:1 in reading divided words into simple sounds using much repetition; no overall strategy or specific curriculum designed for learning disabled children.

Classroom Environment:

Description: Classroom had tiled floor so sound echoed. Quite loud; no other apparent acoustical treatment to reduce noise; all added to a noisy room. Various work stations and cubicles set up so students can work 1:1 or by themselves. Somewhat effective, but noise was distracting to all students. Classroom situated near playground, so much visual stimulation outside classroom window and noise from outside.

Related Services:

At least four students received their related services in class, one had speech therapy, another had a special aide that worked with her in the corner.

Class Visitation Checklist, continued

Other Comments:

School site principal (Lee Parsons) is interested in special education, but has no training or expertise in the field. She did express reservations about excessive mainstreaming of children with disabilities into regular classrooms. Visited one mainstreamed class, teacher seemed interested, but expressed concern that the school had not provided any support or training for dealing with special education students in her regular class.

How This Program Relates to IEP Blueprint:

Program does not meet Tara's blueprint:

• Cognitive and behavioral range of students too wide

• Teacher unable to provide individual attention

• Aide not trained for working with L-D kids

• Question about curriculum

Write down your observations and the answers to your questions. You can write as you watch the class and talk to the teacher. If you "interview" the teacher with notebook in hand and pencil poised, however, the teacher may be intimidated. You might put the teacher at ease by saying something like, "I have a poor memory; do you mind if I take notes while we talk?" If not, try to take notes in an unobtrusive way or wait until you're outside and write down what you remember as soon as possible.

 FORM

A sample Class Visitation Checklist is above; a downloadable copy is available on this book's Companion Page on www.nolo.com. See Chapter 16 for the link. Be sure to keep copies of this important form in your IEP binder.

Find Out About Related Services

Classroom programs are only one component of your child's IEP program. Related services, such as occupational, physical, or speech therapy, are also very important. (Related services are explained in Chapter 2.)

Gathering information about related services will be a little different from gathering information about programs. You'll still want to talk to your child's teacher, the school evaluator, the district special education administrator, other parents, your PTA, and local parent groups for disabled children to find out about related services that will meet your child's needs. But the similarities end there.

Service providers, such as physical therapists or reading specialists, usually work one-on-one with individual children or in small groups. So visiting these specialists in action may not be possible. Instead, when you talk to people about the services available, ask about the background, training, and experience of the specialists. Candid conversations with other parents will probably be your most helpful source of information.

Keep detailed notes of your conversations and include them in your IEP binder.

Compare Your Blueprint With the Existing Program and Services

Once you have information about your school district's programs and services, compare what's available with what you believe your child needs. Obviously, if the school provides programs and services you feel will meet your child's needs (as fleshed out in your blueprint), the IEP process will go more smoothly. On the other hand, if there is a gap between what your child needs and what is available, you will likely have to convince the IEP team that the school options are inappropriate.

You'll need to detail the shortcomings of the programs and services offered by the school district—the classroom visitation checklist will be of real help here. Be as specific as possible: Is the problem the frequency or location of a service, the pupil-teacher ratio, the qualifications of the teacher or service provider, the class makeup, the teacher methodology, the curriculum, or other important features?

Make a comprehensive, side-by-side comparison of your blueprint and what you know about the school's options, and put the details on the bottom of the class visitation checklist.

Generate Additional Supporting Information

Once you've reviewed your child's school file, developed your blueprint, reviewed the school evaluation, evaluated your child's progress, and gathered information about program and service options, you may need further data to support your goals. This material will be invaluable in preparing for the IEP meeting.

Help From School Personnel

Contact any teachers, evaluators, or service providers who you think are likely to support your position. You can do this by phone or in person. Explain the programs and services you want for your child (the items you included in your blueprint) and why you feel they are appropriate. Note any discrepancy between what you want and what you believe the school district has available. Ask for their ideas and opinions about what you plan to propose.

Ask if the teacher, evaluator, or service provider would be willing either to write a statement supporting what you want for your child or to state that position at the IEP meeting.

If you talk to someone who supports your point of view but doesn't want to put anything in writing, follow up the conversation with a confirming letter. (See Chapter 4.) For example, you might say, "Thank you for the chance to chat today. I appreciate your frankness and was glad to hear that you agree that Max needs an aide in order to function effectively in the regular class."

Be aware that a confirming letter can put the teacher in an awkward position. If the teacher says one thing to you (and you confirm it in a letter) and then says another thing at the IEP meeting, the letter may be important proof of what was originally said—but this may lead to some friction between you and the teacher. If the teacher will not speak frankly at the IEP meeting, however, the confirming letter will be valuable proof of what was said earlier—and might discourage the teacher from changing his or her tune.

No matter what, be sure to keep notes of who said what, including the date, time, and place of the conversation, in as much detail as possible. This is your record in case the school representative gives a different story later on.

Help From People Outside the School

Anyone who knows your child or has some expertise in special education or your child's disability may be of value. This includes your child's doctor, tutor, therapist, or other specialist.

Ask each person to write a letter to the IEP team stating:

- how he or she knows your child
- the specific expertise he or she has
- any specific comments on your child's condition as it relates to the educational experience, and

- any recommendations for your child in terms of program, services, or other IEP components.

EXAMPLE: "Teresa needs extensive help with small and large motor skills and should work with an occupational and physical therapist at least three times a week."

Independent Evaluations

An independent evaluation may be the best proof of what program and services your child needs. An independent evaluation, like the school district's evaluation, can be as comprehensive or as narrow as your child's needs dictate. In most cases, an independent evaluation will use a variety of tests to evaluate your child's abilities and determine what teaching and program strategies would be most helpful.

RESOURCE

Independent evaluations have many uses. An independent evaluation will be useful—even if your child isn't eligible under IDEA—for figuring out your child's strengths, weaknesses, and educational needs. If your child is eligible under IDEA, it will help you prove that particular programs or services should be included in the IEP. If your child is not found eligible, it will help you develop a written Section 504 plan or come up with your own program to help your child. Section 504 is discussed in Chapter 7.

Under IDEA, you have an absolute right to have your child evaluated independently. Moreover, your school district is required to provide you with information on where you can get an independent evaluation.

RELATED TOPIC

Chapter 6 discusses evaluations in general; Chapter 11 explains how to present an independent evaluation at the IEP meeting.

While IDEA requires the school district to consider the results of the independent evaluation in reaching any decision regarding your child's education, it does not require your school district to agree with the results. While an independent evaluation may include persuasive information, your child's school district can reject the conclusions. You do have the right to go to due process to prove the district is wrong. (See Chapter 12.)

When to Use an Independent Evaluation

You may want an independent evaluation because you need more information about your child or, as we noted, because the school district's evaluation does not support what you want. Before you hire an independent evaluator, make sure you understand the district's position. If the district's position is clear—and you disagree with it—an outside evaluation may very well be needed.

Finding Independent Evaluators

Independent evaluators generally work in private practice or are affiliated with hospitals, universities, or other large institutions. How do you find a qualified independent evaluator? Here are a few tips:

- Ask parents of children with similar disabilities. Check with the PTA or your school district's advisory committee of parents with children in special education.
- Get recommendations from the school. A trusted teacher, aide, service provider, or other school employee may be able to give you some names.
- Talk to your child's pediatrician.
- Call a local hospital, particularly a university medical hospital. A department that employs experts in your child's disability may be able to do the evaluation or refer you to someone who can.
- Call local private schools for disabled children; they often work with credible independent evaluators.

- Check resources on learning disabilities, including local and regional support groups, Web links, and associations, for information on independent evaluators who specialize in children with learning disabilities. A good place to start is the Learning Disabilities Association of America (LDA), an advocacy and educational group with national and state chapters. See Appendix B on this book's Companion Page on nolo.com (you'll find the link in Chapter 16) for information about LDA and other learning disability organizations.

How Not to Find an Independent Evaluator

Evaluators are often psychologists. If you look in the phone book, you will see a long list of psychologists. But choosing randomly from the phone book is a poor method for selecting a reputable and knowledgeable evaluator—the only thing you really know about these people is that they could afford to pay for an ad in the yellow pages.

Selecting the Right Evaluator

Speak to various independent evaluators, and ask the following questions for each person:

- Does the evaluator have significant expertise, training, and experience in dealing with learning disabilities?
- Is the evaluator affiliated with a well-respected institution?
- Were you referred by someone who actually worked with the evaluator?
- Do you trust the person (or institution) who recommended the evaluator?
- Will the evaluator give you references?
- Did the evaluator's references like the results of the evaluator's work and find the evaluator easy to work with?
- Is the evaluator impartial? (An evaluator who has previously done work for—and been paid by—your child's school district may not be truly independent.)

- Which tools and tests does the evaluator use for children with learning disabilities (see Chapter 6)?
- Can the evaluator complete the evaluation and written report well in advance of the IEP meeting?
- Will the evaluator's report recommend specific programs and services that are appropriate for your child's learning disability?
- Can the evaluator attend the IEP meeting, if necessary?
- Is the evaluator familiar with testing, curricula, methodologies, and other strategies for children with learning disabilities?
- Is the evaluator familiar with the 2004 amendments to IDEA, including changes to the eligibility requirements for children with learning disabilities?
- What are the evaluator's fees, and do they include a written report and attendance at the IEP meeting?

The answers to these questions, your own impressions, and recommendations from others are key factors in making your decision. It is also important that the person you choose be able to clearly, professionally, and vigorously articulate his or her position.

Having the Independent Evaluator on Your Side

The reason you are hiring an independent evaluator is to support your goals for your child's education. Be very clear on your plans and perspectives.

EXAMPLES:
- Your son needs a multisensory approach to help him with his learning disability. Be sure the evaluator's recommendations include (1) information showing that he needs that specific program, (2) specifically named multisensory programs, (3) a detailed explanation of the kind of multisensory work he needs (without referring to a named program), and (4) the time and teaching conditions needed for that program (for example, one hour a day, one-on-one with a teacher trained in a multisensory approach for your child's learning disability).

- You want your daughter placed in a private school for children with learning disabilities. Ideally, the evaluator will write, "Lila requires placement in a program with no more than ten children, a small campus, a full-time aide, a teacher qualified to work with learning disabled children, and a class where there are no behavioral problems. The X School in Boston is the only program that can meet Lila's needs."

Independent Evaluators and Learning Disabilities

As you undoubtedly know, learning disabilities can be complicated and difficult to pinpoint. If you anticipate a disagreement about placement or services with your school district, an expert in learning disabilities can be indispensable to you and your child. An independent evaluator skilled in learning disability issues can not only make your case with careful and detailed analysis, but also give you a frank and objective sense of the real differences between the program the school offers and the one you want. A good evaluator won't just help you win your case if you go to due process—he or she will also let you know when the facts are not on your side and you might lose a due process claim. You may not always be happy with the evaluator's conclusions, but it's better to know where you stand before you waste time and money fighting a losing battle with the school district.

In addition, a good independent evaluator will be able to forcefully and clearly address whether your child qualifies as a student with a learning disability. Be sure your evaluator directly addresses the qualifications for learning disability eligibility. See Chapter 7 for a discussion of those qualifications, and be sure your evaluator uses the specific language of the eligibility regulations and supports his or her findings with as much detail as possible.

If the evaluator can't or won't name a specific school or program, then make sure he or she will name the specific components of an appropriate program. Continuing Example 2, above, if the independent evaluator won't say Lila needs to be placed in the X School, he or she should say that Lila needs a program that has the characteristics of the X School.

Of course, it's possible that the data will not support your goals. Good evaluators will not write something they disagree with or make a recommendation they do not believe in. A good evaluator will tell you when the evidence—the testing data—does not support what you want. You want an evaluator who will:

- show you a draft report
- consider your concerns about the draft report
- make specific recommendations about your child's educational status and appropriate programs and related services to meet your child's needs, and
- provide a written rationale for these recommendations.

How an Independent Evaluation Proceeds

Most independent evaluators will meet with you and review your child's school file, the school district's evaluation, and other district material. The evaluator will then explain what testing will be done, secure your approval, do the testing, and prepare a report. Depending on your child's characteristics and needs, the evaluator may also want to observe your child in class and visit some program options.

When to Submit the Independent Evaluation

Just as you want to review the school district's evaluations before the IEP meeting, the school district will likely want to see your independent evaluation before the IEP meeting. Of course, the more time the school has to review the independent evaluation, the more time the administration will have to find data to counter its conclusions. Does this mean you should delay giving the school district your evaluation? While such a strategy has its attractions, the bottom line is that the school district is entitled to the same courtesy that you are.

Waiting to give the district a copy of your evaluation could ultimately prove counterproductive. The district may distrust you and your evaluation. The delay may be grounds for postponing the IEP meeting. And your relationship with the district may be affected. Because you will likely be working together for many years, you will want to maintain a positive relationship, if possible. If one party will be nasty, unfair, or untrustworthy, let it be someone other than you. While there is no hard and fast rule here, providing the independent evaluation (and other key material) a week before the IEP meeting is usually appropriate.

Cost of an Independent Evaluation

Independent evaluations can be quite costly, anywhere from several hundred to several thousand dollars.

But you may not have to pay for the evaluation. Under IDEA, you have the right to an independent educational evaluation of your child (by a person of your choosing) at public expense if you disagree with the school district's evaluation.

IDEA requires that after you request an independent evaluation to be paid for by the school district, the district must, "without unnecessary delay," either arrange to pay for the evaluation or file for due process and prove at the hearing that the district's evaluation was appropriate.

It is therefore important that you formally request in writing that the district provide and pay for your independent evaluation. In this letter, you should also state who you want to do the evaluation and what the evaluation will encompass. Send the letter certified mail, return receipt requested, so that you have proof it was received.

When you request the independent evaluation, the district has the right to ask you why you object to the district's evaluation. You are not required to respond. If you do respond, do so in general terms—for example, "We felt the evaluation done by Ms. Harkins on behalf of the district was not thorough, we have some concerns about whether the administered tests were the right ones, and we're not sure whether she supported her conclusions with evidence." When in doubt, don't explain. If you choose not to respond to the district's request for explanation, simply say that you understand it is your right not to respond. If you choose not to respond, the district cannot delay either paying for the independent evaluation or going to due process. (34 C.F.R. § 300.502(b)(4).)

Finally, you have the right to only one independent evaluation at the district's expense each time the district does its own evaluation and you disagree with it. (34 C.F.R. § 300.502(b)(5).) No matter who pays for the evaluation, you have the right to present the evaluation at the IEP meeting. (34 C.F.R. § 300.502(c).)

One practical problem may be that you may need to have the evaluation done while you are waiting for the district to either pay or go to due process. In this case, you may need to pay the evaluator yourself. This certainly underscores the importance of requesting an independent evaluation early—so that if the district ends up paying for the evaluation, you won't have to put any resources out for it. If you must have the evaluation completed prior to the district's action (to pay or go to hearing), you might discuss with the evaluator whether you can delay payment or pay over a period of time.

Goals

Goals are the nuts and bolts of your child's education: the academic, cognitive, linguistic, social, and vocational achievements your child should accomplish during the school year. An IEP document usually includes many goals.

Objectives Are No More

Special education law used to use the term "goals and objectives" to describe the accomplishments a child would aim for during the school year. In 1997, Congress changed the term "objectives" to "benchmarks," but the meaning remained the same: short-term accomplishments that would help a child achieve a larger goal and measure progress toward that goal.

In 2004, Congress eliminated both terms. The statute now refers to "measurable annual goals, including academic and functional goals, designed to: meet the child's needs." (20 U.S.C. § 1414(d)(1)(A)(i)(II).) The definition is broad enough to give the IEP team latitude to develop whatever aims are appropriate for your child. This chapter includes examples of broad goals, as well as more detailed, short-term goals.

EXAMPLES OF IEP GOALS:

Tim will improve his reading comprehension. Tim will read a four-paragraph story and demonstrate 75% comprehension using objective classroom tests.

Ellen will improve her peer relationships. Ellen will initiate three positive peer interactions each day, per teacher observation.

Juan will master all third grade math skills. Juan will identify sets of ones and tens with 90% accuracy, using appropriate textbook tests.

Jane will improve her writing skills. Jane will write a three-sentence paragraph with subject and predicate sentences, per teacher evaluation.

Mark will improve short-term auditory memory. Mark will be able to listen to a set of ten related items and list them with 75% accuracy.

IDEA requires an IEP program to include a statement of measurable annual goals (20 U.S.C. § 1414(d)(1)(A)) for two reasons:

- to ensure that the child is progressing in the general curriculum, and
- to meet the child's other educational needs resulting from his or her disability.

Goals are important because they are the guts of your child's daily program (and therefore central to the IEP document) *and* because your child's progress in meeting his or her goals will largely determine whether your school district is providing your child an appropriate education.

What Goals Are Not

- Goals are not used for students who are in regular education. They are written for special education students—even special education students who are mainstreamed into regular classes.
- Goals are not part of a contract between you and the school district— that is, the school is not legally liable if your child does not meet the goals specified in the IEP. Goals are simply a way to measure your child's progress and to determine whether your child's program and services are working.
- Goals are not the totality of your child's instructional plan. They are important aims to be accomplished during the school year, but there will be other important components of your child's IEP—such as particular instruction techniques and methodologies, descriptions of the type of services and special help your child will receive, and information about your child's program.

Skill Areas Covered by Goals

IDEA does not dictate what areas goals must address. They can cover a wide variety of skills or topics relating to your child's academic and functional needs, including:

- academic skills, such as math computation, reading comprehension, spelling, and writing

- cognitive skills, such as abstract thinking and memory
- emotional and psychological issues, such as overcoming fears or improving self-esteem
- social-behavioral skills, such as relating to peers
- linguistic and communication skills, such as expressing oneself effectively
- self-help and independent living skills, such as using money, dressing, using transportation and, perhaps, for younger children, using the toilet
- physical and recreational skills, such as improving coordination and fine and large motor skills
- vocational skills, such as work skill development, and
- transition skills, such as exploring work or college options.

Developing Goals

IDEA does not specify how to write goals, what subjects to cover, how many goals to include in the IEP, or how to implement them. These details are up to the IEP team. This gives you the flexibility to develop goals that will be useful in conjunction with the programs and services you want for your child.

This section describes some of the details you'll want to consider when creating goals for the IEP.

FORM

A sample Goals Chart appears later in this chapter. You can also find examples of goals in the sample IEP. A downloadable copy is available on this book's companion page on www.nolo.com. See Chapter 16 for the link.

Child's Present Level of Performance

The written IEP must include a statement of your child's present levels of "academic achievement and functional performance," including how the child's disability affects his or her involvement and progress in the general curriculum. (20 U.S.C. § 1414(d)(1)(A).) This information will demonstrate how your child is doing and where your child needs to improve, which will in turn help the IEP team develop appropriate goals in each subject and behavioral area.

The IEP should spell out your child's current level of skill in each goal area. This "current level" can be described through evaluation numbers or in more general terms. For example, for a reading comprehension goal, a child's present level of performance may state, "Beth scored X on the Woodcock-Johnson; her current reading comprehension is at the mid-fourth-grade level. She enjoys reading, but requires help in maintaining focus." Or, "Matthew has completed his business math class." Make sure that the IEP addresses every area affected by your child's learning disability.

Who Implements Goals

Normally, your child's classroom teacher is responsible for implementing your child's goals. Junior and senior high school students may have a different teacher for each subject area. If the teacher is working with other educational professionals, such as an aide, that person will be responsible as well. For example:

- A speech therapist may be responsible for a child's language goals.
- An occupational or physical therapist may oversee physical education or motor goals, such as handwriting improvement.
- A school counselor or therapist may cover emotional goals.
- A resource specialist or instructor in a special day class may be responsible for a child's goals that relate to a learning disability— for example, to work with the child on improving reading or handwriting. For a junior or senior high school student, the resource specialist may work on reading, math, spelling, or language skills and/or may work on specific class areas (for example, to assist a child who has short-term memory problems by developing strategies for remembering the details contained in the science class textbook).

Completion Dates

Goals are normally written for a one-year period, but this is not set in stone. Some goals may be reached in less than a year—and it may be a good idea to set a shorter time frame in the written IEP.

> EXAMPLE: Lily is in a special day class with no mainstreaming in a regular classroom. Her IEP reading goal has a completion time of one year. Lily's parents feel she could reach her reading goal in a shorter time if she were in a regular classroom. If Lily's parents want her mainstreamed, it might help to set a shorter period for this goal in the IEP.

Measuring Goals

IDEA requires a child's goals to be "measurable." The IEP must describe how your child's progress toward the annual goals will be measured and when "periodic reports" on the progress will be given to you. (20 U.S.C. § 1414(d)(1)(A).)

There are a number of ways to measure goals, including objective testing, teacher or other staff observation, evaluating work samples, or any other method agreed to by the IEP team. Many IEP goals include a quantifiable accomplishment level, such as "Mia will read a four-paragraph story with 90% reading comprehension as measured by the Woodcock Reading Mastery Test" or "Austin will read the assigned novel in his English class and demonstrate comprehension of the novel's themes, describe the main characters, and explain what they represent."

IDEA does not require goals to be quantifiable—that is, capable of being measured in numbers. Of course, numbers can be of value, but not everything of value can be reduced to numbers. For example, how does one measure numerically whether goals were met in areas relating to emotions, psychology, self-help, or vocational skills?

EXAMPLE: Brian's IEP program states that he will improve his social skills. As a goal, this is stated as follows:

Goal: Brian will improve his ability to interact appropriately with his peers. He will improve his ability to read body and language cues from his peers and respond appropriately in seven out of ten situations as measured by teacher observation and with immediate feedback to Brian by the teacher.

Goals and General Curriculum

IDEA states that a child's goals must allow the child to "be involved in and progress in the general curriculum"—the same curriculum offered to nondisabled children. The IEP team is free to determine how much involvement in the general curriculum is appropriate for a particular child. Indeed, there may be very important reasons why a child is not fully exposed to the general curriculum. Generally, however, Congress wants children with disabilities to have the opportunity to learn the same subjects and skills as all other children their age.

Don't Set Your Sights Too Low

Be wary if an IEP team member from the school district suggests setting your child's goals fairly low. The district may want to set low standards so your child can achieve them without too much help from the school. If the school wants to eliminate a particular support service (such as a one-on-one aide or reading specialist) or keep your child in a special day class rather than a regular class, it might propose goals that your child can meet without this extra help.

Common Core Standards and Special Education

Every state has laws and procedures for what may be called "common core" competencies or "standard-based" competencies; these represent required growth in specific academic and other areas. Each student is intended to meet those requirements. And while a child's IEP can include reasons why the child cannot meet those common core requirements, it is important, of course, that every special education child have the opportunity to do what every other child has the opportunity to do: have access to and succeed in the general curriculum and meet all state standards.

As a parent of a special education child, ask your school to provide you with a written and detailed explanation of the state's requirements surrounding common core. Talk to your child's teacher and all other professionals involved in your child's education and find out their thoughts on how your child can meet all or some of those standards. Finally, be prepared to discuss at the IEP meeting what support, related services, and accommodations are necessary for your child to meet these state requirements

When to Draft Goals

While specific goals aren't discussed, approved, and included in the written IEP until the IEP meeting, it makes sense to draft them ahead of time.

In fact, it is not uncommon for school representatives to write goals in advance. Under IDEA, the school cannot simply present their goals at the IEP meeting, insist that you accept them, and refuse to discuss alternatives. That would violate a basic tenet of IDEA: that the IEP team makes all IEP decisions as a group, at the meeting. Still, you should anticipate that the school district might draft goals in advance. Prepare for the IEP meeting by asking the school district (in writing) to give you a copy of any predrafted goals at least two weeks in advance.

You should also draft goals before the IEP meeting. You do not have to give a copy to the school district ahead of time. However, you can choose to do so. Some advocates argue that you shouldn't do this because it gives the district time to counter your goals. Others argue that if you present your goals for the first time at the IEP meeting, the school might need some extra time to review them—and might postpone the meeting.

In general, I think it's best to provide the school district information in advance, unless the element of surprise is necessary in your particular situation.

Writing Effective Goals

Writing goals for the first time may seem as foreign to you as writing a medical prescription. But don't worry—it's not as tough as it might seem at first. Like much of the IEP process, writing effective goals requires gathering information, asking questions, and a little practice.

Get Your School's IEP Form

Every school district has its own form for the written IEP program. You should get a copy of your school's form and any guidelines or instructions that accompany it. As you begin to draft your child's goals, be sure to refer to the school's current IEP form for guidance.

Use Your Binder and Blueprint

Your dining room table or desk may be overrun with special education papers. If they are not already organized in a binder (as recommended in Chapter 4), take some time to gather them together. Make sure you have the following documents:

- your child's school file
- all evaluation reports
- written reports from professionals, and
- your blueprint.

Start with your blueprint. While the blueprint won't show you how to write specific goals, it will help you think about what you want for your child. The goals you create will be the stepping stones your child uses to achieve these ultimate ends.

Talk to Professionals

Talk with your child's teacher(s), other support staff, your independent evaluator, service providers, and others who know your child. They might be willing to suggest specific goals or at least to review yours. If a specific person will implement or be responsible for your child's goals, be sure to talk to that person.

If this is your child's first IEP, ask the professionals what areas your goals should cover and how to make them as specific as possible. Be sure to explore with them every area that you feel requires goals. Ask them about useful goals for children with learning disabilities. Most teachers and other educators who work with or evaluate children with learning disabilities will be able to provide you with goals that they have found helpful in addressing your child's areas of need.

If this is not your child's first IEP, ask the following questions.

- What previous goals should be retained?
- If previous goals are carried over, why were they not accomplished before? What can be done to better ensure completion this year? Using the progress chart in Chapter 8 will help you monitor goals throughout the year.
- What new goals should be developed?

By talking with your child's teacher and other staff members about goals, you may learn their opinions about your child's placement and services. You may also come to an informal agreement on goals before the IEP meeting, which is always preferable.

Talk to Other Parents

If you know other special education families, ask to see their IEPs, particularly if their child's needs are similar to your child's. Even if your child's needs are different, other parents may have valuable advice to offer about drafting goals that will pass muster with your school district.

Also, check with the PTA, the school district's local advisory committee on special education, and local individuals or organizations that provide help to special education parents for written material on goals. Chapter 15 discusses parent organizations.

Finally, check Appendix B on this book's Companion Page on nolo. com for support organizations and learning disability websites that can provide you with information and help (see Chapter 16 for the link).

List Your Goal Areas

Your job is to develop goals for each skill area that relates directly to your child's needs (see the sample goals listed below). Be as precise as possible. For example, don't simply list "academic achievement" as a skill area— break it down into reading, writing, math, cognitive abilities, spelling, and so on. For junior and senior high school students, list specific academic areas such as biology, algebra, social studies, English, and computer skills. Under social and behavioral goals, you might include separate goals and objectives for peer relations and for self-control.

Connect Goals to a Specific Program and Services

The best goals not only state your immediate expectations for your child's performance, but also provide support for the program and services you want for your child. You should draft them with this result in mind. Whether the school district is offering an appropriate program for your child will depend, in large part, on whether your child can meet his or her goals within that program. On the other hand, if your child can meet those goals without the program and services you want, you probably won't get the program and services. If the IEP team has created appropriate goals and your child is meeting them, that is strong evidence that the IEP is working and, therefore, that the district has met its legal requirements.

When referring to a specific program or service, be as precise as you can. If you can mention the name of a special school or the details of the service, so much the better. If you don't have the exact information, add something that will support your broad IEP program aims. Not all goals are written this way—schools often argue that the goals portion of the IEP is not the place to mention program or services. However, IDEA does not prevent such added language. You should include it in your draft goals and argue for it at the IEP meeting.

The key is to write the goals so that an objective reader will conclude that your child needs the particular program or service you want to meet the goals. Write a variety of goals for each skill area, incorporating specific language and referring to the desired program and services. Then write a second set that describes what you want without referring to specific programs and services by name. For example, assume you want your child in a regular classroom with a one-on-one aide in order to improve her reading comprehension. The ideal goal would be "Mary, in Ms. Jones's regular third grade class at Spencer School, will improve her reading comprehension, using her full-time one-on-one aide." The alternative would be "With the assistance of her one-on-one aide and by modeling her regular peers, Mary will improve her reading comprehension." Or, "With the assistance of his one-on-one aide, Tim will demonstrate understanding of all basic concepts covered in his 10th grade social studies class, including sections on government and the U.S. Constitution." If the school district does not agree that Mary or Tim should be mainstreamed, suggest implicit, instead of explicit, language. For example, the phrases "modeling her regular peers" and "in his 10th grade social studies class" in the examples above suggest (without actually saying) that Mary and Tim will be in a regular classroom.

Sample Goals for Children With Learning Disabilities

The goals developed for your child will be very specific to his or her needs, and will vary in complexity depending on your child's age and ability level.

Goals for children with learning disabilities can cover many areas. The most obvious are academic subjects, but goals may also cover social and behavior issues that relate to the learning disability or to underlying cognitive issues, such as memory and processing difficulties. Goals can also be tied to particular junior and senior high school classes. Some areas for goals for children with learning disabilities include:

- reading
- mathematics
- spelling

- language (reception and expression)
- writing
- speech production
- behavior and socialization
- visual, spatial, auditory, memory, or conceptual problems
- study skills
- fine and gross motor skills, and
- computer skills, including keyboarding.

Reading Goals

Steven will improve his phonemic awareness.

Mark will distinguish initial letter sounds, such as between cat, hat, and sat.

Meg will increase her reading comprehension.

Lucy will read a five-paragraph story at grade level, then describe the main character and list at least five specific details from the story in sequential order.

Todd will increase his reading vocabulary.

Morgan will recognize and define ten new vocabulary words each week.

Jacob will increase his reading vocabulary.

Michael will recognize and define ten new vocabulary words each week as taken from the novel or other readings in his English class.

Mathematics Goals

Jasmine will improve her ability to count.

Shawna will be able to count by ones with 95% accuracy, count by fives with 70% accuracy, and count by tens with 50% accuracy.

Linda will improve her ability to use standard measurements.

Janice will measure by inches and feet, demonstrating 80% accuracy.

Luke will understand geometric concepts.

Marcus will demonstrate understanding of the concepts of geometric shapes, area, and the difference between triangles with 80% accuracy.

Spelling Goals

Cindy will improve her spelling skills.

Rosa will spell correctly ten new spelling words per week as identified by her second grade reader.

Carrie will demonstrate 75% accuracy using a list of spelling words appropriately in a dictated sentence.

Karen will demonstrate 75% accuracy using a list of two-syllable words provided by her teacher.

Language Goals

David will improve his language skills.

Missy will be given five nouns and five verbs and will demonstrate 75% accuracy in identifying which are nouns and which are verbs.

Antoine will be given ten words and will demonstrate 75% accuracy generating short sentences with each of the ten words.

Katie will improve her pragmatic language skills.

Anna will demonstrate 70% accuracy in using sentences to convey correct information about assigned reading topics in her English class.

Writing Goals

Mana will improve her writing.

Given a topic of interest, Jocelyn will describe, in writing, the main idea and three details that support her conclusion about the main idea.

Given a short work of fiction to read, Dylan will describe, in writing, the main character, providing both physical and personality traits.

Claire will demonstrate, with 80% accuracy, the ability to print the letters b, d, l, m, n.

Goals Chart

Skill Area	Reading	Math	Emotional and psychological
Annual Goal	Josh, in his sophomore English class, will improve reading comprehension. He will demonstrate 90% comprehension of the assigned novel in his 10th grade English class	Alex, in his mainstreamed class, will master 4th-grade math skills. He will subtract a one-digit number from a two-digit number with 90% accuracy	Leah, in a class of no more than 12 students in a small and protected educational environment, will reduce her outward anger
Present Performance Level	Josh demonstrates 50% comprehension of the assigned novel	Alex subtracts a one-digit number from a two-digit. number with 25% accuracy	Leah averages five daily angry outbursts as observed
How Progress Measured	Essays assigned for homework, tests, and teacher observation	Teacher material	Teacher and therapist observation and recording
Date of Completion	June 20xx	June 20xx	June 20xx

Goals Chart, continued

Skill Area	Social-behavioral	Linguistic and communication	Self-help and independent living skills (transition services)
Annual Goal	Sarah will improve her peer relationships with the support of her aide and in a class of no more than ten students. Sara will initiate three positive peer interactions per day.	Adam, in his tri-weekly, 45-minute one-to-one speech therapy sessions, will improve articulation.	Nina will meet with the school guidance counselor each month, identify three fields of work that interest her, and arrange, with the counselor's help, to visit a workplace in each field by the end of the year.
Present Performance Level	Sara is unable to initiate positive peer interactions.	Adam produces the s, sh, and c sounds irregularly.	Nina doesn't know what she wants to do when she graduates from high school.
How Progress Measured	Teacher-aide observation and recording	Speech therapist observation and recording	Parent and guidance counselor observation
Date of Completion	June 20xx	June 20xx	June 20xx

Speech Goals

Sam will improve his speech.

Nate's speech therapist will read out loud ten words with a long "e" sound and Nate will repeat those words with 85% accuracy.

Connor will demonstrate 80% accuracy in pronouncing the "th" sound.

Sasha will demonstrate 80% accuracy in pronouncing the "gh" sound.

David will improve his language skills.

Hope will be given ten words orally and will demonstrate 75% accuracy in repeating each word.

(Goals in the area of speech may often be the responsibility of a speech and language therapist, as well as the classroom teacher or aide/ resource specialist.)

Behavior and Socialization Goals

Gemma will improve her relationships with peers and develop specific strategies for improving peer relationships.

After each negative encounter between Dana and a peer, Dana will articulate what happened and why, and discuss specific ways in which she and her peer might approach the same encounter in a more positive and constructive way.

Michelle will correctly recognize, two out of three times, body and other cues from her peers.

Bianca, with the assistance of her behavioral assistant, will recognize when she is becoming angry and will make use of the following strategies: ask to go to a "time out" area, take several deep breaths, or ask for help from an adult to discuss her anger before she acts.

Visual, Spatial, Auditory, Memory, and Conceptual Problem Goals

Keon will improve his ability to maintain visual place.

With the use of visual aids (such as a pointer or bookmark), Tre will read two sentences without losing his place, with 90% accuracy.

Maya will improve her awareness of her immediate environment.

Sonya will develop a simple map of her school, including her classroom, the main office, the gym, and outside areas, and will be able to show her classroom teacher or aide where the items on the map are and how to reach them.

Brad will improve his ability to input auditory information.

Chris will be provided a written description of classroom assignments and then, after the teacher describes that assignment orally, he will explain the assignment.

Nina will improve her short-term memory.

Given a list of five words written on the board and then erased, Dakota will name all five words with 100% accuracy.

Ben will improve his understanding of visual concepts.

Jun will be provided three sets of similar objects (such as a pen and pencil) and will describe their similarities and differences.

 FORM

A sample Goals Chart is above; a downloadable copy is available on this book's Companion Page on www.nolo.com. See Chapter 16 for the link. This chart is intended to give you a feel for what goals look like—including sample entries for present performance level and measuring progress. For more goal examples, go to this book's Companion Page on www.nolo.com. See Chapter 16 for the link.

Preparing for the IEP Meeting

Now that you've gathered your evidence and figured out what kinds of help your child will need, it's time to prepare for the IEP meeting, where you and the school district will hammer out the details of your child's special education program. Preparing for this meeting will make you a better advocate for your child, allow you to influence the IEP meeting agenda effectively, and reduce your own anxieties. In short, preparation increases your chances of success.

If you are attending your first IEP meeting, be sure to read this entire chapter. If you've done IEPs before, you'll want to at least skim this chapter. You might find some new ideas that you can put to use.

While this chapter will help you prepare for the IEP meeting, everything that you've done to this point—gathering your child's school records, having your child evaluated, drafting a blueprint, and so on—will be crucial to the success of the IEP meeting. If you've skipped any earlier chapters, you should go back and read them before reading this chapter.

Schedule the IEP Meeting

IDEA sets out rules about the IEP meeting: (20 U.S.C. § 1414(d).)

- It must be held at a time and location convenient for all parties, especially the parents. The school district cannot simply schedule a meeting on a morning when you must be at work or pick a time without your input. (34 C.F.R. § 300.322(a).)
- It must be held at least once a year.
- It must be long enough to cover all issues.

Do You Need an Interpreter?

The school district must take necessary steps to ensure that you understand the IEP proceedings, including hiring an interpreter if you are deaf or hard of hearing or if English is not your first language. (34 C.F.R. § 300.322(e).) Be sure to let the school district know in advance if you will need an interpreter at the IEP meeting.

Date of the IEP Meeting

As discussed in Chapter 4, the best time for the IEP meeting is during the spring preceding the school year for which you are developing the IEP plan. Before you choose a date, you may have to make several calls to the district administrator and your attendees to make sure all key people can attend. Don't choose a date that won't give you enough preparation time—you'll want to give yourself at least a month to get ready for the meeting.

Sample Letter Requesting More Time for IEP Meeting

Date: February 28, 20xx

To: Ms. Suzanne Warner
        Director of Special Education
        Monroe School District
        892 South 4th Street
        Salem, OR 97307

Re: Karen Jamison, student in first grade class of Drew Bergman

You indicated that we had one hour for my daughter Karen's March 14 IEP meeting. As I mentioned on February 27, I believe the issues we have to discuss will require at least two hours. It would be a hardship on our family to attend two meetings.

I will be calling you within the next few days to discuss this. I appreciate your understanding in this matter.

Sincerely,

Denise Jamison

Denise Jamison
909 Hanson Street
Salem, OR 97307
Phones: 555-3090 (home); 555-5000 (work)

cc: School Superintendent Maria Bander

When a Child With an IEP Transfers to Another School District

IDEA has very specific rules about children who transfer from one school district to another. If a child transfers within the same state, then the new school district must provide, in consultation with the parents, a free, appropriate public education with services "comparable" to that in the child's existing IEP. This comparable program will be in effect until a new IEP is developed. (20 U.S.C. § 1414(d)(2)(C)(i)(I).) If a child transfers to a different state, the same rules apply, except the comparable program will remain in effect until the new school district conducts an evaluation of the child, if the district thinks this is necessary, and a new IEP is developed. (20 U.S.C. § 1414(d)(2)(C)(i)(II).)

The term "comparable" doesn't necessarily mean "identical," but it certainly suggests something close. While you can't insist that your child be provided exactly the same program in all of its particulars, you shouldn't settle for a less effective alternative. For example, if your child had a placement in a regular classroom with a one-on-one aide two hours a week, a placement with comparable services would be a regular classroom with the same aide time, although the new aide may come only twice a week, rather than three times a week.

The new school district must also take reasonable steps to "promptly" obtain your child's records, including the written IEP and supporting documents, from the previous school district. The previous school district must take reasonable steps to respond to the request promptly. (20 U.S.C. § 1414(d)(2)(C)(ii).)

Length of the IEP Meeting

IDEA does not require the IEP meeting to last for a particular length of time. A few weeks before the meeting, you should ask the school administrator how much time has been set aside (two or three hours is common). If the administrator has allotted less time than you think is necessary, explain why you think a longer meeting is needed, particularly if it may eliminate the need for a second meeting. If the administrator insists that the time allotted is enough, put your concerns in writing and send a copy to the superintendent of schools. If you're really concerned, you can file a complaint (see Chapter 13), but there is no legal rule setting a minimum length for the IEP meeting.

Forgoing the IEP Meeting

Once you have your child's yearly IEP meeting, you and the school district can agree to make changes to the IEP without having another meeting. Instead, you can agree on a written document that changes the IEP. Both you and the school district must consent to make changes this way.

IEP meetings can be taxing and often require parents to take time off work, so this can be a good alternative—unless you feel that you need the kind of discussion that typically takes place in an IEP meeting. If you choose to skip the meeting, be sure that your written agreement to change the IEP is clear and precise. You should also ask the school district to give you a new IEP document showing the changes, as required by 20 U.S.C. § 1414(d)(3)(F).

Meeting by Conference Call or Videoconference

The IEP meeting can be held via phone or videoconference. (20 U.S.C. § 1414(f).) (If you are deaf or hard of hearing, the school district will need to set up the meeting so you can use a relay system or TTY.) Both you and the school district must agree to use one of these alternate procedures; the school district cannot set this up without your approval.

While these options offer some advantages, especially if your schedule makes it difficult to leave your home or work to attend a meeting, there are also some potential drawbacks. In a phone conference, it can be difficult to identify who is talking and to clearly hear what is being said. These procedures can also inhibit the kind of freewheeling discussion that can be very important in an IEP meeting.

The IEP Meeting Agenda

Knowing the IEP meeting agenda in advance will help you tremendously as you prepare for the meeting. IDEA requires that you be given the opportunity to participate in and understand the proceedings. (34 C.F.R. § 300.322.) It would not be unreasonable, therefore, to ask that you be told what issues will be discussed.

Most IEP meetings cover the following issues:

- eligibility, if it hasn't already been determined
- your child's current status—his or her progress, whether or not previous goals were met, and what the current evaluations indicate
- specific goals
- specific support or related services, and
- specific program, including the type, makeup, and location of the class.

At least two weeks before the IEP meeting, ask the school district special education administrator for a written agenda or a description of the specific issues that will be discussed at the meeting. After you receive it, check your blueprint to make sure that the issues you've pegged as important will be covered at the meeting. If a crucial item is not on the agenda, let the administrator know, preferably in writing.

Organize Your Materials

Having key material at your fingertips is vitally important in an IEP meeting. You don't want to be fumbling about, looking for that one report or quote that could really help. Following these steps will help you organize the mountain of material.

Review Your Blueprint and All Written Material

Your starting point in preparing for the IEP meeting is your blueprint. You should also gather all written material, such as evaluations, previous IEPs, notes and reports from your child's teacher and other staff members, work samples, and letters to and from your child's school district. These should be in your IEP binder, clearly labeled and organized for easy reference.

Review each document. Bring everything that supports your child's blueprint to the meeting. Also bring any materials that counter the negative points school district representatives are likely to raise.

Highlight Supportive Material

Go through your binder and highlight or underline every important positive or negative statement. You may want to tab certain key statements for easy reference. How do you know what statements to highlight? Focus on the following:

- Test results, staff observations, reports, and other information on your child's current educational status. Highlight descriptive statements, such as "Tom scored at the first grade level on the Brigance Test, Counting Subtest" or "Sheila has difficulty staying focused in class; any activity beyond three–five minutes can be quite taxing for her." Be sure to include all information relating to your child's specific learning problems.

- Recommendations about program placement, related services, goals, and methodology. Look for statements such as "Carla would benefit from 30 minutes of speech therapy a week" or "Jason needs to be in a small classroom in which there are minimal disturbances or acting out behavior." Make sure your material includes recommendations specific to your child's learning disability.

- The consequences of providing or not providing specific placements, services, methodologies, or other program components—for example, "Teri has significant fears about large groups and open space; placing her in a larger class on a big campus will increase those fears and put her at risk for serious emotional difficulties."

As you go through all of your materials, you probably will highlight a lot of what you read, making the task of organizing seem overwhelming. To make it manageable, use different colored highlighters or tabs to differentiate the important from the less important statements or items—such as yellow for very important, green for somewhat important, and blue for less important. You can also make second copies of all significant items and keep them in a separate section in your IEP binder.

Use an IEP Material Organizer Form

Once your material is highlighted, you should take the time to create an additional document that will help you organize and access important information. I call it, for want of a more creative term, an IEP Material Organizer Form.

FORM

A sample IEP Material Organizer Form is below; a downloadable copy is available on this book's Companion Page on www.nolo.com. See Chapter 16 for the link. Use one page for each major issue (for example, programs, related services, and methodology).

An IEP material organizer divides your written information, notes, and reports into important topics (such as related services or methodologies) keyed to your blueprint. As you can see from the sample, the form allows you to find specific information—such as an evaluation report, pediatrician letter, or key statements made by a teacher or other potential witnesses—that support or dispute your blueprint items.

You can divide the IEP material organizer into subtopics that track your child's specific needs and relate directly to your blueprint. For example, under "placement," you might have subtopics like class size, peer needs, type of class, and location of class. Under the related service of a one-on-one aide, you might add the length and number of sessions, the qualifications of the aide, and what the aide will do. Under a curricula/methodology issue such as a reading program, you might include the name of the reading program, when the reading work is done, at what pace, and how reading comprehension will be measured.

Feel free to use the IEP Material Organizer Form to subdivide issues in a way that works for you.

IEP Material Organizer Form

Use this form to track documents and people that provided support for or opposition to your goals.

Issue: Related Service: 1:1 Aide

Document Witness* Name(s)	Binder Location (if applicable)	Helps You	Hurts You	Key Supportive or Opposition Information	Rebuttal Document or Witness Name(s) (if hurts) (If none, what will you say at meeting?)
Lee Portaro (District) 2/1/xx evaluation	1C		✓	Recomm. #s 3, 6, 8, 10 (p. 8)	Brown Evaluation
Suzanne Brown 3/4/xx evaluation (independent)	1B	✓		Narrative (p. 3, ¶s 4, 5). Recomm. #s 1-7, p. 12	
Weekly Teacher Reports	1F	✓	✓	9/6/xx, 10/4/xx, 1/17/xx Support 10/14/xx, 11/5/xx, 2/2/xx Against	Portaro Report: No IEP Agreement on aide
5/2/xx IEP	1A	✓	✓	Narrative (¶s 7, 8) Against Narrative (¶s 2, 5) Support	Portaro p. 3 (¶2)
Dr. Baker (pediatrician) 1/22/xx letter	1G	✓		P. 2, Concerns for psychological impact if no aide	
Phil Anderson (tutor) 2/6/xx letter	1H	✓		Reports positive results with direct work, 1:1 work	
Karla Gamper (District psychologist)	1M		✓	Sees Scott once/month Reports no adverse psych. impact	
Student Work	1P	✓		Scott on 10/5 assignment writes "Don't understand, who cares."	

* A "witness" is someone (teacher, doctor, evaluator, tutor, psychologist) who gives an oral or written opinion regarding your child's needs at the IEP meeting.

Identify Negative Material and Prepare Rebuttals

Keeping in mind your blueprint and goals for your child, what materials hurt your position? Do test results, staff observations, or evaluator recommendations state that your child doesn't need what you want—or needs something you don't want? Do statements such as "Ben does not need any special education services now" or "Leo should be provided one hour of aide time a week" (when you believe he needs one hour per day) or "Nicole cannot function in a regular classroom at this time" (when you're in favor of mainstreaming) appear in the written materials?

Some negative material is less direct. For example, a test result may not reflect the difficulties your child is actually experiencing. If an evaluation concludes that "Sandy is at age level for reading," you might face an uphill climb in convincing the school district she needs additional help. Or a teacher's observation may undermine a placement or service you want. For example, a teacher's statement that "Steven frequently acts out and disrupts classroom activities" may make it very hard for you to have Steven mainstreamed.

Here are some ways to counter negative material:

- Look for anything that directly or indirectly contradicts a troublesome statement or report. For example, an aide's statement that "Steven's behavior is erratic, but with help he can control his behavior and focus effectively and quietly on his work" might help you convince the school that Steven can be mainstreamed.

- Look for professional opinions contrary to the school's position. Usually statements in an independent evaluation can counter school data.

- Are the qualifications of the person who wrote the unfavorable statement appropriate? If a psychologist completed the school evaluation, find out if he or she has expertise in your child's learning disability and the specific subjects of the negative comments.

- Is the negative statement crystal clear? For example, what exactly does the following observation mean: "While Jane does not need a small class, there is some indication that she has a difficult time in a large school environment"? The reference to a large school environment may indirectly support a small class placement.

- Is the unfavorable statement supported by data, testing results, or anecdotal information? If not, be prepared to point that out. For example, if a teacher says that "Mark seems to understand basic math concepts," but Mark's independent evaluation and your experience helping him with homework demonstrate that he can't perform simple multiplication and division, you should challenge the teacher's conclusion.

Use the IEP Material Organizer Form to identify negative statements and rebuttal information. As a general rule, you shouldn't bring up negative statements unless the school district raises them first.

Provide Documents Before the IEP Meeting

In preparation for the IEP meeting, have everything in your binder marked, tabbed, highlighted, and referenced in your IEP material organizer. Also, make copies of material you want to show to school district representatives at the IEP meeting. This includes anything that supports your blueprint or rebuts negative information. The material can be in any form—a letter, report, independent evaluation, teacher's report, work sample, or anything else. You may want to make a copy for each person who will attend the meeting.

Provide the school district with a copy of all material you've generated, such as an independent evaluation. Give these to the district a week before the meeting. This way, school representatives can't argue that they need more time to review your material and, therefore, must postpone the meeting.

Draft Your Child's IEP Program

IDEA requires you and the school district to develop the IEP program as a joint endeavor. This does not mean, however, that you cannot—or should not—draft key portions of what you want to see in the IEP program beforehand. Drafting some language ahead of time can help you organize your arguments and recognize any potential roadblocks to getting what you want for your child.

The major portions of the IEP program are:

- goals
- specific programs and placement
- related services, and
- other items, including curricula, methodology, and a description of the placement.

Can Your School District Write the IEP Before the Meeting?

All IEP team members, including you, must have a full opportunity to discuss all aspects of your child's IEP. This means that the district cannot just present you with a completed IEP at the start of the IEP meeting and tell you to take it or leave it. Like you, however, the district can prepare draft statements ahead of time. School district representatives will probably have discussed the IEP agenda and their thoughts on your child's needs before the meeting—and they have every right to do so.

Writing out your IEP program will not only help you learn your material, but it will also force you to think again about how to make your case for the key issues. When you prepare your draft, you can either fill out a blank school district IEP form—you should get a copy early in the process—or you can simply write out your statements so you're ready to discuss them at the IEP meeting. As the IEP team proceeds, bring up the specific components you want in the IEP program.

You can use your blueprint and IEP Material Organizer Form to help you draft an IEP and be an active participant at the IEP meeting. Chapter 11 explains how to use the IEP form and blueprint to put together the final IEP document—including how to get as much of your blueprint as possible included in the IEP.

Goals

Goals refer to the things you want your child to achieve —usually involving reading, math and language skills, social development, behavior issues, and other cognitive areas of need. Chapter 9 covers goals in detail.

Specific Programs and Placement

Program and placement refer to the exact school, class, and classroom characteristics (number and type of students, teacher qualifications, and so on) you want for your child.

EXAMPLES:
- Placement in the special day class for learning disabled students at Hawthorne School.
- Placement in a special day class for learning disabled children, no more than 12 students, students with no disruptive behaviors, and a teacher qualified to work with learning disabled students; SDC at Laurel or Martin Schools would be appropriate.
- Placement in Tina's home school, the regular third grade class.

Related Services

Related services are developmental, corrective, and other supportive services (such as transportation, one-on-one help from an aide, or special teaching strategies geared to children with learning disabilities) that your child needs to benefit from special education or to be placed in a regular class.

EXAMPLES:
- Jade needs three speech/language therapy sessions per week, each session for 30 minutes, one-on-one with a qualified speech therapist.
- Maria needs a full-time one-on-one aide in order to be mainstreamed in a regular fifth grade class, the aide to be qualified to assist Maria specifically in the areas of reading comprehension, spelling, fifth grade math, and developing positive peer relationships.

Child Profile

School district representatives might balk if you present them with a fully drafted IEP program or blueprint. Instead, you might prepare a statement for the IEP meeting that incorporates important information without necessarily triggering school district opposition. Instead of emphasizing goals, placement, and services, emphasize your child's personality and needs.

> **EXAMPLE:**
>
> Kira has a learning disability that creates problems with auditory memory, spelling, and reading comprehension. She has some emotional difficulties because of her learning disability, which appear in the forms of anxiety, fear of other children, and concern with safety. She has run off campus on a few occasions. When placed in a large class- room, her fears can be increased.
>
> Kira needs a program in which the environment is not overly active, with no children who have behavioral problems. She should not be on a large campus, which might overwhelm her. She needs to be in a classroom of no more than 15 children. She benefits from the Slinger- land method and requires instruction in simple, small steps. She needs one-on-one help with reading for at least two hours a day, and does best when this help is provided in continuous segments that are at least 30 minutes long.

This child profile combines parts of the blueprint with a description of your child and his or her needs. It is not unlike a school district's evaluation, which typically includes a narrative section describing your child. Although you will want to draft the child profile for the meeting, do not give it to the school district in advance. Focus on:

- describing your child (quiet, kind, determined, afraid)
- explaining your child's areas of need, including academic, social, and environmental, and
- weaving in references to specific service and placement needs.

This profile provides another way to incorporate important information about your child into the IEP, which will help you argue for your blueprint goals.

IDEA requires the provision of related services to be based on peer-reviewed research, "to the extent practicable." This means that the IEP team should decide which services are appropriate based on well-established data, gathered according to prevailing methods in the field—not simply on what you or the school district "feel" might work or on what the school district has to offer. Of course, there may not be peer-reviewed research on every potential related service, and there doesn't have to be. If your child needs a related service to benefit from his or her education, that service is required by IDEA—the "to the extent practicable" language protects your right to a necessary related service even if there isn't peer-reviewed research to back it up.

Other Components

Other components of the IEP program include:
- curricula, including how your child will be involved and progress in the general curriculum found in the regular classroom, and whether specific related services or special education are needed to assure your child's involvement and progress in the general curriculum
- teacher methodology and strategies (this is particularly important for children with learning disabilities—and you should be as specific as possible; see Chapters 3 and 5 for more information)
- program modifications or supports required for your child; a program modification might be allowing your child to sit at the front of the classroom or providing a classroom that is acoustically designed to minimize distracting noise
- transition plans, including vocational needs, and
- extracurricular activities such as after-school clubs, lunchtime activities, and sports activities.

RELATED TOPIC
Chapter 2 provides details on each of these components of the IEP.

Establish Who Will Attend the IEP Meeting

Under IDEA, any person with knowledge or expertise about your child may attend the IEP meeting. This includes the following people:

- you
- your child, if appropriate
- a representative of the school district who is qualified to provide or supervise your child's special education and is knowledgeable about the general curriculum
- your child's special education teacher
- your child's regular classroom teacher(s), if your child is or may be in a regular class
- a person who can interpret the evaluations and their impact on instructional strategies
- at your discretion or the discretion of the school district, other people who have knowledge or expertise regarding your child or his or her needs
- if your child is 16 or older, someone who knows about transitional services, and
- if your child received early childhood services (called Part C services in IDEA), a representative of those Part C services can be invited to the meeting at your request. (20 U.S.C. § 1414(d)(1)(B) and (D).)

Representing the School District

Finding out who will attend the IEP meeting on behalf of the school district will help you know what to expect. The school district should give you a written list of attendees, but if you are not told at least two weeks before the meeting, write the district and ask for the following information for each person who will attend:

- name
- reasons for attending
- qualifications and specific title, and
- whether he or she knows your child and, if so, in what capacity.

Prepare a list of all participants, including the positions they are likely to take on your child's special education needs.

Rules on Meeting Attendance

Certain IEP members can be excused from the IEP meeting. If the member's area of curriculum or related services will not be modified or discussed, that person does not have to attend—but only if you and the school district both agree, in writing, to excuse that person. For example, if your child receives physical therapy and that service is not going to be discussed or changed, then the physical therapist need not attend. (20 U.S.C. § 1414(d)(1)(C)(i).) Of course, if you think the service should be discussed or changed, you should insist that the member attend.

Even if someone's area of curriculum or services will be discussed or modified, that person may still be excused, but only if you and the school district consent and the absentee submits written "input into the development of the IEP" to the team before the meeting. (20 U.S.C. § 1414(d)(1)(C)(ii).) In this situation, you should be very sure that the written report is sufficient before you agree to excuse that person. Because IEP meetings are fluid, you cannot always know which issues may come up, what direction the discussion will take, or when a response or comment from a particular team member might be helpful. Proceed with caution when considering excusing an IEP attendee.

FORM
A sample IEP Meeting Participants form is shown below; a down-loadable copy is available on this book's Companion Page on www.nolo.com. See Chapter 16 for the link.

Your Child's Teacher(s)

If your child is in a regular class, his or her current teacher must attend the IEP meeting. Your child's teacher has the most information about your child's education—and the most experience with your child. The teacher may write reports about your child's progress, help write goals, be responsible for seeing that these goals are met, and make recommendations for the next school year.

The teacher can be your best ally or your worst enemy in the IEP process. Either way, the teacher is often the most convincing team member. The teacher's opinion may carry the most weight and influence how far your school district will pursue a dispute. If the teacher supports your position, you have a better chance of success. If the teacher does not, the school district may feel that it would win any due process dispute and, therefore, may decide to stand its ground at the IEP meeting.

Making sure the teacher understands your concerns and is prepared to speak frankly about them is crucial, but not always easy to achieve. Teachers work for their school districts; at times, a teacher's professional opinion may conflict with what an administrator believes to be right or feasible given budgetary or other constraints. A teacher who speaks frankly regardless of what a school administrator thinks is invaluable. It is therefore vital that you keep in contact with the teacher, ask his or her opinion, and indicate your concerns. Be specific, respectful, and always conscious of the teacher's time.

Which Teacher Must Attend the IEP Meeting

IDEA says the IEP team must include "not less than one regular education teacher of the child if the child is or may be participating in the regular education environment." (34 C.F.R. § 300.321(a)(2).) Here a key question is whether the required regular education teacher has to be the child's current regular teacher or simply any teacher. Some districts have interpreted "of the child" to mean a teacher who could be but is not currently the regular education teacher. This makes sense if the child is not currently in the regular education environment, but it doesn't make sense if the child is currently in regular education. In this case, "of the child" should be read to be the child's actual regular education teacher. If that regular education teacher does not attend the meeting, that is a procedural violation and may very well be significant (see our discussion of significant procedural violations in Chapter 2, "The Importance of 'Process").

IEP Meeting Participants

Name	Position/Employer	Purpose for Attending	Point of View
Fred Gomez	Third grade teacher, Kensington School District	Gene's teacher	Supports Gene's placement in regular class; does not think Gene needs aide
Diana Hunt	Psychologist, Kensington School District	Did evaluation	Recommends placement in special day class
Violet King	Psychologist, Independent evaluator	Did Independent evaluation	Supports regular class and aide
Jane Lim	Speech therapist, Kensington School District	Representative of school district	Agrees with need for speech therapy, but not on amount
Phil Chase	Administrator, Kensington School District	Representative of school district	No stated position

School Administrator

In most cases, someone representing the school district will attend the IEP meeting. This may be the district special education coordinator, student services director, county or regional office of education administrator, or school principal. There are all kinds of administrators, just like there are all kinds of parents. The administrator may be a kind, cooperative advocate for your child—or may be a burned-out, unpleasant bureaucrat.

You will be working with the administrator a good deal and will want to know where he or she stands on your child's IEP. Your inclination might be to ask the administrator before the meeting what position the school district will take on key issues for your child. Is it a good idea to do so? Many wise administrators will let you know when they agree with you, but will not let you know in advance if they disagree. That doesn't mean you can't ask, but it does mean you should consider the pros and cons of asking the administrator's position prior to the IEP meeting.

Pros
- You will find out if the administrator agrees with you.
- If you get an honest answer, you'll know what the administrator thinks and how determined he or she is that the IEP plan reflect that position.
- If you disagree with the answer, you may convince the administrator to change his or her mind, or you will have a better idea how to prepare for the IEP meeting.
- You may learn about options you like.

Cons
- The administrator will learn your plans and be able to counter them if the school district takes a different position.
- You may put the administrator on guard, making it difficult for you to communicate with staff, visit programs, and the like.

If you decide to ask and the administrator opposes your goals for your child, consider the following:
- If the administrator says that the school district will not support you on a particular item, he or she may have violated IDEA by making a decision before the IEP meeting. This may be the basis

of a formal complaint against the school district. (See Chapter 13.) This doesn't mean that you should "trap" the administrator into making a decision outside of the IEP meeting. But if it happens, be aware of your rights.

- If the administrator has not made a decision, you may want to share the materials you have that support your position. You might give the administrator some ideas that will allow the district to agree with you. On the other hand, this may help the administrator prepare to rebut you at the IEP meeting. You'll have to judge the odds of making the administrator into an ally versus a well-prepared adversary.

Representatives From Noneducational Public Agencies

Sometimes, representatives from public agencies (other than the school district) may attend an IEP meeting. This generally happens if responsibility for certain IEP services is entrusted to an agency other than the school district. In California, for example, the county mental health department is responsible for providing mental health services, and a representative from that agency will often be present at IEP meetings. In Vermont, a representative of an agency other than the school district will attend to discuss transition services. And if your child has been involved with the juvenile authorities, a probation officer may attend, depending on the laws in your state.

Prior to the IEP meeting, talk with any of these additional folks and find out why they are attending the meeting, what they will do there (such as report on your child), and what position (if any) they plan to take on your child's needs.

School Psychologist and Other Specialists

Depending on your child's condition and needs, other professionals may be involved in the IEP meeting, such as a school psychologist, speech/language therapist, occupational therapist, physical therapist, adaptive physical education specialist, or resource specialist. Most likely there will be someone from the district who has some knowledge about learning disabilities, including evaluations, programs, and services. Like your child's teacher, these specialists may be great allies or formidable foes.

As with the teacher or administrator, speak with the specialists ahead of time to find out their positions on key issues.

One Teacher Too Many

I once represented a child at an IEP meeting where there were a dozen school representatives, including several administrators, the school nurse, and the "teacher of the day." I asked the "teacher of the day" if he knew my client, Laura. The answer was no—he had neither met her nor knew anything about her. I asked him why he was there. Without hesitation he said he was there to "represent the teachers of the area." His involvement—or the presence of anybody else who doesn't have knowledge of your child or the relevant educational issues—would be contrary to federal policy and the purpose of the IEP meeting.

Limits on School Representatives

Are there limits to who can attend the meeting? Federal policy states that a school may not invite so many people as to make the IEP meeting intimidating. State laws and policies, too, may also speak to the issue; California, for example, requires that the IEP meeting be "nonadversarial." A meeting full of district employees may violate these rules.

IDEA requires individuals who attend the IEP meeting at the invitation of the parent or the school district to have knowledge or special expertise regarding the child. If it seems inappropriate for a particular person to attend based on this standard, notify the school in writing of your concern. State why the person is not qualified to attend, why his or her attendance is not necessary or helpful, or why his or her presence may make the meeting intimidating. If the school insists that the person attend, see Chapter 13 on filing a complaint. And at the IEP meeting, state for the record, without being personal, that you feel so-and-so should not be there. When it's time to sign the IEP plan, reiterate your objection.

IEP Meeting Attendance Objection Letter

Date: May 15, 20xx

To: Dr. Sean Gough
        Hamilton School District
        1456 Howard Avenue
        Little Rock, AR 72212

From: Eva Crane
        88 2nd Street
        Little Rock, AR 72212

Re: Amy Crane, student in third grade class of Carol Silberg

I understand that Joan Green, the district's psychologist, will be at Amy's IEP meeting. Ms. Green knows nothing about Amy and appears to have no knowledge that might be of use to the IEP team. I am formally requesting that Ms. Green not attend, unless there is some clear reason that makes her attendance appropriate and necessary for the development of Amy's IEP plan. As you know, IEP meetings can be particularly difficult for parents. We are already anxious about ours and would prefer that you not take action that will heighten our stress level.

If you insist on Ms. Green attending without a good reason, then we will file a complaint with the state and federal departments of education.

I will call you in a few days to find out your decision on this issue. Thank you for considering my request.

Sincerely,

Eva Crane

Eva Crane
88 2nd Street
Little Rock, AR 72212

FORM

A sample letter objecting to a particular person's attendance at the IEP meeting is shown above; you can find a blank downloadable copy on this book's Companion Page on www.nolo.com. See Chapter 16 for the link.

Representing the Parents

While some of the people representing the school district may support your goals for your child, you may want some or all of the following people to attend the IEP meeting on your behalf:

- your spouse or partner
- your child
- others who know your child, such as a relative or close family friend
- independent evaluators or other professionals who have worked with your child, and
- an attorney.

Contact these people well in advance to let them know the date, time, location, and likely duration of the meeting. Make sure they understand the key topics that will arise during the IEP meeting and the issues and solutions they are there to discuss. Let them know the positions of the various school representatives on the key issues. Show them copies of materials that both support and are contrary to your goals.

Remind your attendees that the IEP meeting is informal and that points of view should be stated in a positive but firm way. Disagreements can be spirited, but should remain professional and respectful.

Some of the people you ask to attend—such as an independent evaluator, a pediatrician, or a lawyer—might charge you a fee. Find out the cost ahead of time. If you can't afford to have the person stay for the entire meeting, let the school administrator know in advance that you will have someone attending who needs to make a statement and leave. Before the meeting, ask the administrator to set aside a specific time for that person to speak.

Some people you want to attend might not be able to, or you might not be able to afford to pay them to attend. In either situation, ask the person to prepare a written statement for you to read at the meeting. Some people's testimony may actually be better in writing rather than live—for example, someone who is timid or reluctant to strongly state a position in person might come across better in writing.

 RELATED TOPIC

Chapter 8 discusses items to include in a written statement from your child's doctor or other people from outside the school.

Can an IEP Meeting Be Held Without You?

Your school district has a duty to ensure that you are present at the IEP meeting. It can hold an IEP meeting without your involvement only in unusual situations, and only after following very specific procedures, including:

- notifying you early enough of the meeting to ensure you have the opportunity to attend
- scheduling the meeting at a mutually convenient time and place, and
- finding ways of including you—such as individual or conference telephone calls—if you cannot attend.

The district can proceed without you only if it can prove that it took specific steps to convince you to attend, by keeping records of its attempts to arrange a mutually agreeable time and place by phone, correspondence, and even visits to your home or workplace. (34 C.F.R. § 300.322(d).)

Parents

While work schedules or living arrangements may make attending the IEP meeting difficult, it is generally best if both parents attend, even if you are divorced or separated. If you have differences of opinion, resolve them before the IEP meeting. If you argue with each other during the IEP meeting, you will most likely damage your credibility and chances of success.

I strongly recommend that you attend all IEP meetings. By allowing the IEP to proceed without you, you are giving up your right to be involved—and increasing the chance that an IEP will be developed that doesn't meet your child's unique needs. If one of you cannot attend, be sure to prepare a strong and emotional statement for the other to read.

Sample Statement to IEP Team

To: Morgan Haversham's IEP Team

From: Claudine Haversham (Morgan's mom)

Date: March 1, 20xx

I cannot attend the March 15 IEP meeting, but I wanted you to know that I am very concerned that Morgan might be removed from her regular program. She is such a happy child now that she is mainstreamed. As her mother, I see the joy in her eyes when she gets up in the morning to get ready for school. A placement in a more restrictive environment would be devastating to my daughter. I must be frank and tell you that we will vigorously oppose any efforts to remove Morgan from her current program.

I greatly appreciate your sensitivity to Morgan's needs and your past assistance in making her educational experience a positive one.

Sincerely,

Claudine Haversham

Claudine Haversham

Your Child

A student may attend the IEP meeting if it is appropriate or if the IEP team is considering transition services for a child. (20 U.S.C. § 1414(d)(1)(B).)

When is it considered appropriate for a child to attend? A child who can speak about his or her hopes and needs may be a compelling self-advocate. But be careful—if your child is unpredictable or unsure of the importance of the meeting, you may not want to risk him or her giving a "wrong" answer. For example, you want your child to remain in his mainstreamed program. A school district representative says, "Tell me Tommy, do you want to stay in your class?" You're not going to be happy if Tommy responds, "Nope."

If your child does attend, have him or her focus on feelings and hopes. For example, "Chris, the school evaluator says you had a hard time in Ms. Shaver's class, particularly with other students. Why do you think that was so?" Be sure you know what you child's answer will be.

Bring Someone to Take Notes

Ask a friend or relative to attend the IEP meeting and take notes for you—paying careful attention to who says what regarding important items. Having a note taker can be invaluable, particularly if you anticipate a controversial meeting. See "Final Preparation," below, for information on taping the meeting.

Relatives, Friends, and Child Care Workers

It is important to limit the number of people who attend the IEP meetings—the more people in attendance, the longer the meeting will drag on. Therefore, you'd ordinarily not bring a relative, friend, or child care worker to the meeting. But if someone can present a view of your child that wouldn't otherwise be presented, you might want him or her to come. For example, if your child's regular babysitter can describe how your otherwise shy and reserved child talks nonstop about how he or she loves being in a regular class, it may be powerful testimony.

Generally, a sibling or peer of your child, particularly a young one, should not attend unless he or she is the only person who can speak to an issue or has a really powerful presence. Preparing young attendees will be very important, with focus on the sibling or peer's "feelings" about your child, rather than more formal information.

Independent Evaluators and Other Professionals

Because the conclusions reached by any independent evaluator who has tested your child will probably be instrumental in helping you secure the right services and placement, it is crucial that the evaluator attend the IEP meeting. The evaluator must be able to clearly articulate his or her professional opinion on the key blueprint items, as well as an opinion on all evaluation data. The evaluator must also be prepared to rebut contradictory information presented by the school district.

Other professionals, such as a pediatrician, private tutor, therapist, or psychological counselor, can be important witnesses on your behalf if they know your child and can speak to your child's learning disability and any other key issues affecting the IEP plan. Prepare these individuals as you would prepare an independent evaluator.

You may also have worked with a specialist, an educational consultant, or another professional to address your child's learning disabilities. This person may make the strongest case for including components specific to your child's learning disabilities in the IEP and should certainly attend the IEP meeting.

If the IEP meeting is to determine whether your child is eligible under the learning disability category, be sure that these attending individuals are prepared to discuss in detail the specific requirements for learning disabilities and how your child meets them. See Chapter 7 for reference to the specific language found in those "eligibility" criteria and how to address them.

An Attorney

If you hire or consult an attorney during the IEP process, that person can attend the IEP meeting. You can also hire a lawyer just for the IEP meeting. (See Chapter 14 for information on working with lawyers.) As a general rule, you might want an attorney at the IEP meeting if your relationship with the school district has deteriorated and you anticipate a complicated and difficult IEP meeting.

If you bring an attorney to the IEP meeting, school representatives are more likely to be on guard and less likely to speak frankly. On the other hand, if the school administrators haven't been cooperative and you feel the plan that will emerge from the IEP meeting will be harmful to your child, bringing an attorney shows that you mean business. You're much better off not using an attorney—it does change the entire experience—but if you must, then find one who is reasonable and cooperative.

If you plan to have an attorney at the IEP meeting, you should notify the school district reasonably in advance. Except in unusual situations, you will be responsible for paying your attorney, with little chance of reimbursement. (See "How Attorneys Are Paid," in Chapter 14, for information about attorney fees and reimbursement.)

Final Preparation

As you finish your IEP preparation, consider these additional recommendations.

Taping the IEP Meeting

You (and the school district) have the right to tape record the meeting. While a tape recording may be the best proof of what was said, it may have an inhibiting effect. People don't always want to make a particular statement "on the record." In addition, tape recordings are not always of great quality; participants are not always audible, and it can be hard to discern what was said and who said it.

School Resistance to Tape Recording

The U.S. Department of Education, Office of Special Education Programs, has issued several statements reinforcing the right of parents to tape record IEP meetings. If, once you get to the meeting, the special education administrator says you cannot tape record, state that the district's refusal to allow you to tape is against the law and that you will file a complaint. If tape recording is crucial, your only choice may be to postpone the meeting until this issue is resolved. See Chapter 13 for advice on filing a complaint.

If you decide to tape record, bring a good quality recorder. Bring extra tapes and batteries in case an outlet is not accessible. The school district can tape record even if you object—just as you can tape despite the objections of school representatives. If the school district tapes the meeting, you are entitled to a copy of the tape, and it will become part of your child's file—just as the district can ask for a copy of your tape.

You should notify the district in advance that you want to tape record the meeting.

Reducing Your Anxiety

You will certainly be nervous at the meeting. All parents are, so don't feel bad about it. But do give some thought to what you might do before the IEP meeting to relax: taking a walk or jogging, going out for breakfast, or any other activity that helps you settle your nerves. If you need to get a babysitter or take time off from work, set it up well in advance, so you're not scrambling the day before the meeting.

By preparing—knowing your material, completing your IEP blueprint, drafting your IEP plan, and talking to your IEP participants ahead of time—you will do much to reduce your anxiety.

IEP Preparation List

Things to do before the IEP meeting:
- Find out the date, time, and location.
- Get a copy of the school's agenda.
- Make your own agenda.
- Prepare your IEP Material Organizer.
- Draft an IEP plan.
- Find out who is attending on behalf of the school district.
- Invite and prepare your own IEP meeting participants.
- Give the school a copy of the following:
  - independent evaluations
  - documents such as reports and work samples
  - names and titles of people attending the IEP meeting, and
  - notice of intent to tape record the IEP meeting (if applicable).
- Create a meeting reminder list of items you want to be sure to remember:
  - "Make sure we read statements of Dr. Wilson and Rona (babysitter), who can't attend."
  - "Make sure Dr. Ramirez covers Lydia's physical therapy needs."
  - "We don't have to sign all of the IEP—we can object."

The IEP Meeting

Your IEP meeting is soon. You'll enter the room, sit down, put your binder on the table, take a deep breath, and do just fine. You'll do fine because being nervous is natural, the school administrator probably feels the same way, and, most important, you are prepared for this meeting. You've developed your child's blueprint and drafted an ideal IEP, supported by various documents. You're familiar with the school's IEP form, policies, programs, and services. You know who will attend the meeting and where each person stands on key issues. You have people with you who are ready to help you make your case. Even if you don't have every one of these items nailed down, you'll do your best. And if you can't reach an agreement on some or all of the IEP, you'll know your options.

RELATED TOPIC

Chapter 10 provides valuable advice on preparing for the IEP meeting. Chapter 7 gives you tips on preparing for and attending an IEP eligibility meeting.

TIP

IEP meetings are not always required. Once the annual IEP meeting takes place, you and the school district may agree to make written changes to the IEP without holding another meeting. This can save time, but there may be some risks to proceeding without a meeting. See Chapter 10 for more information on how having an IEP meeting may be the best way to advocate for your child.

Getting Started

IEP meetings can take a lot of time, so it's very important that you be prompt. In fact, you'll want to be at least ten to 15 minutes early so you can get the lay of the land, see the meeting room, and perhaps say a few words to the teacher or school administrator. Also, being early will give you the chance to talk to your participants and make sure they are clear about their roles at the meeting.

What to Bring

Bring your IEP binder and the written material you've gathered, including evaluations, letters, reports, and your IEP Material Organizer Form. Make sure you have extra copies of key documents, such as an independent evaluation.

Get the Notetaker Organized

As recommended in Chapter 10, it's a good idea to bring someone to take notes, particularly if you anticipate a controversial meeting. Make sure you provide your notetaker with paper and pens (unless he or she is using a laptop computer). Remind your notetaker to get the details on important items, particularly those that relate to your blueprint—what was said and who said it are especially important. These notes, particularly on items that you and the school district dispute, will be extremely important should you end up filing for due process (see Chapter 12) or making a formal complaint (see Chapter 13). If you do not have a notetaker, make sure you give yourself time to jot down important statements—don't hesitate to ask participants to slow down or repeat what they said, or to ask for a pause so you can complete your note taking.

Set Up the Tape Recorder

If you're planning to tape record the meeting, set up the equipment and make sure that it's working. Also, make sure you have extra tape and batteries, just in case.

 RELATED TOPIC
Chapter 10 explains how to notify the school district in advance of your intent to tape record the IEP meeting and how to deal with any dispute that arises about taping the meeting.

How the Meeting Will Begin

The IEP meeting is typically led by the school administrator responsible for special education programs, although it may be led by the school site principal, the school district evaluator, or even, on some occasions, a teacher.

Most IEP meetings begin with introductions. School representatives will probably explain their roles at the meeting. You should do the same with your participants. If, for example, a friend will take notes or an outside evaluator will present a report, make that clear.

After introductions, the administrator will probably explain the agenda, how the meeting will run, and how decisions will be made.

If the agenda is different from what you anticipated or omits issues you want to cover, bring up your concerns at the beginning of the meeting. You have the right to raise any issue you want at the IEP meeting. Also, if the agenda appears too long for the allotted time, explain that you don't think there will be enough time to cover everything and ask that certain items be discussed first. If your request is denied, do your best to keep the meeting moving forward.

Hitting the Wall

You may not be able to convince the school district that your position is correct. Unfortunately, there are times when no matter what you say or how persuasive you are, the other side won't budge. Many parents fear that if they are not able to come up with some remarkable statement that will cause the administrator to change his or her mind, there will be some dire consequence. But this is rarely the case, so just make your point and then add your concern about the unresolved matter to the addendum.

While most IEP meetings follow a certain pattern, (discussed in "Writing the IEP Plan," below), don't be surprised if yours seems to have a life of its own, going in directions you did not anticipate. Just make sure your key issues are covered before the meeting ends.

IEP Meeting Dos and Don'ts

Is there etiquette to the IEP meeting? There should be. As in any potentially difficult encounter, try to proceed in a positive way.

Dos

Do respect other opinions.

Do try to include all IEP team members in the process.

Do ask questions in a fair and direct way.

Do state your position firmly, but fairly.

Do explore ways of reaching consensus.

Don'ts

Don't interrupt.

Don't accuse.

Don't make personal attacks.

Don't raise your voice (too high).

Don't question another's motives.

You might begin by saying that you appreciate everyone's attendance, the time and energy they're spending on your child, and their professional dedication. Emphasize that you are determined to discuss all issues in a fair and thorough way, and that you are looking forward to a challenging but ultimately positive meeting in which everyone's point of view is respected.

Simple Rules for a Successful IEP Meeting

Several simple rules can help you get the most out of the IEP meeting.

Know Your Rights

IDEA was created for your child. As you undoubtedly know by now, it gives your child the right to:

- a free appropriate public education (FAPE) in the
- least restrictive environment (LRE), based on an
- individualized education program (IEP).

Parents are coequal decision makers—their opinions are just as important as everyone else's at the IEP meeting.

How to Deal With Intimidating or Nasty Comments

For many parents, dealing with teachers and school administrators in an IEP meeting can be intimidating. You don't want to (but may) hear:

I'm sorry, Mr. Walker, but you're wrong.

I'm sorry, Ms. Richards, the law doesn't say that.

Your evaluation report is incorrect.

Our policy precludes that.

Maybe they do that in another school district, but we don't.

I will not agree to that!

That's enough on that subject!

That's not the way it works.

In most cases, you can ignore these kinds of comments or make a simple response. Try to determine whether the comment is anything more than just an impolite or negative remark. If it is unimportant, say your piece and move on.

"I don't appreciate your tone of voice, Ms. Hanson. I have treated you with respect and expect the same from you. Even if we disagree, we can do it in a civil way. More important, your statement is not correct (or reasonable or productive or conducive to a positive IEP meeting)."

If the comment seems important, you may need to be more assertive.

"Ms. Hanson, I resent your comment and believe you are undermining this IEP meeting. Please understand, I will do what is necessary to ensure that my child receives the program she needs and will bring your behavior to the attention of the appropriate individuals."

If you don't feel calm and your voice is shaky, that's okay, too. Just don't yell or get overly aggressive. If necessary, you may want to raise the possibility of filing a formal complaint regarding something that seems illegal—for example, if the district won't allow you to discuss your independent evaluation. (Chapter 13 covers complaints.) But don't make a threat without first thinking it through. Do you really have grounds to file a formal complaint? Is there any validity to the school representative's comment? Know the difference between an opposing point of view or even a bad style and a patently intimidating statement or action. Is it worth alienating the school district and changing the atmosphere of the IEP meeting? In most cases, you can make your point without threatening to file a formal complaint.

RELATED TOPIC

Chapter 2 explains your child's legal rights under IDEA.

Don't Be Intimidated

You have special knowledge of your child's needs. School personnel are not the only experts. In fact, if you have documents to support each item you want in the IEP plan, you may be better prepared than the school district.

At the same time, don't automatically assume that teachers or other school officials are wrong. There are many dedicated teachers and school administrators who want to provide the best education for your child, have expertise in educating children with disabilities, and have been through this process numerous times before. This doesn't mean you won't encounter opposing opinions or perhaps even run up against someone who is just plain nasty or incorrect. But as a general rule, most of the folks in special education are there because they care for your child and want to provide the best possible educational experience.

Focus on Your Child's Needs— Not Cost or Administrative Constraints

IDEA recognizes that each child's needs are unique and, therefore, that each individual program will be different. If you can show that your child needs a specific service, such as a one-on-one assistance from an aide or two hours of occupational therapy each week, then the law requires it.

If the school district does not have the staff to provide the related service your child needs, such as a speech therapist, then the school should pay for a private therapist.

A child's needs—not cost—should influence all IEP decisions. For example, the school administrator cannot refuse to discuss or provide a service or placement because it "costs too much." Given recent budgetary problems and state deficits, you may hear this comment more frequently. Reduced funding does put school districts in a tough fiscal bind, but neither you nor your child is responsible for that. IDEA still requires a "free" and "appropriate" education for your child.

An administrator may try to get the point across indirectly, by saying something like "If we provide that service for your child, another child will not get services she needs." Don't argue the issue; simply respond with something like this:

> *Mr. Keystone, I do understand and feel the same frustration you do with existing fiscal problems, but it is wrong for you to make my child responsible for your budgetary difficulties. I won't be put in the position of making a choice between my child's needs and the needs of other children. The law is clear that we should be discussing an appropriate education for my child, not the cost.*

If you can't reach agreement, and the school district representative continues to admit that there is an administrative or budget problem, be sure you (or your notetaker) has written this down in case you end up in due process.

This is not to say that cost is never a legitimate issue. Let's say you want your child in Program X and the school offers to put your child in Program Y, which is less costly for the district. You're unable to reach an agreement and decide to resolve the matter through due process. If the district can prove Program Y is appropriate for your child, it will likely prevail at the due process hearing. You won't win a fight for the ideal program when an appropriate one is available.

TIP

Don't describe the program you want as the "best" or "optimum" or "maximum." The school district might use these types of statements as evidence that you want more than the "appropriate" education to which your child is entitled under IDEA. If you feel that a program or service offered by the school isn't right, characterize it as "inappropriate"—this will signal that you don't think the school district is meeting its legal obligations. And always remember to characterize your desired program as appropriate, not "best."

Know When to Fight and When to Give In

Understanding the IEP process and having a clear, step-by-step strategy does not guarantee that every issue will be resolved as you want. It is important to realize when you don't have a case. You may be fully prepared, do a superb job in the IEP meeting, and still not have enough evidence to support your position. Knowing the strength of your case will help you figure out when to fight and when to concede.

Fight for the crucial issues and be more flexible on others. For instance, goals and test protocol may be important, but, ultimately, the related services, placement, and methodology are what matter in your child's education. Spending half an hour fighting over the wording of one goal is probably a waste of time; spending half of the meeting on a major issue like placement is probably worth it.

Ask Questions

You should always feel comfortable asking questions—and there will undoubtedly be times during the IEP meeting when you need more information or clarification. There are several very good reasons to ask questions: to obtain basic information, to persuade someone of your position, or to question a blanket assertion.

Obtain Basic Information

During the IEP meeting, many technical terms will be used. If you don't understand something, ask what it means. It's better to ask—even for the tenth time—than to proceed without understanding.

Most important, find out what these terms mean for your child. Knowing that your child scores at the 42nd percentile on the Wechsler is useless unless it tells you something about your child's abilities and opportunities to improve.

Persuade

Asking questions can be an effective way to persuade people that your position is right and theirs should be changed. State your questions positively, such as "Do you [IEP team members] agree with the recommendations on page eight of Dr. Calderon's report?" or "Ms. Porter, do you agree that Amy should be placed in a regular eighth grade class with a one-on-one aide?"

You may need to establish agreement on preliminary matters before asking these kinds of big questions.

> EXAMPLE: You want a particular IEP member to agree with you on placement. You realize that you must first establish agreement on the evaluation supporting that placement. You first ask, "You read Dr. Harper's report. She states that Carolyn needs, and I am quoting, 'a quiet environment in which there are no behavioral problems or acting out by other students.' Do you agree with Dr. Harper?" The IEP member agrees and you follow up by asking, "Given Dr. Harper's report and our desire that Carolyn be placed in the special day class at the Manning School, do you agree with that placement?"

Someone may chafe at being asked such a pointed question and may feel like they are being cross-examined. One good way to respond would be to say, "I certainly don't mean to cross-examine you and appreciate your reminding me of that. Please understand that I am not a lawyer but a parent. What is important to Carolyn is not the nature of the question but the answer. I will certainly try not to be too formal; would you like me to try to put it another way?"

Challenge Blanket Assertions

Nothing is more frustrating for a parent than hearing lines like these:
- "Unfortunately, we are not allowed to discuss that issue."
- "We don't provide that service."
- "That's not our policy."
- "Sorry, but we can't do that."
- "That's not the law."

If an assertion seems illegal or illogical, ask what it's based on. If the administrator says something vague like "It's our policy," "It's the law," "It's our best judgment," or "It's the way things are," keep asking why. Request a copy of the law or policy.

Sample Responses to School District Statements

Here are some common statements made by school districts at IEP meetings and how you might respond.

Statement: "I don't have the authority to authorize that aide/service/material."

Response: The law requires that a person be at the IEP who has the authority to authorize a service that the IEP team agrees on. You might respond that "IDEA requires that decisions about what services will be provided need to be made at the IEP meeting, and someone with authority needs to be at the IEP meeting."

Statement: "The district supervisor preapproved only one hour of speech therapy/occupational therapy/one-on-one aide per week."

Response: A predetermined IEP decision is an absolute violation of the IDEA (see Chapters 2 and 11). You might respond "Are you saying even though my child needs two hours of speech therapy and we may agree on that, you are not going to provide it?" Make sure you keep detailed notes on who said this and when.

Statement: "You can't add your comments to the IEP form because it's a school document."

Response: This is absolutely contrary to the IEP process and the law that creates the IEP. You might say: "Please tell me where it says that in the law. As a parent, and to be a fully involved decision maker and participant in the IEP, I have a right to see that my thoughts, requests, comments are in the IEP. You don't have to agree with them and you can make it clear on the IEP form that these are only my thoughts."

If possible, refer to your documentation. For example, the district administrator says that, as a general rule, the district doesn't provide more than two hours of a related service per week. An evaluation states that your child needs three hours. Point that out and ask how the district's rule complies with IDEA, which requires that the specifics of a service be determined by the IEP team.

The administrator may say something like "Mrs. Wasserman, that is just the way it is and I won't respond any further to that question."

You'll want to follow up with something like "I'm sorry you won't answer my question; it is a fair and important question and I plan to ask your superintendent or the school board to answer it." If the issue is crucial to your child's education, you may want to file a complaint, as discussed in Chapter 13.

Or the school district may not agree with you on an important IEP component. For example, you feel there is clear support for a specific placement, but the administrator disagrees. Ask for a detailed explanation of the school district's reasoning, supported by appropriate materials.

Note any unresolved matter on your addendum. (See "Parent Addendum Page," below.)

Pay Attention to What's Written on the IEP Form

Make sure you know what statements are entered onto the IEP document and voice any objections immediately—whether it's about a particular goal or a general statement made on the narrative page of the IEP form. (We discuss the narrative page later in this chapter.)

Keep Your Eye on the Clock

Whether the school has allotted two hours or five hours for the IEP meeting, keep track of time. If you are 45 minutes into a 90-minute meeting and the IEP team is still talking in generalities, you should say, "We need to move on to a specific discussion of Cora's goals, placement, and related services."

A good school administrator will keep the meeting on schedule. If not, you should take the lead. Be ready to suggest moving on to the next topic when the discussion on a particular issue has gone on long enough.

Don't Limit Your Options to All or Nothing

At some point during the IEP meeting, you may realize that you will not reach agreement on all issues. For example, you feel your child needs at least two sessions with a reading specialist each week, one hour per session. The district offers one hour-long session. You've done your best to persuade them, to no avail. What do you do?

The school district cannot present you with a "take-or-leave-it" position—for example, "We've offered help from a reading specialist once a week. You want it twice a week. You can either agree with us and sign the IEP or disagree and go to a hearing." Furthermore, the school district cannot insist that you give up your right to due process—for instance, "We've offered help from a reading specialist once a week and that's all we'll offer. We'd advise you to sign the IEP form and not make waves."

Your best bet is to make sure the IEP document specifically states that you agree that a specific service is needed—or that a particular placement is appropriate—and that your child will receive at least what the school district has offered. Then make sure your opinions are reflected on the parent addendum page.

There are no magic phrases you need to use, no legal language required by IDEA. State that you are accepting the district's "offer" but then indicate exactly why the offer falls short and what you believe would be appropriate for your child. For example, your district offers your daughter one hour a week of one-on-one assistance in her 11th grade social studies class so she can meet her reading and language goals. You feel she needs two hours a week. You should state clearly on the IEP (probably on the addendum page) that "Nicole needs two hours a week of one-on-one assistance in her 11th grade social studies class. We have accepted the district's offer of one hour per week, but we do *not* agree that she only needs one hour per week. We reserve the right to go to due process and seek an additional hour of assistance per week."

Don't Be Rushed Into Making a Decision

If you're on the fence about a particular issue, don't be rushed into making a decision. Ask for a break and go outside for a few minutes to think about what the school has offered. If you are concerned that pausing on some issues may mean delay on others, ask for a day or two to make up your mind on a particular issue so that the IEP team can proceed with other items. This may require a second IEP meeting, unless you eventually agree with the rest of the IEP team on the issue. If an item is that important, however, then a second meeting is worth the time. Sometimes, it's easier to figure out what to do once you have gone home and had a chance to think things over.

Become Familiar With Your School's IEP Form

You should get a copy of your school district's IEP form before the IEP meeting. While forms vary, they will almost always have sections on the following:

- present levels of educational performance
- goals (and evaluation procedures)
- related services
- placement/program
- effective dates of the IEP
- summer school or an extended school year, and
- a narrative page or pages for recording various important statements (such as comments on evaluations) or keeping a running account of the meeting discussion. (This important part of the IEP is described in "Writing the IEP Plan," below.)

In addition, IEP forms typically include the following types of information:

- identifying information, such as your child's name, gender, date of birth, grade, and school district, and parents' names and addresses
- the type of IEP (eligibility or annual review) and date of the IEP meeting
- your child's eligibility status and disability category
- the amount of time your child will spend in a regular or mainstreamed program, if applicable
- your child's English proficiency, and
- signatures of IEP team members and parents.

The IEP team may include other important information in the IEP, such as a specific curriculum or teaching methodology, a specific classroom setting, peer needs, or a child profile.

RELATED TOPIC

You can find a sample IEP form on this book's Companion Page on www.nolo.com. See Chapter 16 for the link.

The IEP Form and Your IEP Blueprint

The IEP Form itself and your blueprint (your list of desired program components) will have a similar structure, but won't be identical.

Most of your blueprint items, such as related services and placement, have a corresponding section in the IEP. In some cases, however, you may find that the IEP form does not have space for all the details you included on your blueprint. For example, the IEP form will allow you to specify the kind of program or placement—such as a regular class or special day class—but might not provide space for the details of the placement— such as peer numbers and makeup, classroom environment, and school environment. Other blueprint items, such as methodology and curricula, may not have a corresponding section on the IEP form. And the school administrator may not be familiar with a blueprint like yours.

As you prepare for the IEP meeting, keep in mind that while the IEP Form may not reference all of your blueprint items, IDEA allows the IEP team to discuss and agree on any element it feels is necessary for your child. These types of details can go on the IEP narrative page or, if the school disagrees, a parent addendum page.

Writing the IEP Plan

Usually, someone from the school district will write the IEP plan as the meeting progresses, by checking off boxes on the form, filling in specific sections, and completing a narrative or descriptive page.

You should frequently ask to see what has been written, to make sure it accurately reflects what was discussed or agreed upon. You may want to check every 30 minutes or so, with a simple "Excuse me, but can we break for just a few minutes? I want to see what the IEP looks like so far." If 30-minute breaks seem forced, ask to review the form each time you complete a section. Pay special attention to the narrative page—this will be more subjective than other parts of the IEP.

Your goal is to create an IEP—including the narrative page, goals, placement, and related services—that reflects your point of view.

Under IDEA, the written IEP must include:

- your child's current levels of academic and functional performance
- how your child's disability affects his or her involvement and progress in the general curriculum
- measurable annual goals, including academic and functional goals designed to meet your child's needs
- a statement of the special education, related services, and supplementary aids and services your child will receive, as well as program modifications necessary for your child to meet annual goals and be involved and progress in the general curriculum
- a description of how your child's progress toward those goals will be measured, and when and how that progress will be reported to you
- a statement of any accommodations your child will need when taking state or other systemwide assessments and tests
- if your child is 16 or older, a transition plan
- if your child will not be in a regular classroom or program, an explanation of the reasons for this placement, and
- a description of the program where your child will be placed.

Child's Current Educational Status

If your child is presently enrolled in school, the IEP team will review your child's current educational status, IEP goals, program, and related services. Your child's current status may be reflected in testing data, grades, and teacher reports or observations. If this is an eligibility IEP meeting, the team will review evaluation data; it will do the same every three years (or more frequently), when your child is reevaluated. Discussion of your child's current status may be broad or specific. It may occur at the beginning of the IEP meeting or as you review specific items, such as goals, for the upcoming year.

What goes onto the IEP about your child's current situation is very important. For example, if you are concerned about the current program, you won't want the IEP narrative page to state that "Sam's placement has been highly successful this past year." If such a statement is made and entered onto the IEP document—perhaps on the narrative page—be sure to object, with something like "I'm sorry, but I don't think that statement is accurate, and here's why." Perhaps the ensuing discussion will result in a change of this statement. If not, say, "I certainly cannot agree with it. It should not be on the IEP form as our consensus." If the district insists, then you will have another item for your addendum.

Evaluations

A school district representative (most likely the evaluator) will either read or summarize the school district's evaluation. If the evaluator starts reading the report, ask him or her to synthesize the salient points rather than spend precious time reading it verbatim—especially if you have already seen a copy of the report.

This may be a good time to use your IEP Material Organizer (see Chapter 10) to point to other documents—such as previous IEP plans, an independent evaluation, other reports, teacher notes, and the like—to support or contradict the school evaluation.

If you haven't already introduced the independent evaluation, you will do so once the district has finished presenting its evaluation. You or your evaluator should provide a synopsis of the report, focusing on:

- the evaluator's credentials
- the reason for the evaluation
- the tests used
- the key conclusions regarding the testing, and
- the specific recommendations.

Be sure to highlight the test results and recommendations not covered in the school evaluation. This is also the time to introduce any other supporting material, including letters, work samples, and other professional opinions.

Most IEP forms refer to the evaluations on the narrative page. The IEP plan might specify the sections, results, and/or statements in the evaluations on which you all agree. Even if there is only one statement you all agree on, make sure it gets into the IEP document if it is essential to your child's needs. If the person drafting the IEP plan includes something from an evaluation with which you disagree, make sure your objections are noted.

Sometimes, the evaluation reports are attached to the IEP document. This can work in your favor if you agree with the report. Attaching an evaluation suggests that its findings and recommendations have been incorporated into the IEP.

If an evaluation is not attached or there is some disagreement over the accuracy or usefulness of the evaluation, the narrative page should specify what parts of the evaluations are included or excluded.

> **EXAMPLES:**
> - The IEP team agrees with Sections 1, 2, 4, 6, and 8 of the school evaluation and Sections 3, 5, 9, 10, and 12 of the independent evaluation and incorporates them into the IEP.
> - The IEP team disagrees with the rest of both evaluations and does not incorporate them into the IEP.

You can use the parent addendum page to state the reasons for your disagreement.

Goals

If this is not your child's first IEP, the IEP team will next review the previous year's goals. This discussion is likely to lead to one of four different outcomes:
- You and the school district agree that the goals were met.
- You and the school district agree that certain goals were met, but others were not.

- You and the school district agree that the goals were not met.
- You and the school district disagree on whether the goals were met.

Although you won't be working on placement and services during this part of the meeting, keep in mind that your child's success or failure in meeting the goals will likely affect whether the placement and services are changed. For example, if your child met the goals, perhaps it means the current placement is correct and should continue. Or maybe it means your child is ready to be mainstreamed. If your child didn't meet the goals, he or she may need a smaller class. Or maybe the placement is fine, but more tutoring (a related service) is in order.

The Pros and Cons of Quantifying Educational Progress

Goals frequently refer to numbers to determine whether your child (and the school district) has succeeded—for example, your child might have a goal that says "Mimi will spell three-syllable words with 85% accuracy." These numbers are important indicators of your child's educational health. On the other hand, not all educational goals are measurable. Of course, once you set a numeric goal, your child should strive for it—and you and the school district should fully support that effort—but failing to hit that mark is not necessarily a sign that your child isn't learning. None of us learn in a straight line; progress often takes those classic two steps forward, one step back. And Mimi should not feel she has failed because she spelled those three-syllable words with 78% accuracy.

Once you finish reviewing the previous goals—or if this is your child's first time in special education—it's time to write goals for the coming year. Chapter 9 explains how to draft goals—and recommends that you do so in advance. The school representatives will probably have also prepared some ahead of time.

Remember, you want the IEP team to agree on goals that support the placement and related services you want for your child.

What if you disagree with each other's goals? Try these tips:

- Do your best to convince school members of the IEP team that your goals are consistent with the recommendations made by others, such as the evaluator, the classroom teacher, or your child's aide.
- Ask school members what they specifically disagree with in your goals.
- If you can't agree on all goals, try to reach consensus on some— half a loaf is better than none.
- If attempts to compromise fail, suggest dropping all predrafted goals and coming up with something new.

If you and the school representatives disagree about past or future goals, be sure the IEP document clearly states that. At the very least, record your concerns on your parent addendum.

Transition Services

If your child is 16 or older, the IEP team must discuss transition services, including advanced courses and vocational classes. The IEP team does have the authority to provide transition services before the child reaches 16 if the team determines that is appropriate. (34 C.F.R. § 300.320(b).) There's that vague word again—"appropriate." How do you prove that your child needs transition services earlier than at 16? As with any desired service, you should secure support for that service, in writing or in person. You must show that your child requires assistance with his or her work or educational plans, and that he or she can't wait until age 16. For example, if you have evidence that your child will require significant help in developing independent living skills, you may be able to show that starting training at age 16 may be too late. Or, if your child appears to be heading toward a certain job or educational placement after high school, you may be able to show that he or she will need help as soon as possible to ensure those possibilities.

The IEP team should consider strategies to assist your child in evaluating, securing information about, and taking steps to participate in vocational, employment, independent living, and post–high school educational plans. Your child can investigate transition services in a variety of areas, including looking at potential jobs, learning how to function in the community, accessing other agencies that will provide support for adults with disabilities, and researching college opportunities.

Once your child reaches the age of 16, the IEP must include a statement about his or her transition needs, as those needs relate to your child's courses of study. This means that the team must indicate what advanced placement or vocational courses or classes are necessary to meet your child's unique educational and career needs. Whether your child wants to go to college, do clerical work, or look into computer jobs, his or her studies must provide for ways to explore these possibilities.

The IEP must also include a statement about necessary transition services. This means that the IEP must provide for services that will help your child develop the skills necessary to meet his or her vocational, academic, or independent living plans for the future (after high school ends). Such transition services might include help in developing the skills to create a resume, perform certain jobs, access and use community services (such as public transportation), and find out about job training or college programs.

The IEP must also indicate whether there are noneducational agencies that might provide additional support to your child (such as the department of health or job training agencies), and how your child can access the services these agencies provide. If one of these "outside" agencies fails to provide the transition services described in the IEP, the IEP must reconvene to "identify alternative strategies" to meet the transition objectives of your child as described in the IEP. (34 C.F.R. § 300.324(c).)

As you prepare for the IEP meeting, talk to your child's teacher and other professionals about his or her vocational, college, and independent living skill needs. If your child wants to go to college, what skills will that require, and what institutions or agencies might be available to help your child develop those skills? If your child plans to look for work after high school, what are his or her vocational interests, and how can your child get the training and experience necessary to get into those fields? If your child needs help developing independent living skills, such as using transportation, balancing a checkbook, or keeping house, what kinds of school activities will help?

Related Services

Your discussions regarding related services (and placement, covered in the next section) are likely to generate the most debate. You and the school district may have very different notions of the type and amount of related services that are appropriate for your child. Your child cannot be denied related services because of the school's monetary or administrative constraints. However, the school district may try to argue that your child needs fewer services, or less expensive services, in an effort to stay within its budget.

Under IDEA, related services are the developmental, corrective, and other supportive services, including transportation, that a disabled child needs to benefit from special education. They also include the services your child needs to be educated in a regular classroom. Children with learning disabilities use a wide variety of related services, including one-on-one classroom assistance (for reading, spelling, or math), language and speech therapy, occupational and physical therapy (for fine and gross motor skills), and psychological counseling. Remember, the burden is on the school district to demonstrate that your child cannot achieve satisfactorily in a regular classroom even with the use of some related services. (See Chapter 2.)

Independent evaluators and others who support your position should be prepared to state their opinions in detail—for example, "Given Hank's difficulty in language and reading, he needs to work one-on-one with an aide trained in a multisensory approach for 30 minutes, three times per week." If someone is not there to make this statement, be prepared to point to written materials that show your child's need for the particular related service.

The related services section of the IEP document requires more detail than any other. It's not enough to say "Hank will be assisted in a multi-sensory approach"; the IEP team should specify how often (three sessions per week), how long (30-minute sessions), the ratio of pupils to related service provider (one-on-one), and the qualifications of the aide (trained in a multisensory approach to developing language and reading skills).

The more vague the description, the more flexibility the school district has to give your child something less than (or different from) what he or she needs. Assistance from a one-on-one aide two to three times a week is very different from assistance three times per week. Try to avoid terminology such as "or," "about," "to be determined," or "as needed." When in doubt, be specific; it's that simple.

IDEA now requires the provision of related services to be based on peer-reviewed research "to the extent practicable." (34 C.F.R. § 300.320(a)(4).) Of course, most parents want their children to receive services that are based on sound research. On the other hand, the school district cannot refuse to provide a necessary service just because there is no such research available. The phrase "to the extent practicable" creates a way around the research requirement.

Some advocates worry that this language creates a rationale for school districts to avoid providing related services: "Sorry, we'd like to provide it, but there is no peer-based research." While this fear is real, the bottom line is that IDEA requires the school district to provide a related service if your child needs it, whether there is peer-reviewed research available or not.

Some parents have argued that the "peer-reviewed research" requirement means that districts must provide related services that are heavily reviewed. For example, in several cases involving children with autism, parents have claimed that districts must use "Applied Behavior Analysis" (ABA) because it is strongly supported by peer review. (ABA focuses on systematically applying learning principles, particularly those focused on improving social behavior.) Hearing officers have ruled that there is no specific right to ABA, and that school districts can use other approaches. The mere presence of peer reviews does not require adoption of a certain approach, nor does the absence of such reviews necessarily mean that an approach is not appropriate. (*Joshua A. ex rel. Jorge A. v. Rocklin Unified School Dist.* (E.D. Cal. 2008).)

The bottom line about peer based research: IEP decisions should be based on well-reasoned research, but ultimately, as one court said, the student's IEP team retains flexibility to devise an appropriate program in light of the available research. (*Ridley Sch. District v. M. R.*, 680 F.3d 260 (3d Cir. 2012).)

Other Agencies May Be Responsible for Providing Some Related Services

In some states, certain related services, such as mental health services or occupational or physical therapy, are the responsibility of a public agency other than the school district. Still, these services should be discussed at the IEP meeting, and the school district is responsible for making sure representatives of those other agencies attend the meeting. These other agencies have the same responsibilities as the school district—and therefore the same role to play at the meeting—regarding the services they must provide.

Placement or Program

Placement or program refers both to the kind of class (such as a regular class, special day class, or residential placement) and to the specific location of the program (such as a regular fifth-grade class at Abraham Lincoln School). Placement or program, sometimes referred to on the IEP form as the instructional setting, is central to a successful IEP and an effective educational experience. Placement or program is most often some kind of public program, but IDEA requires placement in a private school if there is no appropriate public option. Placement or program is generally the last item discussed at the IEP meeting.

As explained in Chapter 2, IDEA requires that your child be educated in the "least restrictive environment." This means that to the maximum extent appropriate, children with disabilities are to be educated with children who are nondisabled. Special classes, separate schooling, or other placements that remove children with disabilities from a regular class are appropriate only if the nature or severity of the disability is such that education in a regular class would not be satisfactory, even with the use of supplementary aids and services.

There is no absolute rule that your child must be mainstreamed. For many students with learning disabilities, however, a mainstreamed program will be the least restrictive environment—and the school district has a substantial burden to prove that a different placement would be appropriate.

If you don't want your child mainstreamed, point out that although the law favors regular classroom placement, individual need determines whether a particular placement is appropriate for a particular child. Courts have clearly stated that there is no prohibition to placing a child in a nonregular class—in fact, if a child needs such a placement, it is by definition the least restrictive environment. (See *Geis v. Board of Education,* 774 F.2d 575 (3d Cir. 1985) and *Stockton by Stockton v. Barbour County Bd. of Educ.,* 25 IDELR 1076 (4th Cir. 1997)—for more on court cases and legal research, see Chapter 14.)

If you want your child mainstreamed, you should emphasize your child's basic right to the least restrictive environment. You should also emphasize your child's right to be educated as close to home as possible, in the school the child would attend if not disabled. (Current IDEA regulations at 34 C.F.R. § 300.114–116.) Ultimately, the burden is on the school district to prove that your child should be removed from a regular classroom.

School representatives may be prepared to discuss a specific program in a named school. Or, they may propose a kind of class, such as a special day class, but want to leave the specific location up to the school administration. If this happens, object. The IEP team should decide both the kind of class (such as a special day class for language-delayed children) and the specific location (such as a regular class at King School).

More likely, you and the school administrator will know before the meeting where each of you stands on placement. Still, an open-minded IEP team should fully discuss your child's placement needs. The school administrator will probably state that the IEP team has reviewed your child's record, agreed on goals, resolved related services, and decided that a particular placement is called for—such as, "We recommend placement in the special day class at John School."

Keeping an Open Mind at the IEP Meeting

Your school district should approach the IEP meeting with an open mind, willing to discuss and decide all parts of your child's education plan. When a school district has made up its mind in advance on critical aspects of the plan, such as the class your child will be placed in or the related services that will be provided, the school is hardly fulfilling its obligation. Under the IDEA, a school's premeeting, entrenched position is known as a "predetermination," and it's not allowed.

School districts certainly have the right, as do you, to investigate, consider, and even have opinions about a particular placement, service, or methodology. But when the district has fully made up its mind about what should be in the IEP, it has denied the child's family the opportunity for meaningful input in the IEP decision-making process. (*Doyle v. Arlington County Sch. Bd.*, 806 F.Supp. 1253 (E.D. Va.1992).) For example, take the district administrator who said to a client of mine at the beginning of an IEP meeting, "We believe Mary should be placed in the Jefferson school program and we will not place her in the Wilson school program." Or, consider the school whose attitude at the meeting clearly conveys that the district views any discussion as a mere formality. Though less blatant, such an approach is also evidence of predetermination.

Proving predetermination can be difficult, particularly if the school district says or writes little or nothing before the IEP meeting, and nothing about the district's statements or attitude in the meeting itself is obvious. This is another reason why you should always keep a record of what is said to you, by whom, and when, whether in or out of an IEP meeting. Put together, these tidbits may add up to impressive evidence of predetermination (see Chapter 8).

If you think your district has predetermined an IEP issue, you should file for due process. For example, if you think your child should be placed in a private school and a district employee remarks, before the IEP meeting, that the district does not place children privately, the nature, extent, and impact of those comments would be an issue for a due process mediation or hearing. If, on the other hand, your district has an official policy that clearly predetermines an IEP issue, you should file a complaint (see Chapter 13). If you are not sure which route to take, it is wise to do both.

If you disagree with the administrator's conclusion, state your preference and refer to supportive materials—particularly items that are very persuasive about placement. Then ask (or have your independent evaluator ask) pointed questions, such as:

Ms. Parton, you said Betsy should be placed at Johnson School in the special day class. We believe Betsy should be placed in the regular class at Thompson School with a one-on-one aide. The evaluation by Dr. Jang recommends that placement specifically, and Betsy's current teacher agrees. Can you explain why you disagree?

If the school administrator is not persuaded or does not adequately answer your question, be direct and frank:

With all due respect, I think your answer is vague and does not address the specifics in Dr. Jang's report and your own teacher's comment about Betsy's readiness for a regular classroom. I feel very strongly about this, and we will go to due process on the issue of placement if we have to. I also think that with the documentation and the law on main-streaming, we will be successful in a due process hearing. I really feel like going to hearing is a bad use of school resources and will only make the ultimate move more expensive for you. I just don't understand—given the evidence—why you want to put me and my wife, your district personnel, and, most important, our child through that.

Narrative Page

The narrative page is the place to record information that can't be included by way of a checkbox or is too long for the space provided on the IEP form. The narrative page can include information on any topic covered at the meeting, whether on the IEP form or not. Here are some examples of narrative page statements.

EXAMPLES:

- The IEP team agrees that the school district and outside evaluations are complete and appropriate, and are incorporated into the IEP.
- The IEP team incorporates the child profile provided by Steven's parents into the IEP.
- The IEP team agrees that Melissa needs a school environment in which there are no behavioral problems.
- The IEP team agrees that Henry is beginning to show signs of emotional distress; the classroom teacher will report on a weekly basis to the family about any signs of such distress. The district psychologist will observe Henry in class. The IEP team agrees to meet in three months to review this matter and to discuss the possible need for more formal evaluation or the need for additional related services.
- The IEP team agrees with the recommendations made by Dr. Jones on page 4 of her report.
- Ms. Brown [Destiny's teacher] is concerned about Destiny's lack of focus.
- The IEP team agrees with recommendations 1, 2, 5, 7, and 9 made by Dr. Valdez on page 4 of her report.
- Aiko's parents expressed concern about class size.

Sometimes, the person recording the IEP document may write something that the parents and school personnel disagree about. Make sure the narrative is changed to reflect your disagreement or to indicate that the statement reflects only the point of view of the school personnel. Basically, you don't want the narrative to imply agreement when there is none.

Check the narrative page throughout the meeting to see what has been written. If something is included that you disagree with or something important was left out, raise the issue: "We all agreed that William had a successful year at Kennedy High School and that his mainstreaming helped his sense of self. That sentiment should be included in the narrative page—it is a vitally important bit of information about William."

> ### Include a Child Profile in the IEP Plan
>
> Chapter 10 suggested that you create a child profile to give school officials a perspective on your child beyond numbers and test results. The school administrator may question whether law or policy allows a child profile to be included in the IEP document. IDEA does not prohibit it, so nothing prevents the IEP team from discussing and including a child profile.
>
> Emphasize that your statement about your child will help the school staff implement the goals, and for that reason it should be included in the IEP document. If the school administrator disagrees, ask specifically what is objectionable. Try to convince the team of the importance of the profile. If the administrator continues to refuse, use the parent addendum to include it.

How Decisions Are Made at the IEP Meeting

How does the IEP team make an actual decision on IEP components? Do you vote? IDEA establishes no set method for reaching agreement, so it's really up to the IEP team. The school administrator may not even raise the question of how agreement is reached.

You can request voting, but in most IEP meetings, the team tries to reach consensus through discussion. Asking members to vote may be self-defeating—there are usually more folks on the school district's side of the table than on yours. No matter how decisions are reached, you are an equal partner in the process. If you don't agree on an item, there is no consensus and, therefore, the team has not reached a decision on that topic.

Sign the IEP Document

At the end of the IEP meeting, the school administrator will ask you to sign the IEP document. School officials will be signing the form as well. You don't have to sign the IEP document on the spot. You may want to take it home and return it in 24 hours. This will give you time to decide whether you agree or disagree with each aspect of the plan. It will also give you time to record your concerns coherently on a parent addendum.

Of course, if you have reached complete agreement with the school representatives on all issues and don't need time to mull anything over, go ahead and sign. Read the document carefully, however, to make sure the statements and information accurately reflect the IEP team's intentions. Also, make sure that the team covered everything on your agenda and resolved all important issues.

If you do take the IEP document home, be sure that other participants have already signed off on each item to which they agreed.

Every IEP form has a signature page with a variety of checkboxes, including:

- a box to indicate you attended
- a box to indicate that you were provided your legal rights
- a box to indicate your approval of the IEP document, and
- a box to indicate your disapproval.

There may also be boxes to show partial approval and indicate that you do or do not plan to initiate due process.

Make sure to check the right boxes. If you partially agree, check the partial agreement box—but carefully and clearly write next to it: "Approval in part only; see parent addendum."

You must state your position clearly on the IEP. There are no legally required phrases to use—plain and direct English will do fine.

Full Agreement

Congratulations! Check the correct box and sign the form.

Nearly Full Agreement

It's possible that the IEP team will agree on all important items concerning related services, methodology, and program or placement, but disagree on some secondary issues, such as goals or statements in an evaluation. In this situation, you have two choices:

- You can check the box to indicate your approval and sign your name. This might make sense if the issues on which you disagree are minor and you want to foster a good relationship with the school district.

- You can check the box to indicate partial approval, list the items you dispute (on the signature page if there's room or on the parent addendum), and sign your name.

Sample

Date: April 24, 20xx

Signature: *Lucinda Crenshaw*

I agree with all of the IEP except for:

- items 3, 4, and 6 on the district's evaluation
- goal numbers 2 and 5.

You Don't Have to Accept "All or Nothing"

Remember that the school district cannot present you with an "all or nothing" choice. For example: "We're offering two sessions of occupational therapy. If you don't agree to the two sessions, there will be no occupational therapy for your child." You can agree to the two sessions without giving up your right to seek more.

Partial Agreement

In this situation, you agree on some, but not all, of the big issues (related services, methodology, and program or placement). You should check the box to indicate partial approval, state that your disagreements are on the parent addendum, spell out your disagreements on the parent addendum, and sign your name.

Sample

Date: April 24, 20xx

Signature: *Lucinda Crenshaw*

I agree with all of the IEP except for those items listed on the parent addendum page, designated as "Attachment A" and attached to the IEP.

Nearly Total Disagreement

In this case, you don't agree on any of the major items concerning related services, curricula-methodology, and program or placement, but do agree on certain goals, parts of the evaluation, and minor items. Again, you can check the box to indicate partial approval, state that your disagreements are on the parent addendum, spell out your disagreements on the parent addendum, and sign your name.

Total Disagreement

In some instances, there is total disagreement. If so, sign your name after checking both the box acknowledging that you attended the meeting and the disapproval box. You could also refer to the parent addendum page.

At this stage, your options are informal negotiations, mediation, or a due process hearing.

 RELATED TOPIC

See Chapter 12 for information on due process, including your child's status when there is no IEP agreement.

Parent Addendum Page

When you disagree with any aspect of the IEP deliberations, including specific items such as related services, a statement on the narrative page, a portion of the school's evaluation report, or even the administrator's refusal to discuss an item you raised, make sure to state your position clearly. You or your notetaker should keep a list of every issue you dispute on a separate piece of paper.

A parent addendum page is an attachment to the IEP where you can record these disagreements and give your point of view. There is no IDEA requirement for an addendum page, although your district's IEP form may have one. The addendum page need not be a formal document—a blank piece of paper will do.

You will most likely complete the addendum page at or near the end of the meeting. The content of the addendum page is vastly more important than its format. Your statement should:

- relate specifically to issues concerning your child's education and the IEP meeting; don't use the addendum to state general complaints
- be in plain English, and
- state specifically your point of view on all key items of dispute.

You should indicate on the signature page that you disagree with part of the IEP document and refer to the attached addendum page for the detail of the disagreement.

Date: _____

Parent Signature:** _____

** See Addendum page (designated as "A") for a statement regarding what we are agreeing to and not agreeing to. My signature above is to be read only in conjunction with the statement on "A."

Less Frequent IEP Meetings: A New Model

As both parents and educators know, IEP meetings can be tiring, difficult, and sometimes contentious, and can involve a lot of paperwork. They take up a lot of time for teachers, administrators, and you. Congress has received complaints about this, and has decided to establish a pilot program to find out what happens when IEP meetings are held less than once a year. The program calls for participating districts to establish comprehensive, multiyear IEPs to last for up to three years. Here are some details on the program:

- The Secretary of Education can approve up to 15 proposals to establish pilot programs across the country.
- Participation is **optional**. If your state or school district is chosen for the pilot program, you can opt out if you wish.
- The Secretary of Education is supposed to submit an annual report to the House of Representatives' Committee on Education and the Workforce, describing how effective the multiyear IEP program has been and making recommendations as to whether it should be implemented more broadly.
- Though these reports were supposed to be submitted beginning in 2006, none have been submitted yet because no districts have applied to participate in a multiyear IEP pilot program.

Based on the lack of response from districts to the multiyear IEP pilot program, it does not appear that multiyear IEP's are the wave of the future. Most likely, districts will continue to hold annual IEP meetings for special education students.

If your state or district establishes a program, you should participate only if you are absolutely confident that this kind of procedure makes sense for your child. Ask your district for details about how the pilot program will work.

If your school's IEP form includes an addendum page, use it; otherwise, mark "Attachment A" at the top of a blank piece of paper and write something like the following:

Sample Heading for Addendum Page

Parent Addendum Page of Cara and Marcus Stack
IEP for Beatrice Stack
March 12, 20xx

You have an absolute right to state your position, but if, for some reason, the school district does not allow you to attach an addendum, indicate on the signature page that you do not agree with everything in the IEP document, and that you want to attach an addendum but the school administration will not let you. Mail your addendum to the school—certified mail if you can (keep copies)—with a cover letter stating that you asked to include this at the IEP meeting, were denied by the administrator, and are now sending it to be attached to the IEP. Then, file a complaint. (See Chapter 13.)

EXAMPLES OF ADDENDUM STATEMENTS:

- The district does not agree with the recommendations of Dr. Jordan's independent evaluation, but has refused to state why. We believe that her evaluation is valid and should be fully incorporated into the IEP as representing useful and valid information about Tonya.
- We do not agree with recommendations 3, 6, 9, and 14 of Dr. Lee's evaluation of January 21, 20xx. We do agree with the rest of her report.
- The IEP team agrees with sections 3, 7, 8, and 9 of the school's report and all of Dr. Friedman's evaluation, but the school will not put this agreement into the IEP. We believe those agreed-to sections should be incorporated into the IEP.

- Dr. Pentan of the school district stated that we have no right to include a child profile in the IEP. IDEA does not say that. If the IEP team agrees, the profile can be part of the IEP. We believe the profile provides valid and important information regarding Fernando.

- While the teacher reported that Drake increased his reading comprehension (this relates to goal #4 on page 2), we have observed at home, over a long period of time, that his reading comprehension seems substantially below the test results.

- We don't agree that Sandy's goals were met, because the evaluation of the goals was inaccurate.

- The district offered multisensory work one time a week, 20 minutes per session. Moira needs three sessions per week, each session to be 40 minutes long, conducted one-on-one with an aide trained in one of the multisensory approaches. This is supported by the May 2, 20xx report of Dr. Shawn Waters. We accept the one session and give permission for that to begin, but this acceptance is not to be construed as agreement about the amount of the related services, only agreement as to the need.

- The IEP team agrees that Nick be placed in the regular fifth grade class at Kennedy School. We agree with placement in the regular fifth grade class at Kennedy School, but we believe Nick needs an aide to meet his needs and allow him to achieve satisfactorily in that regular class.

- We believe that the regular ninth grade program at Roosevelt School is the only appropriate placement for Toni. We believe placement in the special day class at Roosevelt as offered by the school district is inappropriate. We agree to placement in regular classrooms at Roosevelt for three periods a day, although such agreement is not to be construed as agreement on partial mainstreaming. We will proceed to due process on the issue of full-time mainstreaming in regular ninth grade classes at Roosevelt.

Resolving IEP Disputes Through Due Process

The purpose of this book is to help you successfully develop an IEP plan for your child, and thereby make this chapter irrelevant. But by the nature of the IEP process, disagreements do arise—and some cannot be resolved informally.

Under IDEA, you have the right to resolve disputes with your school district through "due process." (20 U.S.C. § 1415.) There are two ways to resolve disputes through due process: mediation and/or a hearing.

In mediation, you and representatives of the school district meet with a neutral third party, who tries to help you reach a compromise. The mediator has no authority to impose a decision on you—the mediator's job is to help you and the school district come up with a mutually agreeable resolution to your dispute. You are not required to mediate, but it can be a very good way to resolve your dispute—and avoid the time, expense, and anxiety of a due process hearing.

If you cannot reach an agreement in mediation or if you'd prefer to skip mediation altogether, you can request a due process hearing where you and school district personnel present written evidence and have witnesses testify about the disputed issues before a neutral third party, called a hearing officer. Much like a judge, the hearing officer considers the evidence, makes a decision, and issues a binding order. If you or school district representatives disagree with the decision, either side can appeal to a state or federal court.

Due process is available to resolve factual disputes—that is, when you and your child's school district cannot agree on eligibility or some part of the IEP plan. If the school district has violated a legal rule—such as failing to hold an IEP meeting, do an evaluation, meet a time limit, or provide an agreed-to part of the IEP—you must file a complaint rather than use due process. (Complaints are covered in Chapter 13.)

There are many types of due process disputes that might arise for children with learning disabilities. Some of the more common areas of conflict are:

- evaluations: whether the evaluations used to test for a learning disability are appropriate and/or accurate
- eligibility: whether the child qualifies as a child with a specific learning disability

Don't Delay Filing for Due Process—You May Lose Your Rights

IDEA requires you to formally file for due process within two years after you knew or should have known of the dispute. (20 U.S.C. §§ 1415(b) (6) and (f)(1)(C).) Time limits like these are known in the legal world as "statutes of limitations." If you do not file within the two-year limit, you lose your right to file for due process.

There are two exceptions to this two-year limit:

- If your state has a different statute of limitations, the state's statute will apply. Check with your school district, state department of education, and/or a parent support organization in your state to find out about time limits. (See the appendix for contact information.)
- If the school district misrepresents to you that it has resolved the dispute, or withholds information from you that is required by law, the two-year time limit will not apply. (20 U.S.C. § 1415(f)(3)(D).) For example, you ask for a specific related service and the school district tells you, at the IEP meeting, that its evaluator did not decide whether your child needed such a service. If the evaluator in fact recommended that your child receive the service but you didn't learn of the recommendation for a while, the two-year limit might not apply.

It would be fairly unusual to have a dispute with the school district that you weren't aware of for a lengthy period of time. After all, most due process matters involve a disagreement over services or placement, and these disputes are usually evident right from the start—and certainly by the IEP meeting. The school either agrees to mainstream your child, provide a one-on-one aide, and meet your child's other needs, or it doesn't. It's generally a good idea to start considering a due process proceeding as soon as you know you have a disagreement that can't be resolved with another IEP meeting.

- placement: the district wants to place the child in a special day class or nonregular placement, while the family believes the child's learning disability needs can be met in a regular classroom with support

- methodology: the parent wants a specific methodology (such as a multisensory approach) and the district disagrees, and
- related services: the parent wants one-on-one help or other support services (language/speech therapy, occupational therapy, and so on) and the district disagrees about the need for services or the amount of services to be provided.

Before Due Process: Informal Negotiations

Before invoking due process, you may want to try to resolve your dispute through informal discussions or negotiations with the school. While resolving some problems might require formal action, many of these issues can be settled informally.

In addition, some disputes may not even qualify for due process because they do not involve factual disputes. For example, you and the school principal may disagree about when you can visit the classroom or why the evaluator had to reschedule your child's testing. Because you can't take these disputes to due process, you'll have to hash them out informally or not at all.

The school district must set up a negotiating meeting after you file for due process. (See "Resolution Session," below.) Although this occurs only after a hearing request is filed, you may still be able to resolve the dispute.

Pros and Cons of Informal Negotiation

Informal negotiation (including alternative dispute resolution, or ADR) is useful for several reasons. It if works well, it may save you stress, time, and money. It will also help you maintain a more positive relationship with the school district, and will keep problems from escalating. Finally, informal negotiation is easier to pursue than due process.

Even if you eventually pursue your due process rights, it might be a good idea to start with informal negotiation. This will show that you are reasonable and fair minded, and don't immediately look to an adversarial method of settlement. Informal negotiations will also help you understand the school district's position, which will be valuable if you end up in mediation or at a hearing.

In limited situations, however, it might make sense to go immediately to due process. For example, you should skip the informal negotiations if:

- You need an immediate resolution of an issue that affects your child's well-being, safety, or health. For example, if you think your child needed psychological counseling for depression but the district disagrees, you may not have time for informal meetings.

- The school administrator is so unpleasant or inflexible that you just don't want to deal with him or her. For example, you want your tenth grader in a regular academic high school setting, but the administrator is pushing for a special class comprising only children with learning disabilities, and has said that the district won't budge under any circumstances.

- The IEP meeting made it clear that it would be a waste of time to try to resolve things informally. For example, you want three hours a week of speech therapy for your child, the district's evaluation recommends one hour, the administrator has said that the district will not go beyond the one-hour recommendation, and you know other parents who have faced similar situations without success.

- You're facing a time limit. For example, your daughter is already years behind in reading and each day she goes without a reading specialist will set her back even farther. Informal negotiation will almost always eat up some time—and may not be successful. By trying to handle the dispute informally, you will likely use up weeks or even months before the more formal due process steps begin—weeks and months when your child will not have that daily help she needs.

- You want to push the school district toward a settlement. For example, they have hinted that they are considering giving your child three hours a week of one-on-one aide time for reading problems, but have not taken any concrete steps to set it up. Even if you try to resolve things informally, you might want to file for due process to motivate the school district to settle informally.

Remember, however, that pursuing due process, with its time limits and requirements, will also put pressure on you.

Alternatives to Informal Negotiations and Formal Due Process

Informal discussions with the school district and formal due process aren't the only ways to resolve disputes. Other methods, such as building parent coalitions and becoming involved in the local political process, can also be effective. These options are discussed in Chapter 15.

In addition, IDEA provides that a state or local school district can establish "alternative dispute resolution" (ADR) procedures for parents who choose not to use due process. In ADR, you meet with a neutral third party who is under contract with a parent training center, community parent resource center, or appropriate alternative dispute resolution entity. (20 U.S.C. § 1415(e)(2)(B).) The purpose of the meeting is for you to explore alternative ways to resolve your dispute and for the third party to explain the benefits of mediation. This ADR meeting is intended to be nonadversarial, while mediation is the first step in formal due process. Be aware, however, that using ADR may delay resolution of the dispute—so if you need immediate action or the time limit for pursuing due process is coming up, you might want to skip this step.

If you're interested in ADR, call your school district or state department of education to find out if ADR is available.

Basics of Informal Negotiation

To begin informal negotiations, call or write your child's teacher, school principal, or special education administrator and ask for a meeting to discuss your concerns. You can raise the issues in your phone conversation or letter, but ideally you'll want an appointment to discuss the problem face to face.

Before the meeting, prepare a clear written description of the problem and a recommended solution. Also, find out if any school personnel support you. If so, ask them to attend the meeting or ask for permission to present their opinions at the meeting.

Here are some tips to keep in mind:

- During the meeting, emphasize problem solving, not winning.
- Try to structure the negotiation as a mutual attempt to solve a problem.
- Avoid personal attacks on school personnel.
- Respect the school's point of view even if you disagree.
- Acknowledge the school representatives' concerns. Even if you strongly disagree, you don't lose anything by saying, "I understand your concerns, but I think we can address those by doing …."

Be respectful, but firm—for example, you can say, "It is clear we disagreed at the IEP meeting. I am open to trying to solve this informally, but I will not hesitate to pursue my due process rights if we cannot." When you enter the meeting, you should know what you are willing to compromise and what is not negotiable. If you know your bottom line, you'll have an easier time presenting your point of view and evaluating what the school district has to say.

Good Books on Negotiation

Getting to Yes: Negotiating Agreement Without Giving In, by Roger Fisher and William Ury (Penguin Books). This classic book offers a strategy for coming to mutually acceptable agreements in all kinds of situations.

Getting Past No: Negotiating in Difficult Situations, by William Ury (Bantam Books). This sequel to *Getting to Yes* suggests techniques for negotiating with difficult people.

After Meeting Informally

If you do not resolve your dispute informally, send a letter briefly stating the problem, the solution you think makes sense, and what you are considering next, such as contacting an attorney, pursuing mediation or a due process hearing, or filing a complaint with your school board or the state department of education.

If you resolve your problem informally, it is very important to follow up the meeting with a confirming letter.

FORM
A sample letter confirming the results of an informal negotiation is shown below; a blank downloadable copy is available on this book's Companion Page on www.nolo.com. See Chapter 16 for the link.

If the meeting does not resolve the problem to your satisfaction, then you may proceed to due process (either mediation or a hearing) or file a complaint.

Use the Law to Make Your Case

As you try to persuade your school district—in writing or in person—that you are correct, cite the legal authority for your position, if possible. Referring to a section in IDEA or even a court decision may help convince the school district that you're in the right. See Chapter 14 for tips on legal research.

Resolution Session

Once you or the school district files for due process, the school district must schedule a meeting, formally called a "resolution session," to try to resolve the dispute before mediation or a hearing. (20 U.S.C. § 1415(f), 34 C.F.R. § 300.510.) The rules for this session are as follows:

- You have the right to attend.
- Members of the IEP team who have knowledge about the dispute must attend.
- Someone who has the authority to make a decision on the school district's behalf must attend.

- The meeting must be held within 15 days after the school district receives notice of your due process request.
- The school district may not bring an attorney to the meeting unless you bring an attorney.
- If you resolve the dispute at the meeting, it must be put in writing and signed by both you and the school district representative. The written agreement can be enforced by any state or federal court.
- Either party can void the written agreement within three business days (weekends and holidays don't count) of signing it. The party who voids the agreement doesn't have to give a reason, and the other side doesn't have to approve the decision.
- You can waive the resolution meeting and go straight to mediation or a hearing, but only if the school district agrees. You cannot decide on your own to forgo the meeting.
- If you participate in the resolution meeting, but the district has not resolved the issue to your satisfaction within 30 days of filing your due process request, you can go on to a mediation or hearing. (34 C.F.R. § 300.510(b)(1).)
- If the district does not hold the resolution meeting within 15 days of receiving notice of your due process request, or if the district fails to participate in the resolution meeting, you can ask a hearing officer to begin the timeline (that requires a hearing decision within 45 days after the initial 30-day resolution period expires). (34 C.F.R. § 300.510(b)(5).)
- Important: If you decide not to go to the resolution meeting, you may have your case dismissed. If the school district is unable to obtain your participation in the resolution meeting—and it can document that it made "reasonable" efforts to do so—then after the 30-day period, the district may ask the due process hearing officer to dismiss your case. (34 C.F.R. § 300.510(b)(4).)

Letter Confirming Informal Negotiation Results

Date: June 1, 20xx

To: Michael Chan, Principal
     Truman High School
     803 Dogwood Drive
     Paterson, NJ 07506

Re: Tasha Kincaid, Sophomore

I appreciated the chance to meet on May 28 and discuss Tasha's placement. I also appreciated your point of view and the manner in which we solved the problem. I want to confirm our agreement that Tasha will be placed in the regular academic track at Truman High School with one hour per day of resource specialist help in math, English, and Social Studies for the upcoming school year. [If you have already requested due process, add: Once you have confirmed this in writing to me, I will formally withdraw my due process request.]

I greatly appreciate the manner in which you helped solve this problem. Please tell all of Tasha's teachers that I would be delighted to meet with them before school starts to discuss effective ways to work with Tasha.

Thank you.

Sincerely,

André Kincaid

André Kincaid
4500 Fair Street
Paterson, NJ 07506

555-3889 (home); 555-2330 (work)

Typical Due Process Disputes

Remember, due process (mediation or hearing) is used to resolve only factual disputes, not disagreements over what the law requires or allows. Here are some common IEP factual disputes:

- eligibility for special education
- results of an evaluation
- goals
- specific placement or program
- related services
- proposed changes to your child's current IEP program, and
- suspension or expulsion of your child.

Certain kinds of disputes are simply not appropriate for due process. Such due process claims will usually be dismissed by the agency in charge of mediations and hearings. These disputes include:

- requesting a specific teacher or service provider by name for your child
- hiring or firing school staff
- assigning a different school administrator to your case, or
- requesting that a specific person represent the school district in the IEP process.

These concerns may be addressed through non-IDEA activities, such as parent organizing (see Chapter 15) or informal negotiations with the school.

When to Pursue Due Process

Due process can be hard; it takes time, energy, and sometimes money, and it can be quite stressful. When you consider whether to go forward, you should be careful and objective. Consider these six factors:

- **The precise nature of the problem.** You will have to pinpoint exactly what your disagreement is about—and make sure it is a factual dispute. For example, if you feel your child's education is generally not working (and you have not yet gone to an IEP meeting), or you object to the attitude of the school administrator, your concern is not yet ready for due process. If, however, your child has fallen behind in a regular class and you want him or her placed in a special class but the IEP team did not agree, you have a problem that qualifies for due process resolution.

Don't File for Due Process Until After the IEP Meeting

Many parents make the mistake of requesting a due process hearing before the issue is considered at an IEP meeting. Unless there are very unusual circumstances—for example, a threat to your child's health or well-being—you must go to an IEP meeting and reach an impasse there before you can request due process.

- **The importance of the issue to your child.** Placement or related service disputes are often central to your child's educational well-being. On the other hand, disputes over goals or evaluation conclusions may not be significant enough to merit due process, because they do not directly impact your child's placement and related services.
- **The strength of your case.** Can you win? Is the district's position unreasonable, when you step back and consider the arguments from every angle? What evidence do you have to support your position? What evidence undercuts it? What are the qualifications of the people making supportive or contrary statements? Remember that the district is required to provide your child with an appropriate education, not the best possible one. After the IEP meeting, review and update your IEP Material Organizer Form (discussed in Chapter 10) to evaluate the evidence for and against you. If you want other opinions on the strength of your case, consider these sources:
  - Nonschool employees, your independent evaluator, an outside tutor, or an attorney. Describe the disputed issue, your evidence, and the evidence against you, and ask if they think you have a good chance of winning.
  - Other parents, particularly those who have been through due process with your school district. How does the school

district react? Is the school likely to take a hard line position or might it offer a compromise after you show you are determined to go forward?

- Local parent and disability organizations. (Chapter 15 discusses how to find and work with a parents' group.) If you need help finding a local group, start by contacting a national organization (see the list in Appendix B on this book's Companion Page on nolo.com).

- **The bottom line concerns for the school district.** For any disputed issue, the school district will have some bottom line concerns—notably, the cost and administrative difficulty of providing what you want. For example, the school administrator may be willing to compromise on a dispute between two public school program options, rather than pay for costly private school placement. The school's bottom line may affect your bottom line—and how far you'll go to get it.

- **The cost of going forward.** Due process witnesses (including independent evaluators) and attorneys will charge for their time. You can be reimbursed for attorney fees, but only if you win at the hearing. (See Chapter 14 for information on using an attorney and attorneys' fees.) Even if you win at the hearing, however, you are unlikely to be reimbursed for the cost of having an independent evaluator testify. (See "The Cost of an Independent Evaluator Appearing in Due Process," below.)

- **Time considerations.** Remember, you must file for due process within two years of learning of the dispute or within your state's statute of limitations, if it has one. (See "Don't Delay Filing for Due Process—You May Lose Your Rights," above.) Don't take too long to weigh your decision or spend too much time trying to reach an informal resolution.

Who Can File?

Though the great majority of due process requests are filed by families, districts also have the right to file. Generally, districts initiate due process when:

- a student is in a costly private program and the district wants to be excused from paying for that program
- a family refuses to consent to an initial evaluation or reevaluation, or
- the district truly believes that a student's current program is wrong and needs a due process decision to change the program.

The burden of (responsibility for) proving a due process case is on the party who files. When the district initiates due process it will have that burden; when you file, you have that burden.

Whether the district files for due process or you do, the timelines and procedures governing the hearing stay the same.

Your Child's Status During Due Process

During due process, your child is entitled to remain in the current placement until you reach an agreement with the school, settle the matter through mediation, receive a due process hearing decision that neither you nor the school district appeals, or get a final court decision. This is called the "stay put" provision. (20 U.S.C. § 1415(j).) "Stay put" can be a complicated legal right. If you are concerned about whether your child is allowed to stay put in a particular situation, see an attorney or contact a nonprofit disability rights organization right away.

> EXAMPLE: Your child is in a regular sixth grade class, with a one-on-one aide, two hours a day. At the IEP meeting, the school district offers a special day class, not a regular class, for seventh grade. You want your child to continue in a regular class. You are unable to reach an agreement at the IEP meeting. You initiate due process, during which time your child is entitled to remain in a regular classroom with the same amount of help from the aide until the matter is resolved.

> **Exceptions to the Stay Put Rule**
>
> IDEA entitles your child to remain in his or her current placement pending due process unless your child carries a weapon to school or a school function, or knowingly possesses, uses, sells, or solicits illegal drugs while at school or a school function. In these situations, the school district can change your child's placement to an appropriate interim alternative educational setting for up to 45 days, or suspend your child for up to ten school days. (20 U.S.C. § 1415(k).) See Chapter 2 for more information on discipline for students in special education.

Using a Lawyer During Due Process

Using an attorney in due process certainly escalates the adversarial nature of the dispute, but by the time you've reached due process that is probably not your primary concern. Using an attorney may also speed things along and increase your chances of success.

In mediation, an attorney will present your case and counter the school district's arguments. In a hearing, an attorney should prepare witnesses, submit exhibits, make the opening statement, and direct the proceeding. An attorney can also play a less active role, such as giving advice and helping you organize your case material, without attending the proceeding. Once you hire an attorney, he or she will contact the district to let them know about his or her involvement in the case.

To prepare for and attend a one-day mediation session, an attorney will likely charge from $1,000 to $2,500; much depends on the complexity of the case (and therefore preparation time for the attorney) and how long the mediation takes. The cost for a two-to-three-day hearing may range from $5,000 to $10,000 or more. It is not unusual for an attorney to spend ten to 25 hours preparing for a three-day hearing. If you use an attorney for advice only—for example, to help organize your case—your legal costs will be lower.

RELATED TOPIC

See Chapter 14 for a thorough discussion of attorneys and legal fees.

Check Out Free or Low-Cost Legal Services

The school district must provide you with a list of free or low-cost legal services available in your area. See Chapter 14 for advice on finding and working with an attorney.

Attorney Fees in Mediation

During mediation, you should ask the school district, as part of your proposed settlement, to pay your attorney fees. Your legal fees are one of many bargaining chips you can use to negotiate a settlement in mediation. However, the school district doesn't have to pay your fees, just as it doesn't have to agree to any particular settlement terms. Because mediation (and any settlement you reach as a result of it) is voluntary, the school district may or may not agree to pay attorney fees. Remember, a mediation is usually a settlement in which neither party gets everything it wants; attorney's fees may be one of those things you are willing to forgo in order to get something more important.

The school district's decision will depend largely on how strong your case is and how motivated the school district is to settle. The school district may try to avoid having to reimburse you by agreeing to provide the education you want if you agree to drop your demand for attorney's fees. You will need to assess the strength of your case to decide whether you are willing to forgo your legal fees. If your case is very strong, the school district may decide that they are better off paying your attorney's fees now rather than later, when they will be much higher. Your attorney can advise you of the pros and cons in this situation.

Courts have ruled that attorney's fees in mediation can be awarded to parents.

Attorney Fees in a Due Process Hearing

If your case goes to hearing and you win, you will be entitled to reimbursement of your attorney fees. If you lose the hearing, you're responsible for your own attorney fees, but you will not have to pay the school district's attorney fees absent unusual circumstances (see below). This is often referred to as the "prevailing party" rule. If you win, or "prevail," you will be reimbursed for your attorney's fees.

If you win on some issues but not on others, you will be reimbursed for the time your lawyer spent on the winning issues (but not for time spent on the losing issues).

Liability for the School District's Legal Fees

The 2004 amendments to IDEA create a new risk for parents: You may have to pay the school district's legal fees if you file for due process for "any improper purpose," defined as an intent to harass, cause unnecessary delay, or needlessly increase the cost of litigation. In addition, your attorney may have to pay the district's fees if he or she filed for due process or filed a lawsuit and the action was "frivolous, unreasonable, or without foundation." (20 U.S.C. § 1415(i)(3)(B).)

These new rules are intended to discourage parents from filing unfounded or frivolous actions. Congress believed that some parents (and their lawyers) were filing actions even if they knew their claims weren't valid, in order to try to force a settlement. If the school district's potential legal costs to fight the claim were higher than the cost of giving in, the district might decide to settle rather than paying a lawyer to fight it out, even if the parents' claim was unfounded.

These provisions are controversial. Of course, parents should always think very carefully before filing for due process, and shouldn't file just to harass or delay. On the other hand, plenty of parents have had to fight their school districts at every turn just to get the services to which their children are legally entitled, and these parents shouldn't have to worry about having to foot the school district's legal bills.

Even with these new rules, however, there remains a big difference between filing a difficult or even losing case and filing one that is frivolous or unreasonable. I believe that courts will be very reluctant to dampen the rights of children and their families, and so will require compelling evidence of parental misconduct before ordering a family to pay the district's fees. This was the position taken by a judge who heard a case involving a family's request for reimbursement of private school tuition. The family had not given timely notice to the district that they were placing their child in the private school, which could have allowed the judge to reduce or deny their reimbursement request. The judge decided that they were not entitled to reimbursement because the district had offered an appropriate placement, but didn't saddle the family with having to pay the district's attorney fees because the family had some basis for believing that they could receive reimbursement (*Taylor P. ex rel. Chris P. v. Missouri Dept. of Elementary and Secondary Educ.*, 48 IDELR 242 (W.D. Mo. 2007).)

Of course, you don't want to have to respond to the school district's request for fees, defend your intentions to a judge, and possibly even face a separate hearing on the issue before you are vindicated. With that in mind, here are some examples of filings that may cross the line:

- **Harassment.** You request IEP meetings every two months, request reevaluations numerous times each year, come to the school daily to complain, and file for due process several times a year.

- **Unnecessary delay.** You stall IEP and/or due process procedures without any legitimate reason.

- **Increasing costs.** You and your lawyer file unnecessary motions and otherwise take steps that prolong the litigation, without any legitimate purpose.

- **Frivolous actions.** Your attorney files for violation of a right that doesn't exist under IDEA or is patently beyond the scope of the law. For example, you ask that the teacher remain after school for two hours every day to help your child with homework.

- **Unreasonable actions.** You seek a placement or service that is not at all reasonable. For example, your child has a very mild learning disability and all of the experts (including your own) recommend a regular classroom placement with two-hour pull-out sessions with an aide once a week. You request that your child be placed in a private, residential program and refuse to budge from your position.

- **Actions without foundation.** You have no evidence or support for what you are seeking. For example, you want private counseling for your child, but there is no evidence that your child has any psychological difficulties.

While well-meaning parents who act in good faith should not run into trouble under these rules, you should proceed very carefully. Talk to a special education attorney to make sure you are nowhere near violating these provisions.

Reduced Attorney Fees

If you prevail and are entitled to have your attorney fees paid by the school district, a judge can order that you receive a reduced amount. The amount can be reduced if: your attorney unreasonably extended the controversy, your attorney's hourly rate exceeds the prevailing rate in your community (charged by attorneys with similar experience and expertise), your attorney spent excessive time and resources on the case, or your attorney did not properly inform the school district about the nature of the dispute.

These failings would typically be committed by your attorney (not you), so you should not be responsible for paying any amount the court disallows. You should discuss this possibility ahead of time, before you hire a lawyer. If the attorney doesn't know about this rule, it suggests a lack of knowledge about special education law in general. (See Chapter 14 for pointers on hiring an attorney.)

Other Legal Advocates

There are many nonattorney advocates who are quite skilled in due process. Their fees are usually lower than a lawyer's fees, but you are not entitled to reimbursement of an advocate's fees if you prevail in a hearing.

Special education attorneys, nonprofit law centers, and disability and parent support groups may know the names of special education advocates in your area.

How to Begin Due Process

You must formally request due process in order for a mediation or fair hearing to be scheduled. Due process requests are sometimes referred to as due process complaints, the term used in IDEA. Note, however, that a due process complaint (filed when you and the school district have a factual dispute) is different from a complaint regarding a legal violation (covered in Chapter 13).

Filing a Written Request

You must provide specific written information about the dispute to initiate due process. There can be no hearing or mediation until you complete this first step. (20 U.S.C. § 1415(b)(7), 34 C.F.R. § 300.508(b).) You must provide this written notice to the school district *and* send a copy to the state department of education branch responsible for special education. (You can find the contact information through the federal Department of Education website, at www.ed.gov.)

Your written request must include the following information:
- your name and address
- your child's name and address
- the name of your child's school
- a description of the disputed issues, "including facts relating to the (issues)"
- your desired resolution—what you want for your child's education, as well as reimbursement for your due process costs, such as attorney's fees, witness fees, and independent evaluation costs, and
- whether you want to mediate or to go directly to a hearing (this is not required, but I recommend including it).

Most due process matters involve a disagreement between you and the school district over a particular disputed item—for example, you want a particular placement or service, but the school district won't provide it. You may also believe the school district has violated procedural rules under IDEA. For example, if the school district does not hold a yearly IEP meeting, does not process your request for an initial evaluation, or does not allow you to bring anyone with you to the IEP meeting, you should raise those issues in your due process request.

When putting together the required information, it's best to be precise. You can use a short list to describe the existing problem and your proposed solution. IDEA requires each state to develop a model form to assist parents in filing for due process. Ask your school district or state department of education for a copy.

Keep a copy of your due process request for your records. It's best to send this request "certified mail, return receipt requested," so you'll have proof of the date it was received.

Sufficiency of the Written Request for Due Process

In my experience, at least in California, due process hearing officers often ask for very detailed written requests. Even when advocates, parents, and lawyers provide all the detail required by 34 C.F.R. § 300.508(b), it has not always been enough. I strongly urge you to carefully read 34 C.F.R. § 300.508(b) and cover all areas listed there. When in doubt, include more rather than less. If you run into a hearing officer who rejects your complaint for insufficiency and you think you provided more than enough detail per 34 C.F.R. § 300.508(b), remember this: 34 C.F.R. § 300.508(d) states that a complaint "must be deemed sufficient" unless, within 15 days of receipt of the complaint, the other party formally notifies the hearing officer that it believes the complaint is insufficient. In other words, the hearing officer should not make a determination about sufficiency unless the other side formally states that it believes the complaint is insufficient.

If the hearing officer finds your complaint does not meet the "sufficiency" requirement, he or she will often give you an opportunity to amend your complaint. The officer may even point out where the deficiencies are. You will also be allowed to amend your complaint if the other side agrees in writing to let you do so. (34 C.F.R. § 300.508(d).)

Letter Requesting Due Process

Date: March 1, 20xx

To: Phillip Jones
Due Process Unit
Wisconsin Department of Education
8987 Franklin Avenue
La Crosse, WI 54601

Re: Steven Howard

Our son, Steven Howard, is a fourth grader at Clinton School in La Crosse. His school district is the Central La Crosse Elementary School District, 562 5th Avenue, La Crosse, Wisconsin.

We are formally requesting due process, beginning with mediation. We believe that Steven requires a full-time, one-on-one aide in order to be fully mainstreamed in next year's regular fifth grade class at Clinton School. The school district has refused to provide that aide.

We believe an appropriate solution would include, but should not be limited to, the following:

- A qualified full-time academic aide, to work one-on-one with Steven in the regular fifth grade class at Clinton School for the coming school year.

- Reimbursement for all attorney's fees, witnesses, independent assessments, and other costs accrued for the February 14, 20xx IEP meeting and subsequent due process.

Please contact us at once to schedule the mediation.

Sincerely,

William Howard   *Kate Howard*
William and Kate Howard
1983 Smiley Lane
La Crosse, WI 54601

555-5569 (home); 555-2000 (work)

FORM

A sample Letter Requesting Due Process is shown above; you can find a blank downloadable copy on this book's Companion Page on www.nolo.com. See Chapter 16 for the link.

Other Notice Requirements

The party that receives a due process request (which may be you or the school district, depending on who files for due process) can object that the request does not meet the requirements discussed above. The objecting party has 15 days after receiving the request to send the other party and the hearing officer a written statement explaining why the request is insufficient.

Within five days of receiving this written statement, the hearing officer must decide whether the initial request is adequate. If it is not, the filing party can amend the request, but only if the other party agrees *and* has an opportunity to have a resolution session, or if the hearing officer consents. If the filing party needs time to file an amended request, the timeline for the due process decision will be extended as well.

Of course, you can avoid all of these rules by simply filing a clear, sufficient request in the first place. IDEA requires your school district to provide you with written information about your due process rights, procedures, and requirements.

Prepare for Due Process

While a mediation session and a due process hearing are different, preparing for the former will help as you get ready for the latter. The preparation you did for the IEP meeting will also be of enormous help as you go through due process. The recommendations in this section apply to both mediation and the due process hearing.

Organize Your Evidence

First, pull out your child's file and the reports, evaluations, and other documents in your IEP binder (Chapter 4), your blueprint (Chapter 5), and your IEP Material Organizer Form (Chapter 10).

Make a list of the disputed issues. Using a blank IEP Material Organizer Form, write next to each disputed issue the witnesses, documents, or facts that support your point of view—and those that oppose it. You should make a separate list of all of your potential witnesses and think about who the district's witnesses will be.

Now find every piece of evidence you have that supports your position. Review your binder, original material organizer forms, and notes from the IEP meeting. Focus not only on reports and evaluations, but also on comments made at the meeting. Gather all your supportive evidence together or tab it in your binder and highlight key statements. Make photocopies of all written materials that support your point of view to have available during the mediation or hearing.

Now work on the school district's case—that is, figure out what evidence contradicts your point of view. Think about any evidence you can use (including comments made during the IEP meeting) to rebut the district's likely arguments.

Make a List of Expenses

Once you've gathered evidence, make a list of expenses you've incurred throughout the IEP process, such as the costs of:
- independent evaluations
- tutors
- lost wages for attending IEPs
- private school or private related service costs
- personal transportation costs, such as those incurred driving your child to a private school
- attorney fees
- costs for other professionals (such as a private speech therapist or counselor), and
- photocopying.

Note the date a payment was made or cost incurred, name of the payee, and purpose of the expense. Attach all receipts.

At mediation or the hearing, you will want to request payment of these expenses. If the district agrees to pay some or all of them, or if the hearing officer rules in your favor, the receipts are proof that you really spent this money.

Prepare an Opening Statement

At the beginning of a mediation session or hearing, you will need to make an opening statement explaining why you're there and what you want. Some people are comfortable making notes and then talking extemporaneously; others write out a complete statement and read it. Do what's easiest for you. Whatever method you choose, your opening statement should cover these topics:

Your child. Briefly describe your child, including age, current educational program, general areas of educational concern, and disabling conditions. Give a short explanation of your child's educational history.

The dispute. Briefly describe the specific items in dispute—for example, the amount of a related service or the placement.

What you want and why. Summarize what your child needs—for example, speech therapy three times a week in a one-on-one setting with a therapist qualified to work with students with language delays; placement in Sierra School; or the use of the Lindamood-Bell program or the Orton-Gillingham method.

Your evidence. You'll want to end with a strong statement briefly summarizing evidence you have for your position. In some mediations, however, you may decide not to reveal all of your evidence right away. You will have to judge the best approach, based on the situation, the personalities involved, and even your intuition. See "How Much Evidence Do You Reveal in Mediation?" below.

Mediation Specifics

Mediation is the first official step in due process. It is less confrontational than a hearing, and is intended to help you and the school district explore ways to compromise and settle your dispute.

The mediator is a neutral third party, usually hired by the state department of education, who is knowledgeable about IDEA **and** special education matters. The mediator has no authority to force you to settle. If you reach a settlement, however, your agreement will be put into writing and will be binding on you and the district—you both must abide by and follow the settlement.

While mediation is fairly similar from one place to another, the way the sessions proceed will vary depending on the style of the mediator and rules established by your state.

> **RESOURCE**
>
> **Finding mediation rules.** Contact your state department of education to find out the details of your state's laws on mediation. You can find the contact information through the federal Department of Education website, at www.edu.gov.

Mediation must be made available to you at no cost. Mediation is completely voluntary—if you don't want to mediate, you don't have to. If you prefer, you can skip mediation altogether and go straight to a hearing.

If mediation is not successful, any settlement offers and other comments made during the mediation cannot be used as evidence at the hearing or any subsequent legal proceedings. This rule allows you to discuss matters frankly, without fear that your statements will later be used against you.

Pros and Cons of Mediation

You may be asking yourself why you would try mediation, particularly because it ends in a compromise rather than a clear victory for one side or the other. There are some compelling reasons to go to mediation:

- **Know thine enemy.** Mediation gives you a chance to better understand the school district's arguments. Of course, the school district gets the same opportunity to hear about your case, but sharing information in this way may bring you closer to a solution.

- **The school district may be motivated to compromise.** Mediation takes the school district one step closer to a hearing and the possibility of a ruling against the school, with all of the costs that entails (including possible attorney fees). The school administrator may be far more flexible in mediation than he or she was at the IEP meeting, feeling that a compromise now is better than an expensive loss later. Remember, the school will have to pay your legal fees if you win at the hearing (and you will almost certainly not have to pay their fees if you lose).

- **Mediation is constructive.** Mediation requires the parties to work out their disagreements and increases the chances you can retain a positive relationship with your school district. You also keep control over the outcome—you must agree to any solution proposed in mediation. When you go to hearing, the decision making power is out of your hands.

- **Mediation is cheap.** As a general rule, you will have few or even no costs at mediation. In contrast, hearings can be expensive, particularly if you use an attorney.

- **Mediation can provide a reality check.** Even if you don't settle the case, mediation gives you a chance to have a neutral party assess your case and point out its strengths and weaknesses.

- **You get two bites of the apple.** By going to mediation, you give yourself two chances at success. If the mediation is unsuccessful, you can move on to a hearing.

But there are also downsides to mediation, including:

- **Half a loaf can be disappointing.** Ideally, you can settle in mediation and get everything your child needs. In reality, however, mediation usually involves compromise, meaning you will probably settle for less than what you would have gotten if you won at a hearing.

- **Mediation may delay resolution of your dispute.** IDEA requires that a hearing decision be issued within 45 days after the 30-day resolution process period, whether you go through mediation or go straight to a hearing. In reality, however, extensions of that 45-day rule can be granted if you spend significant time in mediation. If you have a real time problem—for example, your child must be placed in a specific program by a certain date or will suffer dire consequences—you may not want to go to mediation. If you decide to mediate, be sure to oppose any requests to extend the 45-day time limit.

- **You do things twice.** If you go to mediation and then a hearing, you will have been involved in two procedures, doubling the time, inconvenience, stress, and possible costs.

Reality Check: What to Expect From Due Process

Parents often expect to get everything their child needs if they go forward with informal negotiations, mediation, a hearing, or even litigation. After all, if you want certain IEP components and you have evidence and arguments to back up your claims, you can look forward to total victory, right? Well, not necessarily. Even if you have a strong case, you may not get everything that you want. What is fair or right and what will actually happen can be very different things.

This is especially important to remember when you consider a settlement offer from your school district (whether through informal negotiations or through mediation). You may be thinking, "I know I'm right and I know a hearing officer or judge will agree, so I'm going to go for the full loaf and reject the school district's offer of 80%." But you have to weigh the school district's offer against the chances of winning at a hearing—and, if you win, whether you'll get more than the school district offered. You also have to weigh the financial, emotional, and educational cost of going forward rather than getting things resolved now.

> **TIP**
>
> **The bottom line about mediation.** Although there are some downsides to mediation, they are almost always outweighed by its benefits. Unless there's some compelling reason to go straight to a hearing—like a serious time crunch or a truly uncompromising opponent—you should give mediation a try. The vast majority of cases I've been involved in are resolved at mediation (or before).

Mediators

The mediator's job is to help you and the school district reach a settlement. The mediator will not decide who is right and who is wrong.

A good mediator will:

- put you and school representatives at ease
- try to establish an atmosphere in which compromise is possible
- be objective
- give you and the school district a frank assessment of the strengths and weaknesses of your positions, and
- go beyond your stated positions to explore possible settlements that may not be initially apparent.

Some mediators play a more limited role—they simply present everyone's positions and hope that the weight of the evidence and formality of the process will lead to a settlement.

Mediation Logistics

Mediation sessions must be held at a time and place convenient for you. They are often held at the school district's main office, but they can be held elsewhere. Some people are concerned that having the mediation at a school office gives the district an advantage, but I have found it usually does not matter.

The length of the mediation can vary, but sessions generally take several hours and often a full day. The mediation sessions almost always take more time than you would think.

Most school districts send the special education administrator and perhaps another person, one who has direct knowledge of your child, to the mediation. While you can bring outside evaluators, aides, tutors, and any other individuals you want (including a lawyer), you will generally want to save them for the hearing. If you bring a lawyer to the mediation, the district will most likely bring one also.

Bringing in experts might make mediation more expensive and difficult to schedule. Whether you should include (or exclude) experts will depend on:

- how forceful the experts can be
- whether there is any chance to change the district's mind, and
- the risks of revealing some of your evidence prior to the fair hearing.

If you expect to go to a hearing and don't want to put all your cards on the table at mediation, don't bring the experts. On the other hand, if you want to settle quickly and your experts can aid in that process, bring them along.

The Mediation Session

You, the mediator, and the school representatives will gather in a conference or meeting room. After brief introductions, the mediator will explain how the mediation process works, stressing that mediation is a voluntary attempt to resolve your disagreement.

Your Opening Statement

You begin by briefly explaining your side of the dispute. Do not hesitate to express your feelings. Your child has important needs and his or her well-being is at stake. Express how worried you are. Explain why you feel the school district has not effectively served your child and how it has failed to provide an appropriate education. It's important to show the mediator how crucial the matter is to you and your child. This does not mean tirades or irrational, off-the-wall monologues. Give your opinion, but don't question the honesty, professionalism, or decency of the school personnel. Don't berate anyone.

Your opening statement should not discuss every possible problem. It should be clear and succinct and run from five to ten minutes.

If the school has committed any legal violations, you can raise these in your opening statement. While legal violations are subject to the complaint procedure (see Chapter 13), evidence of a legal violation may be a powerful addition to your case, showing the school district's disregard or lack of understanding of the law, and possibly the district's lack of reliability. Nothing in IDEA prevents you from raising legal issues in the mediation. While the mediator cannot look to remedy legal violations, the mediator can say to district personnel, "You are in trouble because you clearly violated the law; you might want to think about settling this case now."

How Much Evidence Do You Reveal in Mediation?

"Prepare for Due Process," above, suggests that you describe your evidence as a part of your opening statement. But you may not want to reveal all of your supporting evidence at mediation. By telling all, you may help the school prepare for the hearing. On the other hand, if your evidence is very strong, revealing it may lead to a settlement in your favor. If you're not sure what to do, ask the mediator's opinion in your private meeting. If the mediator feels that the school realizes its case is weak or for some other reason is close to settling, then it may be wise to lay all your cards on the table. Or, if the mediator feels the school is rigid and unlikely to settle, then it may be better not to reveal all of your evidence.

No matter what, you'll want to provide at least a synopsis of your evidence, noting where a professional (teacher, related service provider, administrator, doctor, outside evaluator, or private tutor) has made a clear statement about the disputed issue. Also note the credentials of the person, particularly if he or she is well known and loaded with degrees and experience. Stress all documents or statements by school district representatives that support your position.

School District's Opening Statement

After you make your opening statement, the school district's representative usually presents the district's point of view, perhaps responding to what you have said. Don't interrupt or respond, even though the school's version of the dispute may be very different from yours. Take notes of the main points.

Sometimes the district will choose not to make an opening statement—in that case, you'll move right on to private sessions with the mediator.

After the school representative finishes, the mediator may invite you to add anything you forgot or to respond to the school's statement. If you respond, make it brief and to the point, focusing on why you disagree with the school's position.

Private Sessions With the Mediator

After you and the school representative make your opening statements, the mediator will meet privately with you, then with the school representatives, then back with you, then back with the school representatives, continuing back and forth as necessary. When you meet privately with the mediator, speak frankly. The mediator cannot disclose anything you say to the school representatives, unless you give the mediator permission. Be sure of this by clearly telling the mediator what you want conveyed to the school district and what you want kept between you and the mediator.

In your first meeting, the mediator may want to clarify issues and begin exploring whether you're willing to compromise. As the mediator shuttles back and forth, specific evidence related to each disputed issue may come up. For example, you and the school district may have very different views on the validity of the district's evaluation versus your independent evaluation. You can tell the mediator something like "Please convey to Mr. Roberts that my evaluator is a recognized expert and is clear in her recommendations; the district's expert has limited knowledge of my child's learning disability."

After a few of these private sessions, the mediator should be able to tell you how far the school will go to settle the dispute. At this point, you will have to discuss your bottom line. Think about what is essential, what you can give up, how strong your case is, and how hard a line the school is taking. Make use of the mediator by asking direct questions, such as:

- What do you think the school will do on the placement issue?
- Do they understand that Dr. Parnell said Victor needs placement in the private school?
- What is their bottom line?
- Do you think we have a case if we go to a hearing?
- I want to push for everything; given the district's last offer, how do you think they'll react to a take-it-or-leave-it last offer?

The strength of the evidence and the work of the mediator will convince the district to settle (or not). If the district has moved somewhat from the position it held at the IEP meeting, but some issues remain unresolved, you'll have to decide what to do. You'll have to weigh the importance of the outstanding issues, your willingness to go to a hearing, and the likelihood of ultimate victory.

Bargaining in Mediation

Bargaining is part of mediation. When presenting what you want, make your list as strong and inclusive as possible. Put in everything you could possibly want, including your expenses and even minor items. But know your priorities—including what you can live without and can therefore use as bargaining chips.

EXAMPLE: You feel your child should be in a private school, which costs $15,000 per year. You also want the school district to pay for your private evaluation, which was $1,000. You also have some reimbursement costs, including a tutor, totaling several hundred dollars. Your case is strong enough to go after all of these items. But to settle the case, the district wants you to forgo the evaluation and other costs. Is it worth giving up $1,000 in costs for the $15,000? It depends on the strength of your evidence. No matter how strong your case is, there is always a risk that the hearing could go against you.

Wrapping Up the Mediation Session

After various private meetings with the mediator, there will be four possible outcomes:

- full settlement of all issues: for example, the school district agrees to provide three hours a week of speech/language therapy so your son can strengthen his expressive and receptive language skills
- partial settlement: you agree on some issues and disagree on others—for example, the district agrees to mainstream your 11th grader, provide three hours a week of aide help in English and social studies, but will not reimburse you for your independent assessment, which cost $2,500
- no settlement, but you agree to try again with the mediator at a later date: for example, you want large-print materials for your child, but the district needs to check the process for securing them or you decide to let the matter sit for a week and reconvene to see if one or both parties have moved from their original position, or
- no settlement and no further mediation sessions scheduled: for example, if you want a private school and the district disagrees, the issue will have to go to a hearing officer.

A mediation settlement can contain anything you and the school district agree to—including that the school district will provide all or part of what you want for your child and pay your attorney fees.

Whatever the outcome, you will all return to the meeting room and the mediator will fill out a mediation form. The mediator will write down what the parties agreed to (if anything), what issues are unresolved (if any), and what the next steps will be if full agreement was not reached.

If you don't reach a settlement on all or some issues, there are three options for what happens next:

- you go to a hearing
- you drop the matter, or
- you go directly to court—this highly unusual approach requires you to prove that the problem is so serious you can't spend time at a hearing and need a judge to look at the matter immediately; you will need a lawyer's help (see Chapter 14).

Be aware that it is within the district's right to ask that you drop your request for a hearing in return for settling some of the issues between you. It is your right, of course, to agree to do so or not. The mediation agreement will spell out any agreement you reach on next steps.

Once you and the school district sign the mediation form, both of you are bound by whatever agreement you reached.

Why LEAs Are More Likely to Negotiate in Mediation: Money

If you do not use an attorney in mediation, it is more likely the school district will not as well. However, it might be useful to indicate that you will use an attorney at the due process hearing, which in most cases will mean the district will use one too. (If you win the due process hearing, you will be reimbursed for your legal fees, but if you lose, in almost all cases, you will not have to reimburse the school for its legal fees (see "Attorney Fees in a Due Process Hearing", above). Because of the high cost of lawyers, the district has an incentive to settle before going to hearing.

For example, say you want the district to provide your child with a one on one aide for 15 hours per week with a cost of $1,500 per month or $18,000 per year. If the district loses at hearing, it will have that cost, plus your legal fees, plus their legal fees. And even if the district wins, It will still be paying its own attorney, which may well total the $18,000 it would cost for the aide. You can see that a simple cost analysis would strongly suggest the district settle before going to hearing, because the best case scenario will still cost them quite a bit and the worst scenario will cost them two to three times the cost of the aide. This kind of analysis does not always work—sometimes districts simply feel they must take a stand—but it is certainly worth keeping this in mind.

Due Process Hearing

A hearing is like a court trial, although it won't be held in a courtroom. You and the school district submit evidence in the form of written documents and sworn testimony from witnesses. A neutral third party (called a hearing officer) reviews the evidence and decides who is right and who is wrong. That decision is binding on you and the district. The hearing officer has the authority to act independently of you and the school district—in essence, as a judge. The hearing officer cannot be an employee of the school district or the state educational agency if either agency is involved in the education of your child. (20 U.S.C. § 1415(f)(3)(A).)

States can vary some of the procedural details. For example, Ohio provides that attorneys will act as hearing officers; other states specify qualifications rather than require that officers be members of particular professions. In most states, the department of education provides a list of hearing officers or contracts with a qualified agency to do so. For instance, in California, the state department of education has contracted with another state agency, which in turn hires the hearing officers.

Hearing Officer Qualifications

IDEA imposes several rules on hearing officers. An officer may not be an employee of the state department of education or the school district, and may not have any personal or professional interest that might conflict with the officer's objectivity in the hearing. The officer must have the knowledge and ability to understand IDEA, to conduct the hearing in accordance with appropriate legal standards, and to make and write a decision that complies with standard legal practice. (20 U.S.C. § 1415(f)(3)(A).)

RESOURCE
Contact your state department of education to find out the details of your state's laws on hearings. You can find the contact information through the federal Department of Education website at www.ed.gov.

Settling Your Case Once the Hearing Begins

Hearings are expensive, difficult, and risky for both parties. Recognizing this, some hearing officers will start the hearing by suggesting that you try one more time to settle the case. If both sides are interested, you might even meet, with or without the hearing officer, to try to work out the details. There are no rules for these discussions—it is a lot like mediation in that neither side has to agree to anything. If you do reach a compromise, the hearing officer will write up a formal agreement for you and the school district to sign.

A hearing is used to resolve factual disputes between you and your child's school district, typically disagreements about placement, related services, curricula, or methodologies. See the list of typical IEP due process disputes, at the beginning of this chapter.

Often, a factual dispute includes a legal dispute. For example, say you want your child in a private school and the school district offers a special day class in the public school. The factual dispute is over which placement is appropriate for your child. The legal issue is whether IDEA allows a private school placement when supported by the facts (it does).

Or perhaps the school district wants to place your child in a special school 15 miles from your home; you want your child placed in a regular class at the local school. Again, the factual dispute involves finding the appropriate placement. The legal issue is IDEA's requirement that your child be placed in the least restrictive environment and as close to home as possible.

At this point, you may be thinking, "I thought legal problems were only subject to the complaint process." Here's how it works: In a due process hearing, there may be legal issues that are pertinent to the factual analysis and outcome. In a complaint, you are only claiming that the school district broke the law—there is no factual dispute regarding an IEP issue.

TIP

You can do both. In some cases, you may simultaneously file a complaint and pursue due process. These situations are discussed at the end of Chapter 13.

A witness may testify about a legal issue, or you or the school district may raise a legal issue in your opening statements. In most cases, however, legal issues are addressed in a posthearing brief. (See "Posthearing Briefs," below.) Discussing legal issues at the hearing or in a brief may seem quite daunting. If you anticipate major legal disputes, see Chapter 14 on lawyers and legal research, or contact an attorney for help on this part of the process.

Fear of Hearings

It's natural to be afraid of a due process hearing—after all, it's like a trial and can be difficult and complicated. But many parents conduct hearings. So how do you get through one with your nerves intact? Here are a few tips:

- Be organized.
- Take some time to think through the issues and your evidence.
- Know that everybody else is nervous, too.

Never doubt that you can do it. Lots of parents have had these same fears—and done just fine in the hearing. In preparing for the IEP meeting (and perhaps mediation), you already did a good deal of the hard work.

Your Due Process Hearing Rights and Responsibilities

IDEA sets out many rights and responsibilities you *and* the school district have during the hearing process. (20 U.S.C. § 1415):

- You have the right to be advised and accompanied by an attorney or another person with special knowledge or training.
- At least five business days before the hearing, you and the school district are required to give each other all evaluations and any

recommendations based on those evaluations. If you don't, the hearing officer can exclude all evidence about the evaluations. This five-day requirement is usually also applied to exchanging witness lists—the names, qualifications, and topics of testimony of everyone you and the school district will call to testify at the hearing.

- The party who requested due process cannot raise any issues at the hearing that were not included in the written request unless the other side agrees.

- Before the hearing, you can subpoena witnesses to ensure that they will attend. (Most state educational agencies have subpoena forms.)

- Before the hearing, you have the right to declare the hearing closed or open to the public, including the press. (34 C.F.R. 300.521(c).) In most cases, I'd opt for a closed hearing—there's little to be gained from an open hearing, and it may greatly increase your level of stress.

- At the hearing, you have the right to have your child present (34 C.F.R. § 300.512(c)), but this is usually not advisable. You want the hearing officer to base any decisions on the objective evidence presented, not on conclusions reached by observing your child. Also, you want to protect your child from any emotional harm that could result from hearing what the witnesses or district representatives say at the hearing. In rare circumstances, you may want your child to testify at the hearing. You should then simply call your child as a witness at the appropriate time. (See "Your Child as a Witness," below.)

- After the hearing, you are entitled to a verbatim record of the hearing (in either written or electronic format). The hearing officer will tape the proceedings.

- After the hearing, you're entitled to a written decision, including findings of fact.

- You have the right to appeal a hearing decision to a state or federal court.

Check your state laws and regulations for any different or additional rules or requirements. For example, California requires each party to a hearing to submit a statement of issues and proposed resolutions at least ten days before the hearing. (Cal. Educ. Code § 56505(e)(6).)

Burden of Proof

In *Schaffer ex rel. Schaffer v. Weast*, 546 U.S. 49 (2005), the U.S. Supreme Court decided that the party initiating due process has the burden of proving its case at hearing. While the Court acknowledged that the term "burden of proof" is very difficult to define, this means that the party that files for due process must prove its case. For you, this means that if you file for due process, it's not up to the school district to show that it is providing an appropriate education for your child. Rather, it will be up to you to show that what the school district is offering is not appropriate.

Pros and Cons of a Due Process Hearing

There are several good reasons to request a hearing:

- If you win, your child will receive the education he or she needs.
- If you win, it's unlikely you will have to fight the battle again.
- If you win, your attorney fees will be reimbursed for every issue you prevail on.
- Whether or not you win, you buy time. If your child is currently in a placement you want to maintain, your child is entitled to remain there until the issue is finally resolved—either through the hearing decision or a final court decision, if you appeal.

Of course, there are also some disadvantages to a hearing:

- Hearings are difficult, time-consuming, emotionally draining, and contentious.
- You might lose.
- Your relationship with your school district will likely be strained and formal. Future IEP meetings may be hard. If you lose, the school district may feel invincible.
- If you lose, you won't be entitled to reimbursement for your costs and attorney fees.

Hearing Logistics

A due process hearing must be held at a time and place that are convenient for you. Normally, hearings are held at the school district office and last anywhere from one to several days.

Once you request a hearing, you will be sent a notice of the date and location of the hearing, as well as the name of the hearing officer. You will also be given the name, address, and phone number of the school district representative. You have to send your exhibits and witness lists to this representative as well as the hearing officer.

Preparing for the Hearing

If you go to mediation first, much of your preparation will be done by the time you go to a hearing. But you still have some very important and time-consuming work to do. Give yourself several weeks to prepare, more if you skip mediation and go straight to a hearing.

Know Your Case

Review your child's file (Chapter 4), your binder (Chapter 4), and your IEP blueprint (Chapter 5). Be clear on the disputed issues: what you want, what the school district is offering, and how you disagree.

Determine Your Strategy

At the hearing, you must clearly state your position on each disputed issue and offer evidence to support it. (In your request for due process, you listed the issues.) You will present your evidence in the form of witnesses and documents.

You should have a clear strategy that connects your evidence to the disputed issues. For example, you want your child to have a one-on-one aide, two hours each day, to work on reading comprehension and language acquisition. How can you convince the hearing officer to give you what you want? Hopefully, you have specific evidence about your child's needs, written reports as exhibits, and/or testimony from your witnesses. But there may be other important, if indirect, evidence as well. For example, the school district may not have evaluated your child in a timely manner or may have failed to test in certain areas. Or the district may not have up-to-date evaluation material to prove an alternative to the aide would be sufficient. Or the district may have cut off the discussion of your proposal in the IEP meeting. None of this evidence proves or disproves that your child needs a one-on-one aide, but it does show that the district did not allow the IEP process to proceed appropriately—and, therefore, adds weight to your argument that the district is wrong.

> EXAMPLE: You want your child mainstreamed with a one-on-one aide, but your school district offers a special class. At the hearing, you will have to show that:
> - The school district failed to offer mainstreaming placement.
> - An aide will help your child function in the mainstream classroom.
> - Your child will benefit socially by being in a regular class.
> - A special class will be detrimental to your child because it will not address your child's unique needs—and is contrary to IDEA's least restrictive environment requirement.

Prepare Exhibits of Written Material

Any written document that contains evidence supporting your position or provides information that the hearing officer will need to make a decision can be used as an exhibit. But be choosy—you don't necessarily want to turn over your entire IEP binder. The issues in dispute will guide you. Review all of your documents, looking for everything that supports your position, such as an evaluation or teacher's report. Note the specific page number and paragraph in each document where the supportive statement is made. You have probably done much of this work with the material organizer form you developed for the IEP meeting.

> CAUTION
>
> **Do not submit material that damages your case or reveals private information you don't want known.** The school district may submit evidence that harms your case or points out the gaps in your evidence; obviously, you should not. Remember that the school district and hearing officer will get to examine whatever you submit as evidence—if it contains personal or confidential information you don't want to reveal, you should try to find a different way to make your point or submit only portions of the document.

Example of exhibits typically presented at hearings include:
- IEP documents
- evaluations
- letters or reports from your child's teacher or physician
- articles about your child's disability, appropriate teaching methods, or any other issues in your case
- witnesses' résumés and articles they've written that relate to the issues in dispute, and
- your child's classroom work.

If in doubt, include the item. You never know when you might want to refer to something during the hearing. If you don't include the item when you prepare your exhibit exchange (at least five days before the hearing), you will probably be barred from using it at the hearing.

Arrange your exhibits in an order that makes sense to you, such as the order in which you plan to introduce them or alphabetical order. Place them in a folder or binder with tabs and a table of contents. Be sure to put page numbers on each individual exhibit, too, so you can easily find specific statements.

You'll refer to these exhibits in your own testimony and when you question witnesses. At this stage, it is unlikely that you will have to develop new evidence. But if you do not yet have support for a disputed item, you may need new material—for example, a supportive letter or even an independent evaluation.

Choose and Prepare Witnesses

Witnesses are crucial to the outcome of a fair hearing. Choose and prepare your witnesses with care.

Choosing Witnesses

Double-check your list of *all* potential witnesses, those who support you and those who might testify for the school district (including participants at the IEP meeting). Try to anticipate what each witness can testify about. One witness may be able to testify about several issues, while others may focus on only one disputed matter.

In choosing your witnesses, look for the following:

- The strength of the witness's testimony.
- The witness's experience, training, education, and direct knowledge of your child.
- The witness's willingness to testify under oath. You should consider whether a person is willing to testify at the hearing before you put him or her on your witness list. A witness's favorable or supportive report won't help if that person equivocates at the hearing. In that case, submit the witness's written material and have other witnesses refer to that report.

Sometimes, an important witness refuses to testify voluntarily at the hearing. For example, your child's former tutor—who could testify in detail about your child's reading problems—may now work for the school district and be reluctant to support you in a due process fight over eligibility. In these cases, you may need to subpoena a reluctant witness to testify at the hearing. A subpoena is an order that requires the witness to appear. You can get subpoena forms from your state department of education.

Preparing Witness Questions

Write out a list of questions for each witness. Here is a general outline (of course, the specific questions you ask each witness will depend on what he or she knows about your child):

- Ask the witness to identify him- or herself—for example, "Please state your name, occupation, and place of employment."
- Ask about the witness's experience, education, training, and specific expertise in the area of dispute—you can refer the witness to a résumé or written articles that you included in your exhibits. In a hearing for a child with learning disabilities, the witness might be an expert in reading, language, or strategies used to address learning disabilities. It is important to establish your witness's credentials so that his or her testimony will carry a lot of weight with the hearing officer.
- Establish the witness's knowledge of your child—for example:
  - *"Have you met my son, Philip Lavelle?"*
  - *"Please tell us when, for how long, and for what purpose."*
  - *"Did you also observe him in school?"*
  - *"Please tell us when that was and for how long."*
- Ask questions to elicit your witness's opinion about the issues in dispute, for example:
  - *"You stated that you tested Philip. What tests did you administer?"*
  - *"What were the results?"*
  - *"What do those results mean?"*
  - *"What conclusions did you draw regarding Philip's reading difficulties?"*
  - *"How severe are his difficulties?"*
  - *"In your professional opinion, what is the appropriate way to help Philip improve his reading?"*
  - *"Do you have any specific recommendations regarding Philip's reading needs?"*
  - *"What is your professional opinion regarding Philip's prognosis as a successful reader if he is not provided the help you recommend?"*

TIP

Keys to preparing your witnesses. As a general rule, witnesses must be able to clearly state what your child needs and why, the benefits to your child if those needs are met, and the detriment to your child if they are not.

The Cost of an Independent Evaluator Appearing in Due Process

In the 2006 case of *Arlington Central School District Board of Education v. Murphy*, 548 U.S. 291, the U.S. Supreme Court ruled that when a parent goes to due process and prevails, IDEA does not allow the parent to be reimbursed for the cost of an expert witness. The majority of the court acknowledged that when Congress enacted IDEA it indicated that costs could include reimbursement for expert witnesses and their fees, but the Court found that IDEA does not clearly allow such reimbusement. This means then that even if you win your case in due process, you will not be reimbursed for the cost of having an independent evaluator testify.

Preparing Your Witnesses

Before the hearing, meet with your witnesses and go over your questions. Their answers may lead to new questions you'll want to ask or trigger a new strategy or approach. Explain that after you're done asking questions, the school district representative will cross-examine the witness by asking additional questions.

Some witnesses, particularly any school employees who agree to testify for your child, may be unwilling to meet during school hours. You may have to arrange to meet them at their homes. Others may not want to meet at all. What should you do about witnesses who can help your case but won't talk to you ahead of time? If you can't discuss the case before the hearing, you won't know exactly how the witness will testify, which can be risky. One strategy is to leave the person off your witness list, then hope that the district calls her so you can cross-examine him or her. Of course, if the witness is the only person who can testify about a certain element of your case, then this may not be wise.

Another strategy is to include the person on your witness list but don't ask him or her to testify during your presentation. Then you can either cross-examine the witness (if he or she is called as a witness by the school) or use him or her as a "rebuttal witness," a witness you call after the school district presents its evidence, to counter the testimony of the district's witnesses.

Just before the hearing date, get back in touch with your witnesses to tell them:

- the date, time, and location of the hearing
- what time you need them to arrive to be ready to testify—be sure to let them know that they might not be called on time if an earlier witness takes longer than expected or the hearing officer breaks early, and
- how long you expect their testimony to take.

Preparing Yourself as a Witness

You will most likely be a witness at the hearing. You have valuable information about your child's history, previous programs, and needs; your worries and frustrations; and what teachers have said to you about your child.

Your testimony should cover those matters about which you have first-hand knowledge. Although you can testify about the evaluation done on your child and what the evaluator told you, the evaluator is in a better position to testify about this issue. It's best for your testimony to cover the areas in which you are the expert.

Your Child as a Witness

There may be situations in which you want to call your child as a witness. For example, if your child is in high school, is deaf and wants an interpreter, then the child's testimony about feeling isolated without access to classroom communication may be powerful. But when your child testifies, the other side may try to trick him or her.

You have to be absolutely sure that your child is prepared to testify and understands what the other side may ask. You should also carefully consider whether the benefits of your child's testimony will likely outweigh the negatives. You may want to consult with experts—such as your pediatrician or another adult your child trusts—to make sure that testifying (and particularly undergoing cross examination) would not be harmful to your child.

You can present your testimony in one of two ways: You can respond to questions (just like you will be asking questions of your witnesses) asked by your spouse, a relative, or a close friend, or you can make a statement covering all issues of importance. You can either read your statement or give it from notes. After you're done answering questions or making your statement, the school district representative will cross-examine you.

Your testimony should be clear, specific, and objective. Break down your points into the following areas, using your mediation statement (if you made one) as a starting point:

- a general description of your child, including age, strengths, and weaknesses (your child profile, discussed in Chapter 10, can help here)
- your child's disability and the effects of that disability—for example, your son has a learning disability, and, as a result, he has difficulty with simple computations, reading comprehension, and visual memory
- any secondary difficulties due to the disability—such as emotional problems
- your child's educational history—that is, his or her classes, prior placements, and current program
- the particular issues in dispute and your desired resolution (remember, your child is entitled to an "appropriate"—not an ideal—education; your testimony should explain why the program, related services, and other items you want for your child are appropriate)
- your observations at class visits, meetings with teachers and other professionals, and the IEP meeting (for example, "On February 12, 20xx I visited the second grade class at Tower School and I observed….")
- statements others have made to you that support your point of view, including your reaction to those statements—for instance, "On November 3, 20xx Mr. Mastin of the school district told me there was no room for my child in the second grade class at Tower School; I confirmed this conversation in a letter which is my Exhibit F. Mr. Mastin did not respond to my letter," and

- your child's specific educational needs and the consequences if those needs are not met—for example, "Given the assessment by Dr. Pollack, I believe a placement in a program other than the second grade class at Tower School will have serious emotional and cognitive consequences for my child."

Rules of Evidence

You may have heard of something called the "rules of evidence." These formal rules, which are very specific and sometimes quite arcane, are used in courts to guide judges in deciding what evidence can be included and what must be excluded. These rules don't have to be followed at due process hearings, but the hearing officer can use them as appropriate.

For example, some rules relate to hearsay evidence—information that a witness did not hear or receive directly. "I saw Jack hit Frank" is not hearsay; "Jack told me that Frank hit Bill" is hearsay evidence and can be excluded at a hearing.

Don't worry too much about formal rules of evidence. If the other side "objects" to a question you ask because it violates a rule of evidence, ask the hearing officer to explain the rule and then rephrase your question.

Prepare Questions for School Witnesses

Preparing questions for school witnesses is more difficult than preparing for your own witnesses because you don't know exactly what they'll say. Still, you can probably guess what many witnesses will say, because you heard their opinions at the IEP meeting.

Start by reviewing your files, the transcript or notes of the IEP meeting, and the school district's exhibits (you'll get them five days before the hearing). Then make a list of questions to strengthen your case or at least undermine what the school district's witnesses might say.

EXAMPLE: Your child's teacher said something very important to you when you visited your child's class. You sent a letter confirming what was said ("Thanks for talking to me today. I was glad to hear that you agreed Jake should remain in a regular class with the help of an aide"). The teacher never objected to your confirming letter, but you now believe she will say the opposite at the hearing. Be ready to point out the discrepancy—for instance, "Ms. Jenkins, you testified this morning that you feel Jake should be placed in a special education class. Do you recall when we met on October 15 and you told me that Jake was doing well in the regular class but needed an aide to keep up? You don't recall that meeting? Please look at Exhibit B, my November 1 letter to you."

Exchange Witness Lists and Evidence

Remember, you should submit a list of your witnesses and must submit copies of written exhibits at least five days before the hearing begins. (20 U.S.C. § 1415(f)(2).) Once you have your exhibits (organized in binders) and your list of witnesses, make two copies. Keep the originals for yourself, send one copy to the hearing officer, and send the other copy to the school district representative. To make sure you have proof that the school district received the items at least five days before the hearing, send them certified mail, return receipt requested.

The Due Process Hearing

The hearing normally proceeds as follows:

1. The hearing officer gives an overview of the hearing process. The hearing officer will usually identify and confirm the witness list and the exhibits that you and the school district submitted.
2. The hearing officer turns on the tape recorder, and the formal hearing begins.
3. The parties introduce themselves on tape.
4. You make your opening statement.
5. The school district makes its opening statement.
6. You question (direct examine) your witnesses.
7. The school representative questions (cross-examines) your witnesses.

8. You ask more questions of your witnesses (redirect) if you want, the school representative cross-examines again (called recross), and so on.

9. The school district calls its witnesses with the same pattern of direct examination, cross-examination, redirect, and recross.

10. You call (or call back) any witnesses after the school finishes, if you want. These are called rebuttal witnesses and are used to clarify or contradict testimony raised by the other side. The school district has the same right.

11. You give a closing statement, if you want.

12. The school district gives a closing statement, if it wants.

13. The hearing officer adjourns the hearing.

14. You and the school district submit written briefs discussing the facts presented at the hearing and any applicable law. (See "Posthearing Briefs," below.)

15. The hearing officer issues a written decision.

Make an Opening Statement

You can use the opening statement you prepared for mediation as a starting point, but you will need to change it somewhat for a hearing. At mediation, you can say anything; your aim is to reach a compromise. At a hearing, however, your aim is to prove your case. Your opening statement, therefore, should emphasize what you want for your child and how that is supported by evidence. This doesn't mean you shouldn't include items for which your evidence is weak, but it does mean that you should carefully think about what you're requesting—and how likely you are to get it. The hearing officer will consider not only your evidence, but your credibility. If you ask for something unsupported by any evidence, your credibility may be affected.

Be sure to include these details in your opening statement:

- basic facts about your child, including age, disability, and current educational program
- a clear statement of your child's needs and the dispute that brought you to the hearing, and

- a brief statement that what you want is supported by evidence, such as "Cheryl needs a full-time aide, as we will clearly show with evidence, including the testimony of several different professionals and Exhibits B, D, and M."

Opening statements can be any length, but five to 15 minutes is typical. If you can, don't read a verbatim statement—instead, use notes to guide you in making your points. If you're very nervous, however, it's okay to read a statement. It is important to express your feelings and bring the human element into the hearing. Be careful not to ramble in an unfocused way or attack school district representatives on a personal level, but don't hesitate to make a strong, clear statement of what your child needs.

Questioning Your Witnesses

After opening statements, your witnesses will testify. Think carefully about the order in which you want to present their testimony. You are telling a story, and you need to present the details of the story in an order that will make sense to someone who has little or no prior knowledge of the situation. It's often best to begin with someone (possibly you) who can give general background information about your child. Next, you might want a witness who can present the evaluation data, such as your independent evaluator.

After that, you want to go to the core of the dispute and make your case. For example, say you and the school district disagree on placement and a related service. During the past year, your child was in a regular class, with no assistance. You want your child to stay in that class with an aide; the school district has offered placement in a special day class. Your first witness can give the details of the regular class. The second can talk about why your child needs that class. The third can describe the services offered by the aide. The fourth can explain why your child needs that aide.

Of course, you may have to modify the presentation and go out of order if a witness is available only on a certain day or at a certain time. Or, you may choose a different order to maximize impact. In some instances, the witness who will give the most dramatic and effective testimony should go last, so the hearing officer is left with that impression. Or that person might go first, to set a tone for the rest of the hearing. Only you can decide which strategy will be most effective in your situation.

Keeping Track During the Hearing

You want to have an ongoing record of the testimony during the hearing because you may need to refer back to previous testimony. For example, say the district calls a witness who testifies for 45 minutes on various issues. When you cross-examine, you want to refer back to a specific statement this witness made that contradicted other testimony or ask him or her to clarify something he or she said. You need to be able to refer to earlier statements.

Taking notes is the logical way to keep track; however, it can be difficult to get everything down while also conducting the hearing. Instead, have someone else take notes for you, recording statements of each witness, while you also take notes on key statements. (You can do this on paper or a laptop computer.) If you had a notetaker at the IEP meeting, consider using the same person, who is probably very familiar with the issues by now. You can tape the hearing, but you won't have time to review taped testimony while the hearing is going on. Also, it is more difficult to try to find an exact statement on a tape than to simply refer to written notes. If you don't have a notetaker, be sure to take notes as the other side questions witnesses. Highlight key statements.

How do you use the notes? During your cross-examination you say something like, "Mr. Adams, you testified that, let me see [look at your notes], and I quote, 'I don't think James needs an aide in class.' Is that correct?" If he agrees, then point out evidence that contradicts him, such as "In her testimony yesterday, Dr. Markham stated that you told her on April 29, 20xx that James needed an aide. Which statement should we believe?"

Questioning Reluctant Witnesses

Question reluctant witnesses with care. First, ask the hearing officer to note that the witness is not cooperative. To ensure the person's attendance at the hearing, you should have issued a subpoena. At the hearing, ask something like "Mr. Perez, are you testifying voluntarily?" The response will be something like "No. As you know I was subpoenaed by you."

Another possibility is to begin your questioning with a statement such as "This witness, Mr. Hobson, the fourth grade teacher, would not talk to me prior to the hearing. I am calling him as a hostile witness."

Further Suggestions on Questioning Witnesses

No matter how much you prepare, you won't be able to anticipate exactly how the questioning will go. Be ready to depart from your planned questions. For example, a witness might answer in a way slightly different from what you expected, requiring you to ask follow-up questions. Or the witness may say the opposite of what you expect.

Here are some tips on questioning witnesses:

- Ask for a brief break if you need to gather yourself or consider new questions.
- Keep track of your questions. If you veer off on a line of questioning you had not planned, mark where you are on your list of questions so you can come back to it later.
- Be very, very careful about asking a question unless you know how the witness will answer, particularly of a school witness.
- Don't overwhelm the hearing officer with a ton of facts. Parents tend to try to get everything into the record at the hearing. Know the difference between important facts and minutiae.
- Know when to stop. Stop asking questions when something powerful has been stated. Further questioning will only dilute the impact.
- Don't badger a witness. Ask questions in a firm way and repeat them if necessary. But don't become hostile, belligerent, or belittling.
- Don't play lawyer. You'll do fine with your own style and language.

How to Use Your Exhibits

Have your exhibits available so you can use them when you question witnesses. For example, "Tell me, Dr. Whitland, you said Monroe does not need counseling. Would you please look at Exhibit B, page 4? You reported last year that Monroe had severe emotional difficulties that were interfering with his education. Aren't severe emotional difficulties usually addressed in some kind of psychological therapy?"

Closing Statements

After all the evidence has been presented and all witnesses have testified, the hearing officer will ask if you want to make closing arguments or submit a written brief.

A closing statement, like the opening statement, is a powerful and precise summary of your arguments, but now you can refer to useful testimony from the hearing itself as proof of what you want. For example, you might say, "Every witness we called agreed that Michele needs four sessions each week with a reading specialist; not one of the school district's witnesses contradicted that. This is fully consistent with Dr. Hanover's written report, Exhibit L." Your closing statement might also note that the recommended education is consistent with IDEA, and point out what may happen to your child if the hearing officer rules against you.

Posthearing Briefs

If you agree to submit briefs, the parties, with the help of the hearing officer, will set a short time frame (usually no more than ten days) to submit the briefs. The purpose of the briefs is to highlight the evidence that supports your case and bring any supportive law or legal cases to the attention of the hearing officer.

To develop your brief, first review your notes, your memory, and the evidence. The written brief should point out the evidence that supports your case and the evidence that contradicts the school district's point of view. If there are legal issues, you should review IDEA and any court cases that support your analysis of the law. (See Chapter 14 for advice on legal research.) You may also want to contact a lawyer for help.

It may be quite daunting to think about writing this brief after all the work you've already done, particularly the legal part. If you don't want to hire a lawyer, I strongly recommend that you contact one of the many nonprofit organizations that can help children with disabilities. While they may not be able to represent you at the hearing, they may be able to provide you advice about the brief and even what regulations and cases might apply (if you let them know the legal issues).

Hearing Decision and Appeals

After the hearing, you're entitled to a written decision, including findings of fact. The hearing officer must have "substantive grounds" for the decision, which must include a finding of whether the child has been receiving a free, appropriate public education (FAPE). (20 U.S.C. § 1415(f)(3)(E).) Many courts have found that a school district's violation of IDEA procedures constitutes a denial of FAPE.

Both you and the school district have the right to appeal the hearing decision, theoretically all the way to the U.S. Supreme Court. If you lose, several factors will help you decide whether or not to appeal:

- **Strength of your case.** You should already have considered this as part of your decision to pursue due process. For an appeal, you must look at your situation with a more critical eye. Many reviewing courts will defer to the administrative decision and won't want to rehear the evidence anew. Even if the court takes a fresh look at the evidence, remember that a neutral third party has already ruled against you, which suggests some problems with your case.

Exhausting Administrative Remedies: When You Can Go Straight to Court

In most special education disputes, you have to go to the administrative, or "due process," hearing before you can sue in court. There are times when it may seem better to go straight into court. For example, if you live in a state where the due process hearing decisions don't often favor the student over the school district and where there are courts that are more sensitive to the needs of children with disabilities, it might be best to go directly to court. There are, however, several complications to such a plan: first, you will need an attorney, and second, you are eliminating one of only a few chances to win your case. You might be able to win at hearing, but if you go straight to court, you've eliminated the first chance to win.

Moreover, there are very strict rules about when you can bypass the administrative hearing and go directly to court. The most notable rule is that you have to show that the administrative process would be futile or that there is an emergency that requires remedies (solutions) only available in a court of law. This is often referred to as "exhaustion of administrative remedies." For example, if you want the district to do something immediately (or stop doing something immediately) because your child is in danger but the district won't agree, waiting the 45 days allowed for a due process hearing decision to be rendered would harm your child and only a court could force the district to act immediately. If there is no urgent matter, it is unlikely a court will allow you to forgo the administrative hearing.

In the vast majority of cases, you should be very careful about bypassing the due process hearing. Absolutely, you should discuss this with an attorney well-versed in special education law.

- **Costs of an appeal.** There are various costs in appealing a hearing decision to court, including filing fees, fees for serving papers on the school district, witness fees, and other trial costs (such as copying exhibits). And there's one more cost: potential attorney fees. While nonattorneys can represent themselves in court, I strongly recommend that you hire an attorney. At the very least, have an attorney who specializes in IDEA review your case and advise you of your chances on appeal.

- **Time.** If you or the school district wants to appeal the due process hearing decision, you must do so within 90 days after the decision is issued (not the date you actually receive it), unless your state law establishes a different time limit for such appeals. (20 U.S.C. § 1415(i)(2)(B).) Contact your state department of education or a parental support group to find out about your state's timelines. See Appendix B on this book's Companion Page on nolo.com (you'll find the link in Chapter 16) for contact information.)

Filing a Complaint

A s discussed in Chapter 12, factual disputes with the school district are usually resolved through informal negotiation and due process. But what if you believe that the school district has violated a legal requirement under IDEA? You can use the IDEA complaint process. You can find the regulations regarding complaints at 34 C.F.R. §§ 300.151–153.

"Complaint" or "Due Process Complaint"?

They might sound alike, but there are important differences between a "due process complaint" (see Chapter 12) and a "complaint" as discussed in this chapter. To clarify:

File a **due process complaint** when you have a factual dispute about your child's IEP. For example, you want your child placed in program A and the school district offers program B, your child needs three weekly sessions of physical therapy and the district offers none, or you want your child mainstreamed and the district offers placement in a special day class.

On the other hand, when you believe the district has violated a legal duty—by not following one of the many requirements under IEP—then file a **complaint** as described in this chapter.

When to File a Complaint

The IDEA statute and regulations set out the school district's legal obligations. Excerpts of key sections of IDEA are contained in Appendix A on this book's Companion Page on nolo.com (see Chapter 16 for the link). Here are some common school district actions (or inactions) that are legal violations of IDEA:

- failure to provide a child's records
- failure to do evaluations
- failure to meet evaluation and IEP timelines
- failure to hold an IEP meeting, either an annual meeting or an IEP meeting you request because you want to change your child's IEP
- failure to allow a parent to effectively represent his or her child in the IEP meeting—for example, by limiting who can attend or by intimidating the parent

- failure to follow certain procedures before suspending or expelling a special education student (see Chapter 2)
- failure to discuss all elements in an IEP meeting—goals, placement, related services, and transition plans
- failure to implement an agreed-to IEP—for example, if your child's IEP calls for three sessions of speech/language therapy each week and the school district provides only one session, and
- failure to give notice before changing a child's IEP. Your district cannot change your child's IEP without giving you notice of that change and holding an IEP meeting.

You should file your complaint within a year after the violation occurs. You should also send a copy of your complaint to the school district. To be safe, send this copy—and the complaint you file with a state or federal agency (see below)—by certified mail.

Avoid Factual Disputes With a Carefully Written IEP

Sometimes it's hard to tell whether you're dealing with a factual dispute (and therefore something that is subject to due process) or a legal violation that must be resolved by filing a complaint. For example, let's say your child needs a multisensory methodology. The IEP might refer to a specific multisensory approach, such as Slingerland. If the district does not provide Slingerland, then it has violated the IEP. You should file a complaint.

On the other hand, if the IEP does not specifically require Slingerland, then the dispute may be over what the IEP requires. For example, the IEP says only that your child will have a multisensory approach or (even more vaguely) that the teacher will try to help your child use his or her visual, auditory, and kinesthetic abilities. If the district does not use Slingerland, it has not violated IDEA. Because the IEP did not specifically require Slingerland, this is a factual dispute about what the IEP requires. You can deal with it by filing for due process.

To avoid factual disputes like this, make sure that your child's IEP is clear and precise.

Collective Complaints: There's Strength in Numbers

If your school district is violating the law in a way that affects a group of children, consider filing a complaint together. A complaint filed by more than one family can be that much more effective. Your state department of education has a legal duty under IDEA to monitor all school districts to make sure they are following the law—and to take any necessary steps to force a recalcitrant district to shape up. States are usually more sensitive to what may be a pattern of IDEA violations. If you are able to show that many children are being hurt by the district's failure to follow the law, your state department of education may be quicker to step in and take action. And it's much less costly for a group of parents to hire one attorney to draft and submit a complaint than for each family to hire its own lawyer. See Chapter 15 for a more detailed discussion about the value of parent groups.

Where to File a Complaint

The common violations of IDEA listed above are not the only grounds for a complaint. If you believe your school district has violated IDEA or any state special education law, contact your state department of education (or a locally designated agency) or the U.S. Department of Education, Office for Civil Rights (OCR). Contact information for both can be found through the U.S. Department of Education website at www.ed.gov.

You can file a complaint with either the state or federal education agency. Both handle violations of IDEA, state law, or Section 504 of the Rehabilitation Act of 1973.

RELATED TOPIC

See Chapter 7 for a brief description of Section 504, which prohibits schools from denying access to children with disabilities.

State departments of education primarily focus on IDEA violations, but will also look into complaints regarding Section 504. In contrast, the federal OCR is primarily concerned with Section 504 or discrimination violations, but will also investigate IDEA complaints.

Before deciding where to file a complaint, contact your state department of education and the regional office of the OCR and ask the following questions:

- What kinds of complaints do they investigate?
- What is the deadline for filing a complaint? Section 504 complaints must be filed within 180 days of the last alleged act of discrimination against your child. IDEA complaints must be filed within the time established in your state statute of limitations (discussed in Chapter 12).
- How do they handle complaints? In some states, an IDEA or Section 504 complaint is initially investigated by the school district. If you have a choice, opt for an investigator (who is not associated with your school district).
- What are their timelines for investigating complaints?
- What remedies are available if the district is found in violation of the law? For example, are you entitled to reimbursement for attorney fees or the cost of related services?

What to Include in a Complaint

Your state department of education may have a complaint form for you to use. OCR has one, but you aren't required to use it. (OCR's complaint form is available online at www.ed.gov/about/offices/list/ocr/complaintintro.html.)

Whether you use a form or simply write a letter, include the following information:

- Your name and address (a telephone number where you may be reached during business hours is helpful, but not required).
- Your child's name, the school he or she attends, and the name of the school district.
- As precise a description as possible of the violation, including the date, time, and location. If you cite more than one violation or you have very broad concerns, be as detailed as possible, describing each violation separately. Include a statement that "The school district violated Part B of IDEA."
- The applicable section of IDEA or any state law, if you know it. Key sections of IDEA are cited throughout this book, and

Appendix A on this book's Companion Page on nolo.com (see Chapter 16 for the link) includes excerpts of IDEA. Contact your state department of education (contact information at www.ed.gov) for state special education laws and regulations.

- The remedy you want, including reimbursement for costs incurred due to the district's violations.
- You must sign the letter. (34 C.F.R. § 300.153(b).)

A sample complaint letter is shown below.

Hiring a Lawyer to File a Complaint

Nothing in IDEA prevents you from hiring an attorney to file and pursue a complaint on behalf of your child. If the issues are particularly complex, it might be a good idea to bring in a lawyer. Keep in mind, however, that you are less likely to be reimbursed for your legal fees in the complaint process. While there is always a chance that the school district will pay your attorney fees (particularly if you have a strong case), most families have to pay their own fees if they use an attorney to bring a complaint.

If your state department of education investigates your complaint and finds in your favor, nothing in IDEA prevents the department from requiring the school district to pay your legal fees as part of the resolution. However, IDEA does not require reimbursement, so if you hire a lawyer, it's unlikely you'll be reimbursed for fees.

Notifying the U.S. Department of Education

In addition to filing a complaint, you can notify the U.S. Department of Education, Office of Special Education and Rehabilitative Services, Office of Special Education Programs (OSEP). OSEP won't investigate the problem or issue a decision, but it has overall responsibility for monitoring how states implement IDEA and might consider your comments when conducting its annual review of the programs in your state. You can find contact information at www.ed.gov.

Sample Complaint Letter

February 5, 20xx

John Harrington, Director
Compliance Unit
Special Education Division
Department of Education
721 Capitol Mall
Sacramento, CA 95814

Dear Mr. Harrington:

I am formally requesting that you investigate legal violations by the Valley
Unified School District, 458 4th Street, Visalia, California. I am making this
request pursuant to IDEA and state law, which gives me the right to file a
complaint if I believe the school district has violated IDEA.

The facts in this matter are as follows:

I requested an IEP meeting on October 14, 20xx, just after my child was
determined eligible for special education. The school district did not
contact me to schedule an IEP meeting until February 2, 20xx, at which
time I was told that the meeting would be March 5, 20xx. By doing this,
the school violated Part B of IDEA, which provides that an IEP will be held
within 30 days of a determination that a child needs special education
and related services. I request that an IEP meeting be held within 15 days
of the conclusion of your investigation. I also request reimbursement
for the cost I incurred to hire a private physical therapist because of the
school district's failure to address my child's needs.

Please contact me to confirm receipt of this request, set up times for me
to meet with your investigator, and establish timelines for completing the
investigation.

Sincerely,

Becky Masteron

Becky Masteron
6004 Green Street
Visalia, CA 95800

What Happens When You File a Complaint

After you file your complaint, the investigating agency will most likely:

- meet with you to discuss the case
- give you an opportunity to provide additional written or oral information
- review evidence and records
- meet with the school district
- give the school district an opportunity to present its side of the story, and then
- issue a decision.

IDEA requires that the state issue its decision within 60 days after the complaint is filed. This requirement can be extended if there are "exceptional circumstances" or if the parties go to mediation to resolve the complaint. (34 C.F.R. § 300.152.)

If the agency finds that the district violated IDEA, the agency will make recommendations that the school district must follow to comply with the law. The decision can be appealed to the U.S. Secretary of Education.

Finally, the line between a factual due process complaint (discussed in Chapter 12) and a legal complaint (discussed in this chapter) may not always be clear. For example, in your child's current IEP, the district may have agreed to continue providing a specific related service that it provided last year, but it stated in the most recent IEP meeting that your child now needs less of that service. In this case, you might file a due process complaint because you have a factual dispute—for the current year, the parties cannot agree on the related service. But you might also file a legal complaint if the district stops providing the related service altogether. When it is not absolutely clear whether you should file a due process complaint or a legal complaint, do both.

Due Process and Complaints

You can simultaneously go through due process and file a complaint alleging a legal violation. If the district is found to have violated the law, you would certainly want the hearing officer to know. Indeed, if timing permits, you may want to file your complaint first so you can submit the decision as an exhibit at the due process hearing. Note, however, that the portion of your complaint that involves a factual dispute can be set aside to be resolved through due process. (34 C.F.R. § 300.152(c).)

Lawyers and Legal Research

L awyers (also called attorneys) can play an important role in the special education process. While the purpose of this book is to guide you through the IEP process without an attorney, there may be times when you might need to hire or at least consult one.

This chapter covers:

- how a lawyer can help with the IEP and other IDEA procedures
- whether you need a lawyer
- finding an effective lawyer
- how lawyers are paid
- resolving problems with your lawyer, and
- doing your own legal research.

How a Lawyer Can Help

Generally speaking, a lawyer can help you in one of two ways: A lawyer can provide advice and assistance as needed throughout the IEP process while you do most of the work, or a lawyer can be directly involved as your formal representative.

Here are some of the specific tasks a lawyer can help you with:

- securing your child's school files
- requesting an evaluation or an IEP meeting
- helping you find specialists and programs for children with learning disabilities
- preparing for the IEP eligibility meeting
- preparing for the IEP program meeting—including drafting goals, your child's profile, and program and service descriptions; reviewing supportive evidence and materials; suggesting who should attend and what material will be most effective; and providing pointers that will help you present your ideas persuasively
- attending an IEP meeting (remember to notify your school district before the meeting if your lawyer will attend)
- reviewing evaluations and IEP forms before you sign them
- researching a specific legal issue that applies to your situation

- helping you informally resolve a dispute with the school district
- assessing the strength of your case, if you're considering filing a complaint or pursuing due process
- preparing for and attending mediation and the due process hearing
- writing a posthearing brief
- preparing a complaint for you to file with the appropriate educational agency, and
- representing you in court.

You may choose to have a lawyer do everything from beginning to end in the IEP process or only handle certain tasks. For example, you might want to attend the IEP meeting yourself but have a lawyer review the IEP document before you sign it.

Do You Need a Lawyer?

Because lawyers can be expensive—and because hiring a lawyer definitely makes the IEP process more adversarial—you'll want to think carefully before bringing one in. Here are some factors to consider:

- **Complexity of the case.** The more complex your case is, the more likely it is that you could benefit from some legal advice. If your dispute involves complicated placement and service issues, for example, it might make sense to bring in a lawyer. Fighting about the difference between two and three hours a week of occupational therapy is pretty straightforward; a dispute over whether your child's learning disabilities require a private school may justify the use of an attorney.
- **Strength of your case.** If you really don't know whether you have a good case against the school district, consider scheduling a consultation with a recommended attorney. A good attorney should tell you how strong your case is and, therefore, whether your situation justifies hiring him or her.
- **Your time and energy.** If you work full time, are a single parent, or have a difficult schedule, you may want someone else to take

charge. On the other hand, if you have the time and energy to represent yourself and your child, hiring an attorney may not be necessary.

- **Your budget.** Attorneys aren't cheap. Can you afford the help? Even though you might be entitled to reimbursement for your legal costs, you must assume your legal costs may not be recouped. (See "How Attorneys Are Paid," below.)

- **Your self-confidence.** The purpose of this book is not only to help you advocate for your child, but also to give you the confidence to be an effective advocate. Still, you may prefer to hire a lawyer rather than waging the battle on your own.

- **Who represents the school district.** If the school district is using an attorney, you may want the same protection and leverage.

- **Your relationship with the district.** Hiring an attorney may change your relationship with the school district. When you involve attorneys, the atmosphere becomes more formal and potentially combative. School personnel will likely be more guarded and may view you as a troublemaker or squeaky wheel. Of course, if you are at the point where you may need an attorney, your relationship with the school district has probably already changed. Ultimately, your child's welfare is more important than maintaining a cordial relationship with the school district. And, as attorneys have become more common participants in IEPs and due process, most school districts have become quite used to us, if not fully happy to see us.

Finding an Attorney

Special education attorneys are not as numerous as personal injury or business lawyers. It is also unlikely that attorneys working in more standard areas of law—such as wills and estates, criminal law, family matters, or corporation law—will know anything about special education law.

You may be tempted to hire the attorney who did your will, your sister-in-law who just graduated from law school, or the attorney whose ad in the phone book promises the lowest rates. But special education law is highly specialized. Hiring an attorney who does not know the law or have experience in special education will significantly increase your chance of failure and can ultimately cost you more rather than less. When you pay an attorney, you are paying for all the time spent on your case, including time spent on research. You don't want to pay an attorney for on-the-job training, nor do you want to hire an attorney who won't be able to master the subject matter and legal issues quickly enough to serve you and your child well.

Should Your Lawyer Be an Expert in Learning Disabilities?

If you find a qualified special education attorney who has handled many cases for children with learning disabilities and has a solid working knowledge of learning disabilities, you've found the best of two worlds. Most special education attorneys will likely have had cases involving learning disabilities. If you find a special education attorney who is not that conversant with learning disability issues, but you feel he or she is the right lawyer for your case, ask how the lawyer will develop the learning disability arguments in the case. Remember, your lawyer doesn't have to be an expert in learning disabilities, but should have enough working knowledge to be able to understand the issues, prepare witnesses, and make the necessary factual and legal arguments required in the hearing.

If you are unable to find a special education attorney—which is more likely if you live in a less populated area—your attorney is not likely to know much about learning disabilities. You and others who know your child's needs will have to bring your attorney up to speed. Ultimately, you and your experts will make or break your child's case in mediation or a hearing, not your lawyer. However, your lawyer will need to understand enough about your child's learning disability to know what questions to ask and what answers to seek.

Compile a List of Potential Attorneys

To find the "right" lawyer, you'll need to compile a list of potential candidates. Here's how:

- Ask other parents in the school district.
- Ask your pediatrician or other health care professionals.
- If you are working with or know learning disability specialists, ask them.
- Ask school district personnel—the district is required to maintain a list of special education attorneys and other advocacy resources for parents.
- Contact your state special education advisory commission. IDEA requires each state to have a special education commission, composed of educators and parents, which advises the state about special education. The commissioners should have numerous special education contacts.
- Contact your state department of education and ask for referrals.
- Contact a nearby Parent Training and Information Center (PTI). (See Appendix B on this book's Companion Page on nolo.com.)
- Contact a local disability rights advocacy organization. (See Appendix B on this book's Companion Page on nolo.com.)
- Contact a low-cost or free legal clinic, such as legal aid—while most offices focus on common civil issues (such as domestic disputes or evictions), some offices do special education work for low-income people.
- Use your personal network—friends, colleagues, neighbors, or coworkers who know special education lawyers or who know lawyers who can recommend good special education lawyers.

Call the Attorneys on Your List

Once you have a list of recommended attorneys, you can either narrow it down to one or two individuals who were enthusiastically recommended or make initial contact with everyone on your list.

Nonprofit Legal Clinics

There are nonprofit organizations that provide legal assistance in special education, disability rights, or what is generally called "public interest law." Your school district should have a list of disability-specific or special education nonprofit legal clinics in your area. Also see the organizations listed in Appendix B on this book's Companion Page on nolo.com.

There are advantages and disadvantages to using a nonprofit legal clinic rather than a private attorney. Advantages to using a nonprofit include:

- The attorneys probably have worked in special education and handled many cases.
- Nonprofits often do not charge for their services, or have significantly reduced rates.
- Nonprofits, particularly disability-focused offices, have special knowledge and often a strong passion about the issues.

But there are disadvantages to using a nonprofit:

- Demand is often greater than supply; you may have to wait some time for an appointment, even to have someone assess your case.
- Nonprofit organizations often have limited resources—some focus on either precedent-setting cases (unusual disputes) or cases that will have an impact on a large number of children—and may not handle individual cases.

Try to have a brief phone conversation or ask for a short meeting. Some attorneys will briefly chat with you over the phone to determine the nature of your case and whether or not you need an attorney. Other attorneys may have you speak with an assistant, complete a form describing your case, or make an appointment to come in and talk about the case. Some attorneys will not talk to you without at least a minor retainer or fee; others will not charge for the first discussion. Before making an appointment, find out the following information:

- the attorney's fee
- how the attorney will review the case and decide whether or not you should proceed

- how much the initial review costs, and
- whether you can talk briefly to decide if it's worth sending in a retainer. (If your case is complicated, this might not be an option— you can't expect an attorney to listen to an hour-long explanation of your child's situation during an initial screening call.)

Meet With the Best Candidates

Make an appointment with those candidates who seem like the best prospects. Naturally, if there is a fee for the initial intake, you may only want to see a few attorneys. Be sure to ask what records the attorney needs to evaluate your case.

When you meet with an attorney, you should ask about your specific case, of course. You should also ask about the attorney's:

- years of experience
- specific experience with special education and learning disabilities
- experience with your particular legal issue (such as a due process hearing)
- knowledge of special education law and the IEP process
- experience with your school district
- general style—is the attorney confrontational or cooperative (for example, does the attorney like mediation or think it's a waste of time?)
- references (you may ask for references when you first call), and
- fees.

Does the attorney clearly answer your questions about fees, experience, and your specific legal issues? Does the attorney objectively assess your chances in due process? If the lawyer makes you uncomfortable, think carefully about whether the lawyer's expertise and success rate are worth putting up with a difficult style.

Will the attorney provide the type of help you want? Is the attorney willing to advise you now, but hold off on full participation unless and until you need it? If the attorney wants to take over the case but you only want a consultant, you have the wrong attorney.

Will the attorney be accessible? This is important: The most common complaint about lawyers is that they don't return phone calls, respond to faxes or email, or make themselves available when a client calls. Discuss the attorney's response time. While no attorney should be expected to respond instantly, you shouldn't have to wait more than a day or two, except in rare circumstances.

How Not to Find a Special Education Lawyer

There are several bad ways to find a special education lawyer. Avoid these traps for the unwary:

- **Heavily advertised legal clinics.** While they may offer low flat rates for routine services such as drafting a will, most make their money on personal injury cases. I am not aware of any such clinics offering special education help.
- **Referral panels set up by local bar associations.** Bar association panels do only minimal (if any) screening before qualifying lawyers as experts in certain areas. While you might get a good referral from these panels, it is highly unlikely there will even be a special education attorney listed.
- **Private referral services.** When it comes to services that advertise on TV and billboards, forget it. It is highly unlikely they offer any special education help.

Ask for a Case Evaluation

A good attorney will evaluate the evidence before giving you any advice. After reviewing your case materials, a good special education attorney should be able to:

- tell you the strength of your case
- explain the process
- evaluate your documents and potential witnesses
- tell you if additional supportive material is needed

- estimate the cost of hiring an attorney for due process or beyond
- estimate how long your case may take
- provide insights into school district personnel, particularly if the attorney has worked with the district before, and
- provide a cost-benefit analysis of hiring the attorney to represent you versus using the attorney as an adviser only.

A Word on an Attorney's Style

Some attorneys are pleasant, patient, and good listeners. Others are unpleasant, impatient, and bad listeners. Although you may want the former, you may get the latter. Whatever the style of your attorney, make it clear that you know the attorney is busy, but you expect him or her to treat you courteously, explain matters, keep you fully posted about what is happening, and include you as an active partner in the process. An effective professional relationship must be based on mutual respect.

Furthermore, the attorney should contact you regarding any decision to be made, whether scheduling a meeting, deciding on tactics, reviewing a key issue, or considering a possible resolution of the dispute.

If at any time you don't understand what your attorney has said, requested, or planned, ask for clarification. If the answer isn't clear, ask again. Although you hired the attorney for professional expertise and knowledge—and therefore have relinquished a certain amount of control—it does not mean you should be kept in the dark.

How Attorneys Are Paid

How you pay your lawyer depends on the type of legal services you need and the amount of legal work involved. Once you choose a lawyer, ask for a written agreement explaining how fees and costs will be billed and paid. In some states, a written agreement is required by law; even if it isn't, you should always ask for one. A good attorney will provide you with a written contract (whether you ask or not). Be sure to tell the lawyer how much you are able (and willing) to spend—if you and the lawyer agree on a cap or limit on legal fees, that should also go into your fee agreement.

Your Responsibility in Working With an Attorney

Your attorney should be responsive and courteous, and keep you informed. But the client-attorney relationship is a two-way street. Keep the following in mind:

- Vague questions are likely to receive vague responses; be clear and specific when you discuss matters or ask questions.
- No matter how good an attorney is, the quality of the case—that is, the strength of the evidence—is the key to success. Your attorney cannot transform a bad case into a good one.
- You have responsibility for controlling your legal bill. Be especially aware of time. If you talk to your lawyer for 30 minutes, you will normally be billed for 30 minutes, even if you feel you were "just chatting."
- You cannot call up an attorney, chat for five minutes, and have your problem resolved. I frequently receive phone calls that go something like this:

    "Hello. I have a question about special education. Do you know special education law?"

    "Yes."

    "My daughter has an IEP on Thursday. She is learning disabled and I want her placed in a private school. The school district has offered a special day class. What do you recommend?"

If I tried to answer that question without knowing all of the facts, I would be doing a disservice to myself and the caller. And the caller is being unfair. I will try to answer simple questions over the phone from first-time callers—such as, "Can you tell me if a school has to do an evaluation of a child before the child enters special education?"—but most questions are more complicated than that. It is unfair to assume that an attorney can either provide a simple answer to a complex question or provide free advice.

One final suggestion: Courtesy and respect for the attorney's time go a long way. It can be very off-putting to get a call from someone who presumes that I am prepared to provide free advice. On the other hand, when strangers call and say something like "Can I take two minutes of your time?" or "Do you have a moment? I'd be happy to pay for a brief call," I will do my best to try to answer the caller's questions, without any thought about my fees.

As your case progresses, you'll want to make sure you receive a bill or statement at least once a month. A lawyer's time adds up quickly. If your lawyer will be delegating some of the work to a less experienced associate, paralegal, or secretary, the delegated work should be billed at a lower hourly rate. Make sure this is stated in your written fee agreement.

Lawyers' Billing Methods

Lawyers charge for their services in three different ways.

Hourly rate. Most special education attorneys charge by the hour. In most parts of the United States, you can secure competent representation for $200–$400 or more an hour. Many clients prefer an hourly rate to a flat fee (discussed next) because you pay only for the actual time the lawyer spends on your case. Comparison shopping among lawyers can help you avoid overpaying, but only if you compare lawyers with similar expertise. A highly experienced special education attorney (who has a higher hourly rate) may be cheaper in the long run than a general practitioner (at a lower rate). The special education attorney won't have to research routine questions and usually can evaluate your case quickly.

Legal Time	
How much time your attorney will spend on your case depends on the nature of your dispute. Here are some general guidelines for the amount of time it might take a good lawyer to do common legal tasks in the IEP process:	
• initial review of your records and interview with you	2–3 hours
• helping you with the IEP process —developing a blueprint; contacting evaluators and school personnel; drafting goals	3–5 hours
• attending the IEP meeting	2–4 hours (per meeting)
• preparing for and attending mediation session	3–8 hours
• preparing for and attending hearing	10–35 hours

Flat rate. A flat rate is a single fee that will cover all the work the lawyer has agreed to do—for example, prepare for and attend the IEP meeting or prepare for and conduct the hearing. You are obligated to pay the flat fee no matter how many hours the lawyer spends on your case, assuming the lawyer does the work. A flat fee can be quite economical if the fee is reasonable and you anticipate a lot of work. On the other hand, if the case is resolved early in the process, you may end up paying much more than you would have paid in hourly fees. Most special education attorneys charge by the hour and may be unwilling to work on a flat fee.

Contingency fee. Contingency fee arrangements are rarely used in special education cases. A contingency fee is a percentage of whatever money the party wins; if you don't win anything, the attorney gets nothing. Because almost all successful special education cases require the school district to provide a program or service rather than pay an award of money, don't expect a special education attorney to work on contingency.

Legal Costs

In addition to the fees they charge for their time, lawyers bill for a variety of expenses they incur. These costs, which can add up quickly, may include charges for:

- photocopies
- faxes
- postage
- overnight mail
- messenger services
- expert witness fees
- court filing fees
- long distance phone calls
- process servers
- work by investigators
- work by legal assistants or paralegals
- deposition transcripts
- online legal research, and
- travel.

Some lawyers absorb the cost of photocopies, faxes, online legal research, and local phone calls as normal office overhead, but that's not always the case. When working out the fee arrangement, ask for a list of costs you'll be expected to pay. If the lawyer seems intent on nickel-and-diming you or hitting you with a $5 per page fax charge, you should bring it up. While this may not reflect the attorney's skills or ability to win a case, it does raise some red flags about how he or she does business.

Reimbursement for Legal Fees and Costs

If you hire an attorney *and* you prevail in due process (at a mediation or hearing), you are entitled to be reimbursed by the school district for your attorney fees and other due process costs. (20 U.S.C. § 1415(i)(3).)

But your right to reimbursement can be limited. First, you are not entitled to reimbursement for the fees you paid an attorney to attend the IEP meeting, unless the meeting was required as part of due process. This might happen if the hearing officer orders a second IEP meeting to discuss matters that were improperly omitted from the first meeting.

Second, you are not entitled to reimbursement if the school district makes a settlement offer ten days before the due process hearing, you reject the offer, *and* the hearing officer finds that what you actually won in due process is no better than the school district's settlement offer. If the hearing officer finds that you were substantially justified in rejecting the settlement offer, however, you are entitled to full reimbursement. What constitutes "substantially justified" is not defined in IDEA.

Third, the hearing officer can reduce the amount of attorney fees to which you are entitled if the officer finds that any of the following are true:

- You unreasonably protracted or extended the final resolution of the controversy.
- The attorney's fees unreasonably exceed hourly rates charged by other attorneys in the community for similar services.
- The time and services provided by the attorney were excessive.
- The attorney failed to provide certain information to the district required by law. (20 U.S.C. § 1415(i).)

You should carefully discuss these reimbursement issues with your attorney before you evaluate any settlement offers or decide to request a fair hearing.

CAUTION

Remember IDEA has important rules regarding your liability for legal fees. See Chapter 12 for more information.

Reducing Legal Fees

There are several ways to control legal fees.

Be organized. Especially when you are paying by the hour, it's important to gather important documents, write a short chronology of events, and concisely explain the problem to your lawyer. Keep a copy of everything you give to the lawyer.

Be prepared before you meet your lawyer. Whenever possible, put your questions in writing, and mail, fax, or deliver them to your lawyer before all meetings or phone conversations. Early preparation also helps focus the meeting so there is less chance of digressing (at your expense) into unrelated topics.

Carefully review lawyer bills. Like everyone else, lawyers make mistakes. For example, 0.1 of an hour (six minutes) may be transposed into 1.0 (one hour) when the data is entered into the billing system. That's $200 instead of $20 if your lawyer charges $200 per hour. Don't hesitate to question your bill. You have the right to a clear explanation of costs.

Ask your lawyer what work you can do. There are some things you can do to save time. For example, you could go through the school's record and highlight key statements. Or you could talk with important witnesses to find out their attitudes about key issues in the case. Some attorneys may be comfortable with your doing substantial work; others won't. Be sure to discuss this ahead of time.

Listen to your lawyer. Certainly, lawyers deserve some of the criticism that comes their way; there's a reason why lawyers are the subject of a separate book of *New Yorker* jokes. But large legal bills are sometimes the result of clients losing track of time and/or ignoring advice. I have had clients to whom I have carefully, clearly, and repeatedly explained why I thought pursuing a particular argument was a waste of time or had little chance of success, yet the client persisted in pressing forward, despite my advice. When the argument ultimately failed, all that was left was a legal bill. As a client, you should not be afraid to question your attorney's recommendation. But part of what you're paying for is reasonable and objective advice—and when your attorney says not to waste time on an issue, you should probably listen.

Resolving Problems With a Lawyer

If you see a problem brewing with your lawyer, don't just sit back and fume. Call or write your lawyer. Whatever it is that rankles—a high bill, a missed deadline, or a strategic move you don't understand—have an honest discussion about your feelings. Be prepared to state your concerns and listen objectively to your lawyer's side of the misunderstanding.

If you can't frankly discuss these matters with your lawyer or you are unsatisfied with the outcome of any discussion, it's time to consider finding another lawyer. If you don't, you may waste money on unnecessary legal fees and risk having matters turn out badly.

Here are some tips on resolving specific problems:

- If you have a dispute over fees, the local bar association may be able to mediate it for you.
- If a lawyer has violated legal ethics—for example, had a conflict of interest, overbilled you, or didn't represent you professionally—the state agency that licenses lawyers may discipline the lawyer.
- Where a major mistake has been made—for example, a lawyer missed the hearing deadline for submitting the witness list and exhibits—you might even consider suing for malpractice. Lawyers carry malpractice insurance.

Remember, while there will be times when you question your attorney's tactics, you have hired someone because of his or her expertise and experience. Before confronting the attorney, ask yourself whether the attorney misfired or you are overreacting.

If you decide to change lawyers, be sure to end the first professional relationship before you start a new one. If you don't, you could find yourself being billed by two lawyers at the same time. Also, be sure all important legal documents are returned to you. Tell your new lawyer what your old one has done to date and pass on the file.

Your Rights as a Client

As a client, you have the right to expect the following:

- courteous treatment by your lawyer and staff members
- an itemized statement of services rendered and a full explanation, in advance, of billing practices
- charges for agreed-upon fees and nothing more
- prompt responses to phone calls and letters
- confidential legal conferences, free from unwarranted interruptions
- up-to-date information on the status of your case
- diligent and competent legal representation, and
- clear answers to all questions.

A final word on attorneys: We live in a time when public attitudes about attorneys are negative, to some degree rightfully so. There are, however, many conscientious attorneys, particularly in the special education field. A high percentage of the special education attorneys I've run across in my 25 years of practice have been compassionate, able, and decent professionals.

Doing Your Own Legal Research

Using this book is a good way to educate yourself about the laws that affect your rights as a parent of a special education child. Chapter 2 has already provided you with much of the key legal language of IDEA. Because the laws and court decisions of 50 states are involved, however, no one book can give you all the information you might need.

There's a lot you can do on your own, once you understand a few basics about law libraries, statute books, court opinions, and the general reference books that lawyers use. Some basic legal research skills can help you determine how strong your case is and the best and most effective way to go forward. Whether the issue is private school placement, the type or amount of a related service, an evaluation question, or an eligibility issue, IDEA and judicial decisions can help you judge the strength of your case.

Using the Library

Look for a law library that's open to the public—there may be one in your main county courthouse or at your state capital. Law librarians, who increasingly have experience working with nonlawyers, can help you find the appropriate resources. Publicly funded law schools generally permit the public to use their libraries, and some private law schools grant access to the public, sometimes for a modest fee.

If you can't find an accessible law library, don't overlook the public library. Many large public libraries have sizable legal reference collections, including state and federal statutes. Also, if you work with a lawyer, ask about using the research materials at your lawyer's office.

EXAMPLES:
- You want your child to be placed in a private school that has an identical program to the one available in your school district. Legal research should lead you to the conclusion that your position isn't a winning one. The law is clear: There is no right to a private school in this situation.
- Your child needs a multisensory approach to address a learning disability. You do some research and find that IDEA does not require the IEP team to include a teaching methodology, but you also find cases stating that, if the evidence supports the need, the hearing officer can rule in your favor.
- Your child is going into the tenth grade and continues to have significant difficulties with handwriting and using the computer keyboard. Your child also has had some behavioral

problems and was suspended in the ninth grade. The district wants to place him or her in a special class for learning disabled students at a small alternative high school. You visit a law library and discover that in the case of *Sacramento City Unified School Dist., Bd. of Educ. v. Rachel H.*, 14 F.3d 1398 (9th Circuit 1994), the court established rules for determining whether a child is entitled to be mainstreamed, including:

- the academic and nonacademic benefits to the child
- the effect of the placement on the teacher and other students, and
- the cost of the aids and services needed to mainstream.

The materials you can research include:

- IDEA statutes and regulations (excerpts are in the appendix)
- state statutes
- court cases interpreting IDEA and other relevant statutes
- explanatory documents, such as the U.S. Department of Education policy guidelines and correspondence—these documents do not have the authority of a statute or court case, but they reflect the department's analysis of the law.
- hearing decisions (available through your state department of education and the *Individuals with Disabilities Education Law Report*, discussed below)—although these are binding only on the parties to that specific hearing, they may be of value to you in showing how hearing officers make decisions in your state, and
- law review and other articles about IDEA and special education issues.

CAUTION

Get the right IDEA. When doing your own research, be sure that you have the latest version of IDEA (the 2004 reauthorization) and the most recent regulations (issued in 2006). Key sections of both are available on this book's Companion Page on www.nolo.com. See Chapter 16 for the link.

Individuals with Disabilities Education Act (IDEA): Where to Find It

Like all federal laws, IDEA is found in a multivolume series of books called the United States Code (U.S.C.), which is available in most libraries or online. The U.S.C. consists of separate numbered titles, each covering a specific subject matter. IDEA is found in Title 20, beginning with Section 1400. Appendix A on this book's Companion Page on nolo. com includes a copy of key sections of the IDEA statute (see Chapter 16 for the link).

You can find annotated versions of the U.S.C., which include not only the text of the IDEA but also summaries of cases that interpret IDEA and a reference to where each case can be found. Annotated codes also list articles that discuss IDEA. Annotated codes have comprehensive indexes by topic and are kept up to date with paperback supplements (called pocket parts) found inside the back cover of each volume or in a separate paperback volume. Supplements include changes to IDEA and recent cases.

Your school district is required to provide you with copies of federal law—that is, the statutes and regulations of IDEA. Your school district, however, is not required to inform you of any legal decisions on IDEA. One source of up-to-date information, including policy guidelines on the IDEA, is the U.S. Department of Education (www.ed.gov). But that's not the only source.

Special newsletters provide extensive detail about most fields of law. Special education has one such publication called the *Individuals with Disabilities Education Law Report* (IDELR). It is published by LRP Publications (contact information is in Appendix B on this book's Companion Page on nolo.com (you'll find the link in Chapter 16). IDELR issues a bimonthly highlights newsletter, along with IDEA court rulings, hearing decisions, Department of Education policy statements, and other publications. IDELR has a subject index, making it easy to locate the specific cases you want to review. At a current cost of more than $1,000 per year, IDELR is aimed at special education lawyers and school districts.

Some law libraries subscribe to IDELR—call the nearest law libraries and ask. Some school districts also subscribe. If this fails, contact a local nonprofit special education or disability organization in your area and ask if they receive IDELR.

State Statutes

As noted in Chapter 2, each state has passed a law that parallels or even exceeds the rights under IDEA. You should take a look at your state's special education laws, which are available in many public libraries and all law libraries.

Most states also make their statutes available online. (See "Online Legal Research," below.) In some states, statutes are organized by subject matter, with each title, chapter, or code covering a particular legal area—for example, the vehicle code or the corporations code. Most states have some kind of education code. In some states, statutes are simply numbered sequentially without regard to subject matter, which means that you'll have to use the index to find what you need. State codes are like the federal U.S.C., with annotated volumes, indexes, and pocket parts.

Some states have their own regulations implementing special education laws; check with your state department of education for information about these regulations. You can find the contact information for your state on the U.S. Department of Education website (www.ed.gov).

Court Decisions

When Congress passes a law, it cannot address every possible situation or clarify what each section of the law means. It is the job of a court— federal or state—to interpret the applicable laws and apply them to particular facts. The court will often explain, clarify, and even expand or limit what actually appears in a statute. These court decisions are often referred to as "case law."

Court decisions are published in state or federal reporters. Each decision has a name and a citation, indicating the volume, name, and page of the reporter in which it appears, the court that issued the decision, and the year of the decision. With the citation, you can locate the printed decision.

EXAMPLE:

The first special education case to reach the U.S. Supreme Court was *Board of Education v. Rowley.* It concerned a deaf child who needed a sign language interpreter in her regular classroom. The U.S. Supreme Court said she didn't need one, because she was passing from grade to grade (even though not having an interpreter caused her to miss 40% of classroom communication).

The case was first decided by a federal trial court: the case citation is 483 F.Supp. 536 (S.D. N.Y. 1980). This means that the case can be found in volume 483 of a reporter called the Federal Supplement, starting at page 536. The court that issued the decision was the federal court for the Southern District of New York. The case was decided in 1980.

That decision was appealed, and the case citation of the appeal is 632 F.2d 945 (2d Cir. 1980). This means that the decision of the appellate court can be found in volume 632 of the Federal Reporter (2d Series), starting at page 945. The court that ruled on the appeal was the Second Circuit Court of Appeals. The appeal was decided in 1980.

The citation for the U.S. Supreme Court decision is 102 S.Ct. 3034 (1982). The decision can be found in volume 102 of the Supreme Court Reporter, starting at page 3034. The court decided the case in 1982.

Although IDEA gives you or the school district the option of appealing a due process decision to a state court, most cases involving a federal law such as IDEA are decided by the federal courts. Each state has a unique case reporting system, but decisions are usually found in regional reporters. For example, in the case of *State v. Bruno, 673 A.2d 1117 (Conn. 1996)*, the decision was published in volume 673 of the regional law reporter called the Atlantic Second Series and begins on page 1117. The case comes from the state of Connecticut and was decided in 1996.

Finding Cases About Learning Disabilities

Every decision a court issues is specific to the facts of that case. Even though a case addresses the same underlying legal concepts as yours, it might be very different, factually, from your child's situation. When you come across a case involving a learning disabled student, remember that the facts of the case will dictate the extent to which it applies to your child and your claims.

You'll find learning disability cases that interpret every aspect of IDEA, including evaluation, educational methodology, eligibility, placement, services, suspension, and expulsion. Because the facts of each case are different and because IDEA requires an appropriate education for each individual child, you will not find any court saying that a particular kind of methodology or placement is always required for students with learning disabilities. Instead, the court will decide whether IDEA procedures and rules were followed in the context of a particular factual situation and for one particular child.

On rare occasions, a court will make a very broad and important decision. For example, in a famous case in 1986, a federal court ruled that IQ tests were not valid for determining whether African American students have learning disabilities. (*Larry P. v. Riles*, 793 F.2d 969 (9th Cir. 1984).) It is very unusual, however, for a court to make this kind of blanket ruling.

If you use IDELR, you can find cases on learning disabilities in the *Topical Index/Current Decisions*. Each *Topical Index/Current Decisions* book will cover those cases reprinted in particular IDELR volumes. Most of the *Indexes* cover two to three volumes. The topics are arranged alphabetically. You can find learning disability cases under the heading "Specific Learning Disability," which in turn is divided up into subcategories such as Educational Methodologies, Eligibility Criteria, Identification and Evaluation, Placement, and so on. Cases are listed under each of the subcategories.

IDELR reprints not only court case decisions but also decisions made by due process hearing officers (usually referred to as SEA or state educational agency decisions) and the federal Office of Civil Rights, or OCR, which investigates § 504 complaints. IDELR also includes

IDEA policy analyses by the U.S. Department of Education, Office of Special Education Programs (OSEP). Court decisions will have the most potential impact, but the SEA, OCR, and OSEP decisions and policy determinations, particularly the OSEP letters, can be of real value to you and your child. The OSEP letters on policy indicate how the department interprets IDEA; they have a broader application because they deal not so much with particular facts, but with policy and the meaning of IDEA.

RESOURCE

Further Reading on Legal Research. *Legal Research: How to Find & Understand the Law,* by Stephen Elias and the Editors of Nolo (Nolo), gives easy-to-use, step-by-step instructions on finding legal information.

When you research cases, make sure the case you find has not been overturned or replaced by a more recent court decision. You can check this through a set of books known as Shepard's. A friendly law librarian might have the time and patience to guide you through this process—if not, Nolo's *Legal Research* book has an easy-to-follow explanation of how to use the Shepard's system to expand and update your research.

When you find a court decision, there will be a short synopsis of the decision at the beginning. This synopsis not only will help you determine whether the case is relevant to your situation, but also will tell you what the court decided. After the case synopsis there will be a list of numbered items, each item followed by a short summary. The numbers (1, 2, 3, and so on) refer to the location in the written decision where that legal issue is discussed.

Keep in mind that your situation may or may not relate exactly to a particular court decision. It will depend on how similar the facts are and whether your situation and the legal decision involve the same sections of IDEA. The more alike the facts and pertinent parts of IDEA, the more you can use the decision to your advantage. But the existence of a case that supports your position does not mean that the school district has to apply or even abide by that decision. It is certainly a very persuasive precedent, but it is just an example of how one court has ruled in a similar situation.

Letter Encouraging School Board Settlement

Date: April 20, 20xx

To: Howard Yankolon, Superintendent
Eugene School District
15578 South Main Street
Eugene, OR 97412

Re: Clara Centler, student in Westside School, 5th grade

I appreciated your efforts at the April 14, 20xx IEP meeting; as you know, we are in disagreement about Clara's need for a one-on-one aide so she can be mainstreamed.

I have requested a hearing. I have also done some research on this matter and determined that the facts and the law in the U.S. Supreme Court's decision in *Sacramento City Unified School Dist., Bd. of Educ. v. Rachel H.* are almost identical to our dispute. I strongly believe that with the Supreme Court's direction in that case, it would be a real waste of time and district money to go to due process.

I am therefore requesting that you consider this and meet with me to discuss a possible settlement of our differences.

Sincerely,

Stuart Centler
Stuart Centler
78 Pine Avenue
Eugene, OR 97412
Phones: 555-5543 (home); 555-0933 (work)

If the decision was reached by the U.S. Supreme Court, the federal court of appeals covering your state, your federal district court, or your state supreme court, the case represents the law in your area. Decisions in other federal circuits can be useful as long as there is not a different legal standard in your circuit.

If you find a case that is similar to yours and the decision is a good one, think about discussing the case in a letter to your school district, explaining why you believe you will prevail in due process.

CAUTION

Do legal research with care. Analyzing case law and the meaning and reach of legal statutes can be complicated. Make sure you know what you're talking about before you cite the law. While you can learn a good deal, becoming expert at legal research requires care, time, and training. Proceed carefully and use what you learn with caution.

Online Legal Research

Every day, a growing number of basic legal resources are available online. If you are comfortable using the Internet, you may find doing research online easier than using books. Online documents often have links that let you jump from one topic to another, and you can access many different documents at one sitting without ever leaving your chair. If you don't have Internet access at home, check with your local public library to see if they offer free Internet access to your community.

The sources below provide access to a variety of legal information:

- **www.nolo.com.** Nolo's Internet site contains helpful articles, information about new legislation, and a legal research tool you can use to find state and federal statutes.
- **www.law.cornell.edu.** This site is maintained by Cornell Law School. You can find the text of the U.S. Code, federal court decisions, and some state court decisions. You can also search for material by topic.

- **www.gpoaccess.gov.** This site provides the entire Federal Code of Regulations.
- **www.statelocalgov.net.** This comprehensive site provides links to state and local government websites. Look here to find a link to your state's department of education, your county government's site, and perhaps even a website for your city or town.

In addition, Appendix B on this book's Companion Page on nolo. com includes a section entitled "Legal Resources on Special Education." These resources include websites that offer a wealth of legal and practical material on special education (see Chapter 16 for the link).

Parent Organizations

The first word in IDEA is "Individuals." Special education law and philosophy are based on the individual child, which makes it difficult to approach special education from a collective or group perspective. Each IEP is different. That is why this book focuses on strategies and procedures for parents who are acting alone.

There are, however, situations in which a group of parents working together can have a tremendous impact on a school district and the programs available for children with learning disabilities. Because the "specific learning disability" category under IDEA is the largest, you are going to find some parents in your school district whose children have learning disabilities. When a group of parents approaches a school to recommend changes, the school is more likely to take notice. A parent group can also serve as an invaluable resource for information and support as you navigate the special education process.

Join a Parent Organization

There are many ways to find an existing parent group. You can start by getting in touch with the local PTA. In addition, most school districts have a parent advisory committee (sometimes referred to as CACs or Community Advisory Committees) specifically formed for special education matters. If you haven't already done so, contact your school district to find out about that committee. Usually, these committees are composed of special education professionals and other parents. If you can't find information on a local group, try the state level. Appendix B on this book's Companion Page on nolo.com (see Chapter 16 for the link) contains a state-by-state list of Parent Training and Information Centers (PTIs). PTIs are parent-to-parent organizations that can provide advice, training, and even advocacy help.

Because a majority of children in special education have learning disabilities, you may be able to find a local parents' group that deals only with learning disability issues. You should also take a look at Appendix B on this book's Companion Page on nolo.com (see Chapter 16 for the link) for a list of national organizations serving children with learning disabilities. You can contact them to determine if there are any local, regional, or state affiliates.

A parent organization can help you in several ways:

- There is strength in numbers. School districts often pay more attention to four parents versus two, and ten parents versus five.
- A parent group can provide you with all kinds of important information about the school administrator, staff, existing classes, the local IEP process, and outside support professionals, such as independent evaluators, private service providers, private schools, and attorneys.
- A parent group can offer you plenty of information and resources, can suggest successful educational strategies and methodologies geared to your child, and even give you sophisticated information about IDEA and its legal mandates.
- A parent group can provide the emotional support you will need as you wind your way through the special education process.

> **CAUTION**
>
> **Community advisory committees may include school district representatives.** School personnel regularly attend meetings of these committees, so parents may find it difficult to speak frankly. This is not to say you shouldn't trust or include school personnel, but you should recognize that there may be times when the presence of school personnel inhibits honest discussion of certain issues. If this is the only organization in your area, consider forming an independent parent organization.

Form a Parent Organization

If your community doesn't have a parent organization, the existing group is too tied to or influenced by the school district, or the existing group doesn't meet your needs, you can organize a new group. How do you begin?

First, consider how wide or narrow you want your focus to be. If you want to form a specialized group that deals only with learning disabilities, you may have to sacrifice size for specificity. If you open your group up to parents whose children have any type of disability, you'll have a larger group, with more general goals. The strength that comes from a large group can often offset the challenges that come with a diversity of concerns. But even if you can only put together a small group, you should find it helpful. You don't need a lot of people. A handful of parents can be quite effective.

Sometimes a few simple phone calls will lead to very useful recommendations. Here's how to get started and prepare for your first meeting:

- Invite all possible parents who fit within your chosen scope.
- Ask them for agenda ideas, focusing on common issues and concerns.
- Ask them for the names of other parents to invite.
- Ask your child's teacher or pediatrician for names of other parents to invite.
- Ask the PTA and your school district to announce the meeting or to include information on it in any mailings.
- Place an announcement in your local newspaper.
- Contact local disability organizations. They may be able to connect you with other parent support groups in your state. They may also be able to advise you if you encounter problems. (Appendix B on this book's Companion Page on nolo.com lists learning disability organizations.)

At your first meeting, you can decide on how formal you want to be and on what issues you want to focus. If you take the formal route, you'll need to select a name, elect officers, decide whether to charge dues (and, if so, how much), collect those dues, and establish regular meetings.

No matter how formal or informal you are, you will need to spend some time discussing your purpose and what you hope to accomplish. Do you simply want to establish better ties with the school administration? Do you want to address specific concerns, such as the quality of a particular class, intimidation by school personnel during the IEP process, or certain procedures that you find unfair? Once you decide which issues you want to tackle, you can figure out how to formally contact the district and raise your concerns.

At later meetings, consider inviting guests, such as representatives of the school district or a local special education attorney. The attorney may charge for his or her time. Your dues or an additional contribution from each family can cover the cost. Also, consider developing a newsletter (online is easiest) to stay in touch and share ideas with other parents in your area.

Your Child's Privacy

Before you get involved in a parents' group, you should consider your older child's feelings about privacy. We all know that the teenage years are a time of significant emotional and physical growth, when your child will have to face important social and identity issues. Will your active involvement in a parent group compromise your child's privacy and self-confidence? Does your child want you to take such a high-profile stance? Is your child comfortable with your using his or her name as you become involved in school organizing? There are of course no hard and fast answers—you'll have to talk with your child to figure out how to proceed.

A successful group will develop important contacts with the district, represent a collective strength that can affect district decision making, and provide a way to express specific concerns directly and powerfully.

Get Involved With the School District

Whether you work alone or with a group, there are many ways to improve your child's educational program through direct involvement with the school district. Volunteer at school or in the administrative office, run for school board, or assist in school fundraisers. Generally, this kind of activity gets you involved, opens doors, and allows you to meet the people in charge. This often can foster a good relationship with school personnel, making it easier for you to pick up the phone and call about—and resolve—a problem.

The same advice goes for your parent group. You should meet with the district on a somewhat regular basis, to find out how you can help the school. Build a relationship between your group and the school. Ultimately, you and the school district really do have the same goal: to help your child grow into an effective, productive, and happy adult.

How to Use the Companion Page on Nolo.com

This book has a "Companion" Web page, which you can find at **www.nolo.com/back-of-book/IELD.html**

There you can download, for free, some invaluable resources, including forms, letters, and checklists to help you through every stage of the IEP process; a sample filled-out IEP form; key special education laws and regulations; information for advocacy, parent, and disability organizations; and a comprehensive explanation of the severe discrepancy model, introduced in Chapter 7. These resources are contained in five appendixes, as follows:

Appendix A: Special Education Law and Regulations

Appendix B: Support Groups, Advocacy Organizations, and Other Resources

Appendix C: The Severe Discrepancy Model

Appendix D: Sample IEP Form

Appendix E: Forms

Using the Forms From the Companion Page

Go to the Companion Page at **www.nolo.com/back-of-book/IELD.html** and click the icon "Download Forms."

To use the form files, your computer must have specific software programs installed. Here is a list of types of files provided by this book, as well as the software programs you'll need to access them:

- **RTF.** You can open, edit, print, and save these form files with most word processing programs such as Microsoft *Word*, Windows *WordPad*, and recent versions of *WordPerfect*.

- **PDF.** You can view these files with Adobe *Reader*, free software from www.adobe.com. Government PDFs are sometimes fillable using your computer, but most PDFs are designed to be printed out and completed by hand.

TIP

Note to Macintosh Users. These forms were designed for use with Windows. They should also work on Macintosh computers; however, Nolo cannot provide technical support for non-Windows users.

Editing RTFs

Here are some general instructions about editing RTF forms in your word processing program. Refer to the book's instructions and sample agreements for help about what should go in each blank.

- **Underlines.** Underlines indicate where to enter information. After filling in the needed text, delete the underline. In most word processing programs you can do this by highlighting the underlined portion and typing ctrl-u.
- **Bracketed and italicized text.** Bracketed and italicized text indicates instructions. Be sure to remove all instructional text before you finalize your document.
- **Optional text.** Optional text gives you the choice to include or exclude text. Delete any optional text you don't want to use. Renumber numbered items, if necessary.
- **Alternative text.** Alternative text gives you the choice between two or more text options. Delete those options you don't want to use. Renumber numbered items, if necessary.
- **Signature lines.** Signature lines should appear on a page with at least some text from the document itself.

Every word processing program uses different commands to open, format, save, and print documents, so refer to your software's help documents for help using your program. Nolo cannot provide technical support for questions about how to use your computer or your software.

CAUTION

In accordance with U.S. copyright laws, the forms provided by this book are for your personal use only.

List of Forms

The following forms come in Rich Text Format (rtf) and Adobe Acrobat (pdf).

Form Title	RTF File Name	PDF File Name
Request for Information on Special Education	SpecialEdInfo.rtf	SpecialEdInfo.pdf
Request to Begin Special Education Process and Evaluation	BeginProcess.rtf	BeginProcess.pdf
Request for Child's School File	FileRequest.rtf	FileRequest.pdf
Request to Amend Child's School File	AmendFile.rtf	AmendFile.pdf
Special Education Contacts	Contacts.rtf	Contacts.pdf
IEP Journal	IEPJournal.rtf	IEPJournal.pdf
Monthly IEP Calendar	IEPCalendar.rtf	IEPCalendar.pdf
IEP Blueprint	IEPBlueprint.rtf	IEPBlueprint.pdf
Letter Requesting Evaluation Report	Evaluation.rtf	Evaluation.pdf
Request for Joint IEP Eligibility/Program Meeting	MeetingRequest.rtf	MeetingRequest.pdf
Progress Chart	Chart.rtf	Chart.pdf
Program Visitation Request Letter	VisitRequest.rtf	VisitRequest.pdf
Class Visitation Checklist	Checklist.rtf	Checklist.pdf
Goals Chart	Goals.rtf	Goals.pdf
IEP Material Organizer Form	Organizer.rtf	Organizer.pdf
IEP Meeting Participants	Participants.rtf	Participants.pdf
IEP Meeting Attendance Objection Letter	Objection.rtf	Objection.pdf
IEP Preparation Checklist	PrepChecklist.rtf	PrepChecklist.pdf
Letter Confirming Informal Negotiation	Negotiation.rtf	Negotiation.pdf
Letter Requesting Due Process	DueProcess.rtf	DueProcess.pdf

Index

⚖ NOLO *Online Legal Forms*

Nolo offers a large library of legal solutions and forms, created by Nolo's in-house legal staff. These reliable documents can be prepared in minutes.

Create a Document

- **Incorporation.** Incorporate your business in any state.
- **LLC Formations.** Gain asset protection and pass-through tax status in any state.
- **Wills.** Nolo has helped people make over 2 million wills. Is it time to make or revise yours?
- **Living Trust (avoid probate).** Plan now to save your family the cost, delays, and hassle of probate.
- **Trademark.** Protect the name of your business or product.
- **Provisional Patent.** Preserve your rights under patent law and claim "patent pending" status.

Download a Legal Form

Nolo.com has hundreds of top quality legal forms available for download—bills of sale, promissory notes, nondisclosure agreements, LLC operating agreements, corporate minutes, commercial lease and sublease, motor vehicle bill of sale, consignment agreements and many, many more.

Review Your Documents

Many lawyers in Nolo's consumer-friendly lawyer directory will review Nolo documents for a very reasonable fee. Check their detailed profiles at **Nolo.com/lawyers**.